THE LIFE
AFTER

3

EXODUS

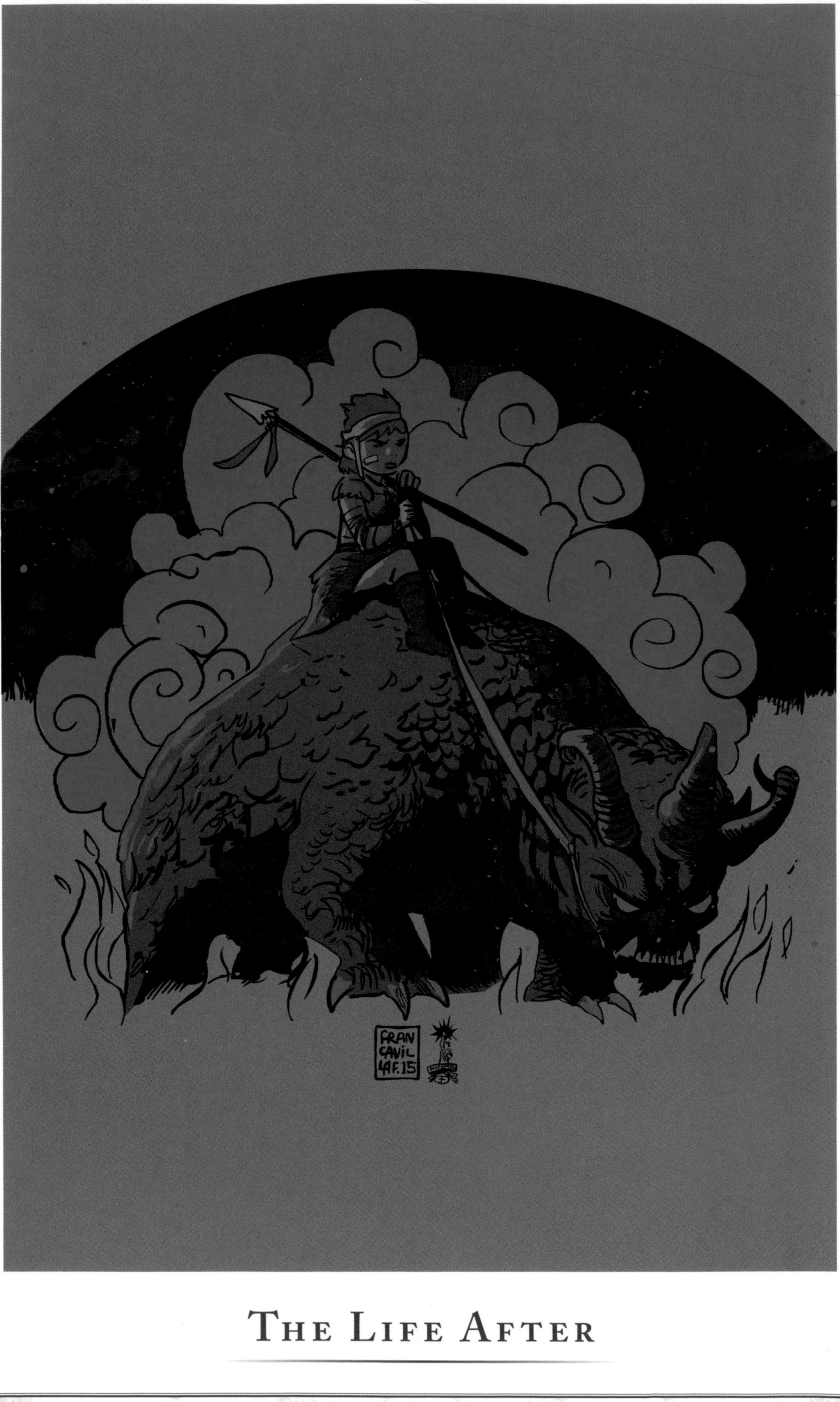

The Life After

THE LIFE AFTER

3

EXODUS

Written by
JOSHUA HALE FIALKOV

Illustrated and colored by
GABO

Lettered by
CRANK!

Color assists by
ASHLEY ERICKSON

Designed by
KEITH WOOD

Edited by
ARI YARWOOD

AN ONI PRESS PUBLICATION

PUBLISHED BY ONI PRESS, INC.

JOE NOZEMACK publisher

JAMES LUCAS JONES editor in chief

ANDREW McINTIRE v.p. of marketing & sales

CHEYENNE ALLOTT director of sales

RACHEL REED publicity coordinator

TROY LOOK director of design & production

HILARY THOMPSON graphic designer

JARED JONES digital art technician

CHARLIE CHU senior editor

ROBIN HERRERA editor

ARI YARWOOD managing editor

BESS PALLARES editorial assistant

BRAD ROOKS director of logistics

JUNG LEE logistics associate

Oni Press, Inc.
1305 SE Martin Luther King Jr. Blvd.
Suite A
Portland, OR 97214
USA

First edition: July 2016

onipress.com • facebook.com/onipress • twitter.com/onipress
onipress.tumblr.com • instagram.com/onipress

thefialkov.com • @joshfialkov
yogabogabo.com • @galvosaur

This volume collects issues #1-5 of the
Oni Press series *Exodus: The Life After*.

ISBN 978-1-62010-321-0 • eISBN 978-1-62010-322-7

Library of Congress Control Number: 2014944756

10 9 8 7 6 5 4 3 2 1

PRINTED IN CHINA

To the quantum to my particle.

(Will that make sense to a five-year-old?)

- Joshua

To hitting the reset button; this time I know where all the good treasures are.

- Gabo

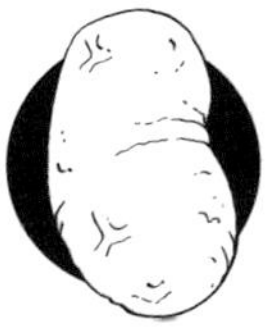

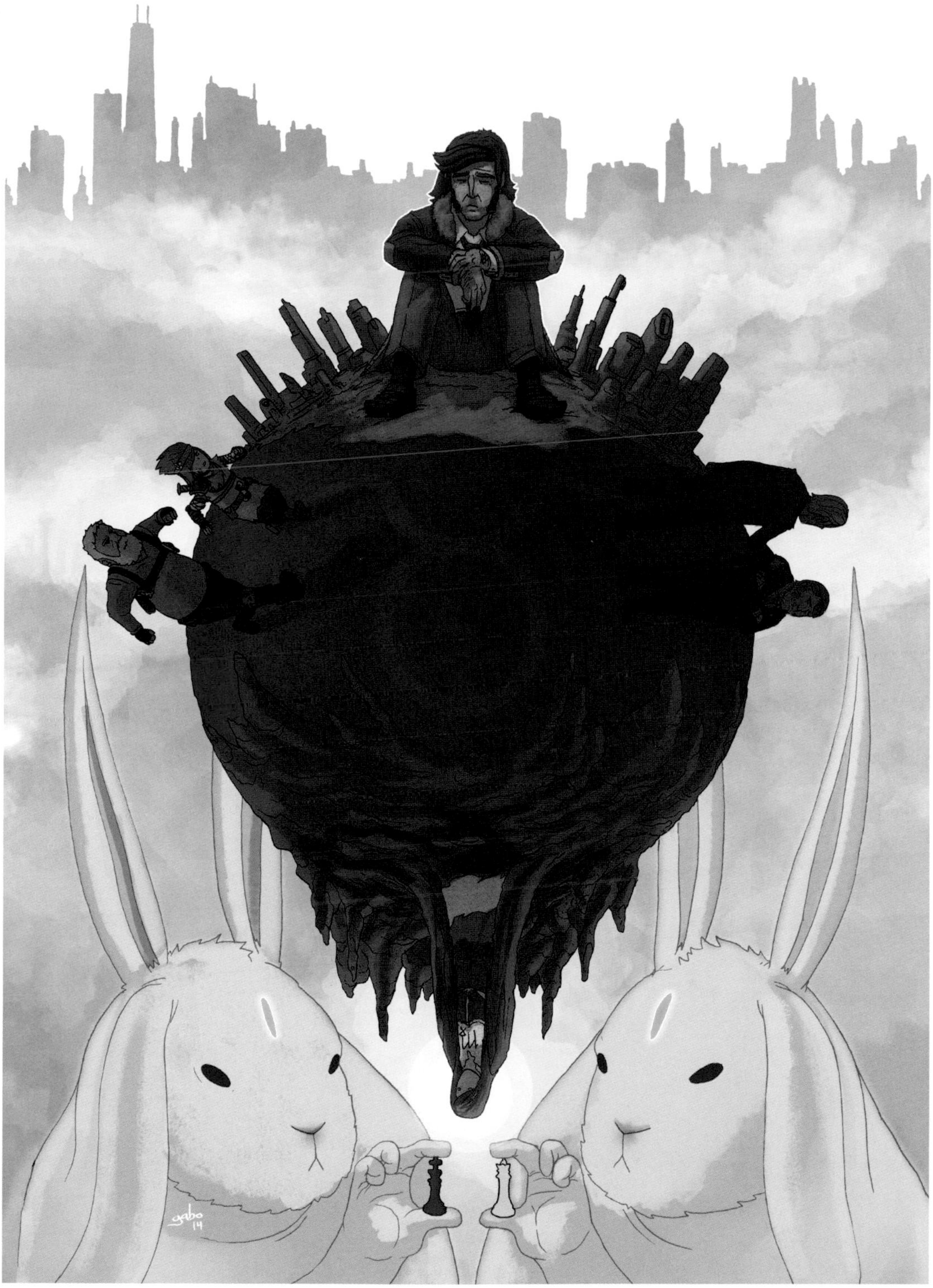

Chapter Eleven

THE LIFE
AFTER

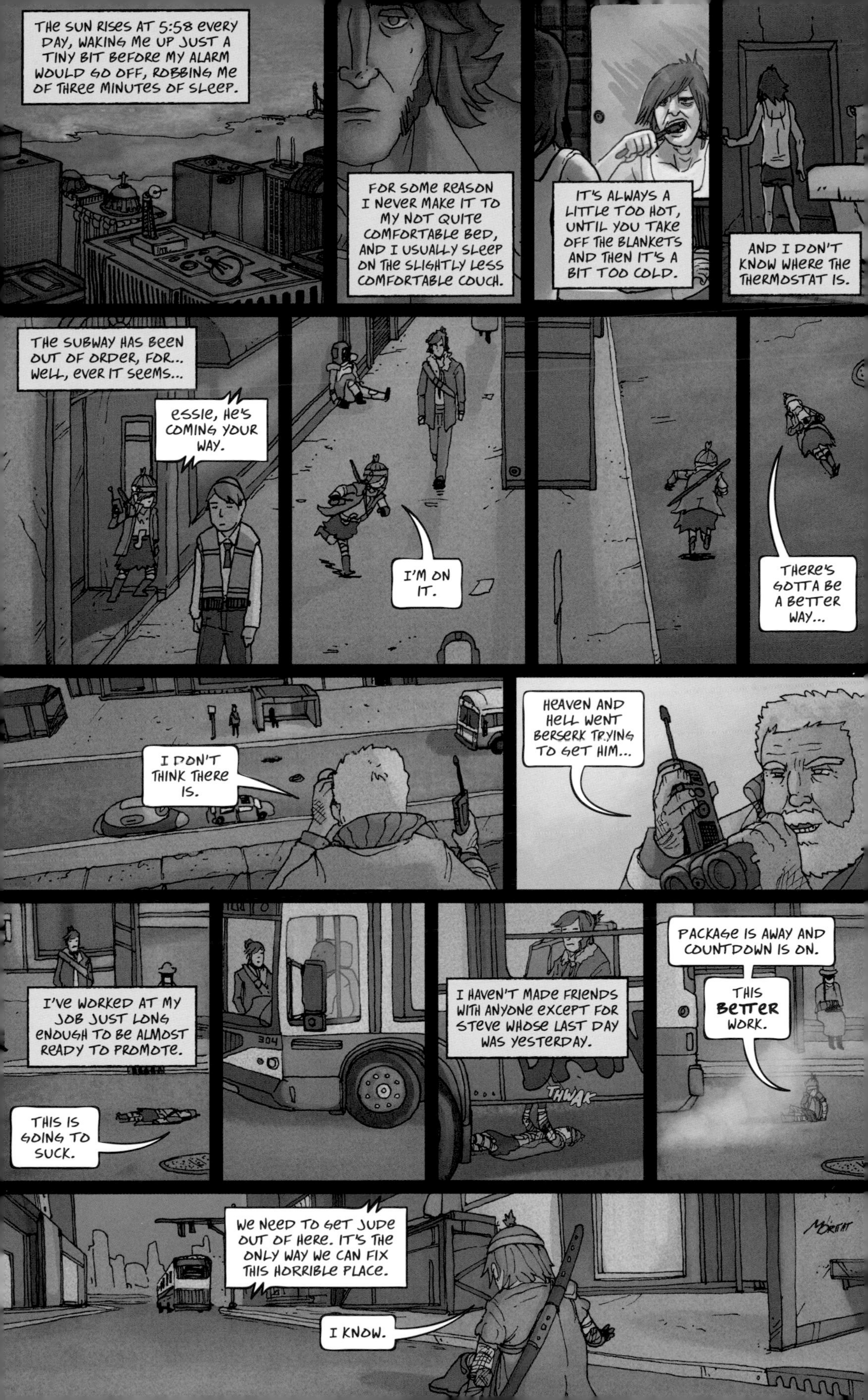
THE SUN RISES AT 5:58 EVERY DAY, WAKING ME UP JUST A TINY BIT BEFORE MY ALARM WOULD GO OFF, ROBBING ME OF THREE MINUTES OF SLEEP.
FOR SOME REASON I NEVER MAKE IT TO MY NOT QUITE COMFORTABLE BED, AND I USUALLY SLEEP ON THE SLIGHTLY LESS COMFORTABLE COUCH.
IT'S ALWAYS A LITTLE TOO HOT, UNTIL YOU TAKE OFF THE BLANKETS AND THEN IT'S A BIT TOO COLD.
AND I DON'T KNOW WHERE THE THERMOSTAT IS.
THE SUBWAY HAS BEEN OUT OF ORDER, FOR... WELL, EVER IT SEEMS...
ESSIE, HE'S COMING YOUR WAY.
I'M ON IT.
THERE'S GOTTA BE A BETTER WAY...
I DON'T THINK THERE IS.
HEAVEN AND HELL WENT BERSERK TRYING TO GET HIM...
I'VE WORKED AT MY JOB JUST LONG ENOUGH TO BE ALMOST READY TO PROMOTE.
THIS IS GOING TO SUCK.
304
I HAVEN'T MADE FRIENDS WITH ANYONE EXCEPT FOR STEVE WHOSE LAST DAY WAS YESTERDAY.
THWAK
PACKAGE IS AWAY AND COUNTDOWN IS ON.
THIS BETTER WORK.
WE NEED TO GET JUDE OUT OF HERE. IT'S THE ONLY WAY WE CAN FIX THIS HORRIBLE PLACE.
I KNOW.

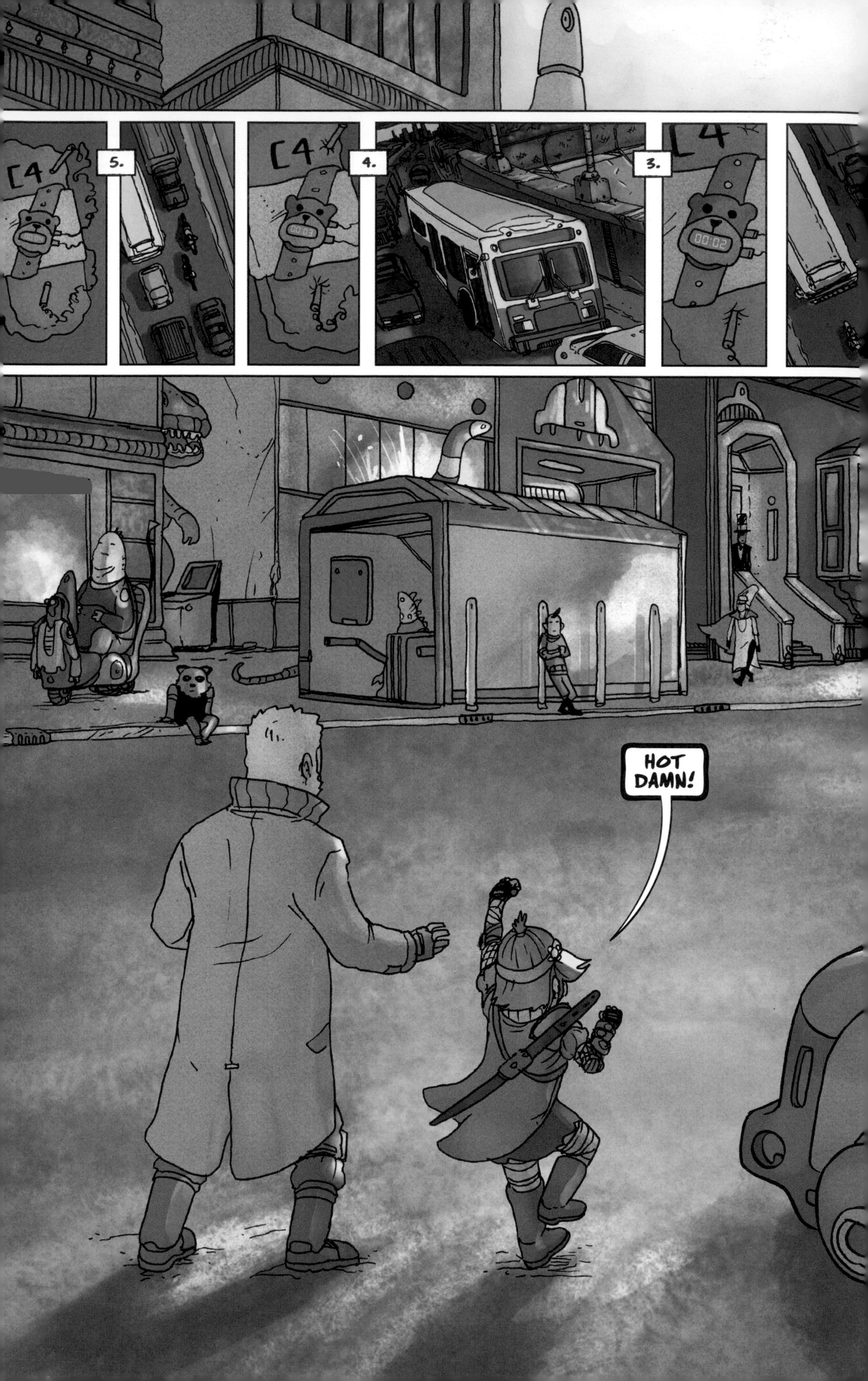

5.
4.
3.
HOT DAMN!

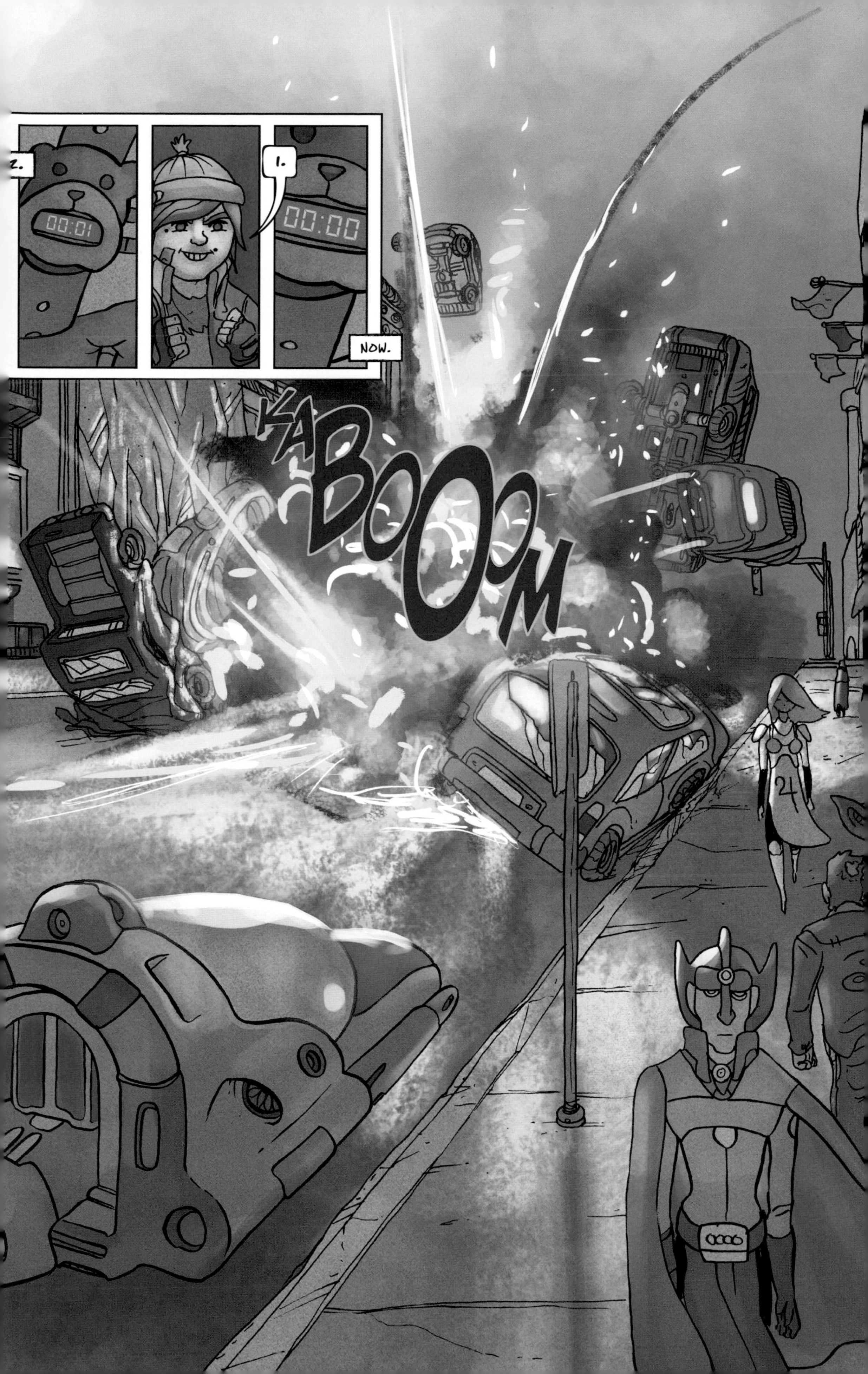
2.
00:01
1.
00:00
NOW.
KABOOOM

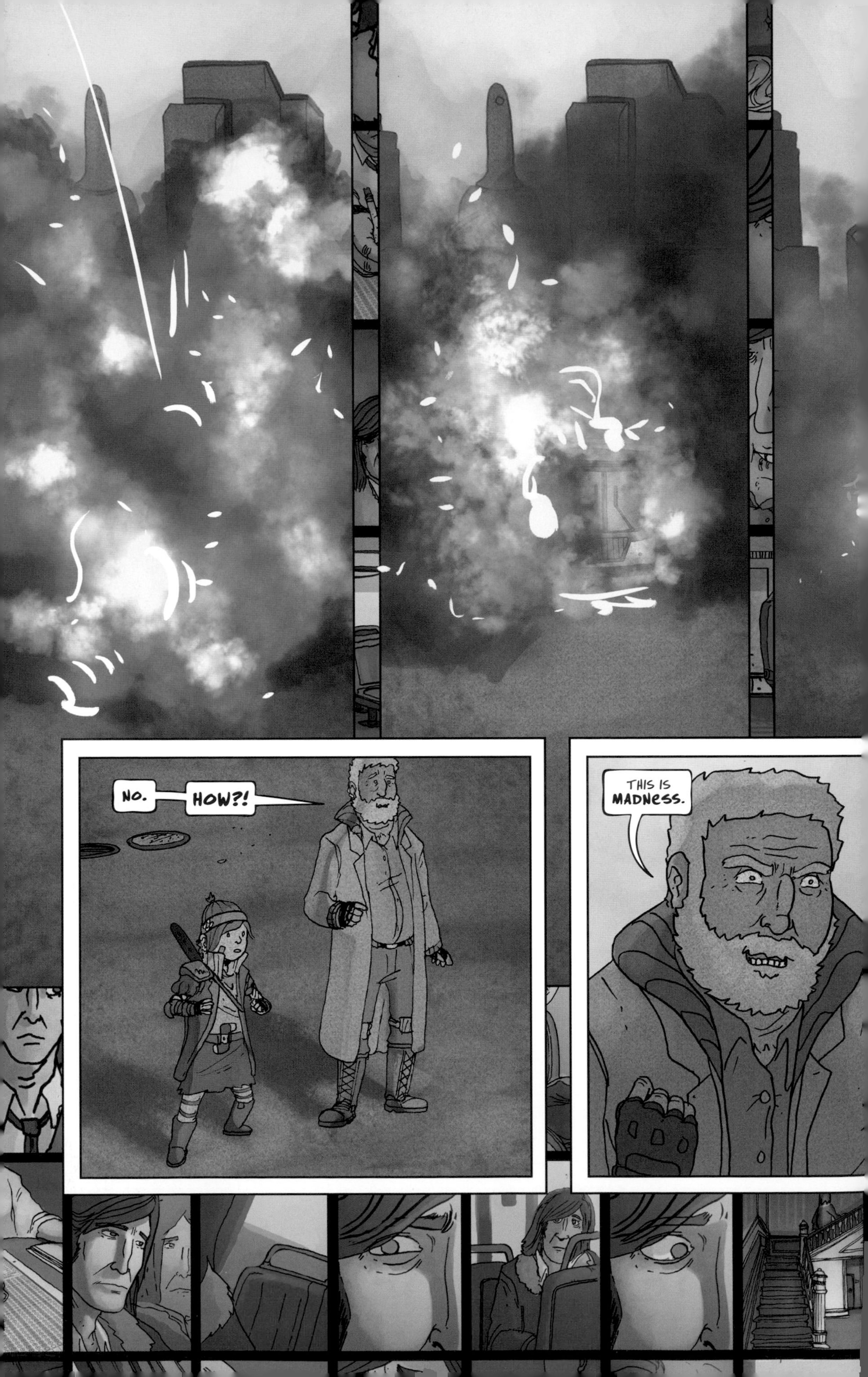
NO.
HOW?!
THIS IS MADNESS.

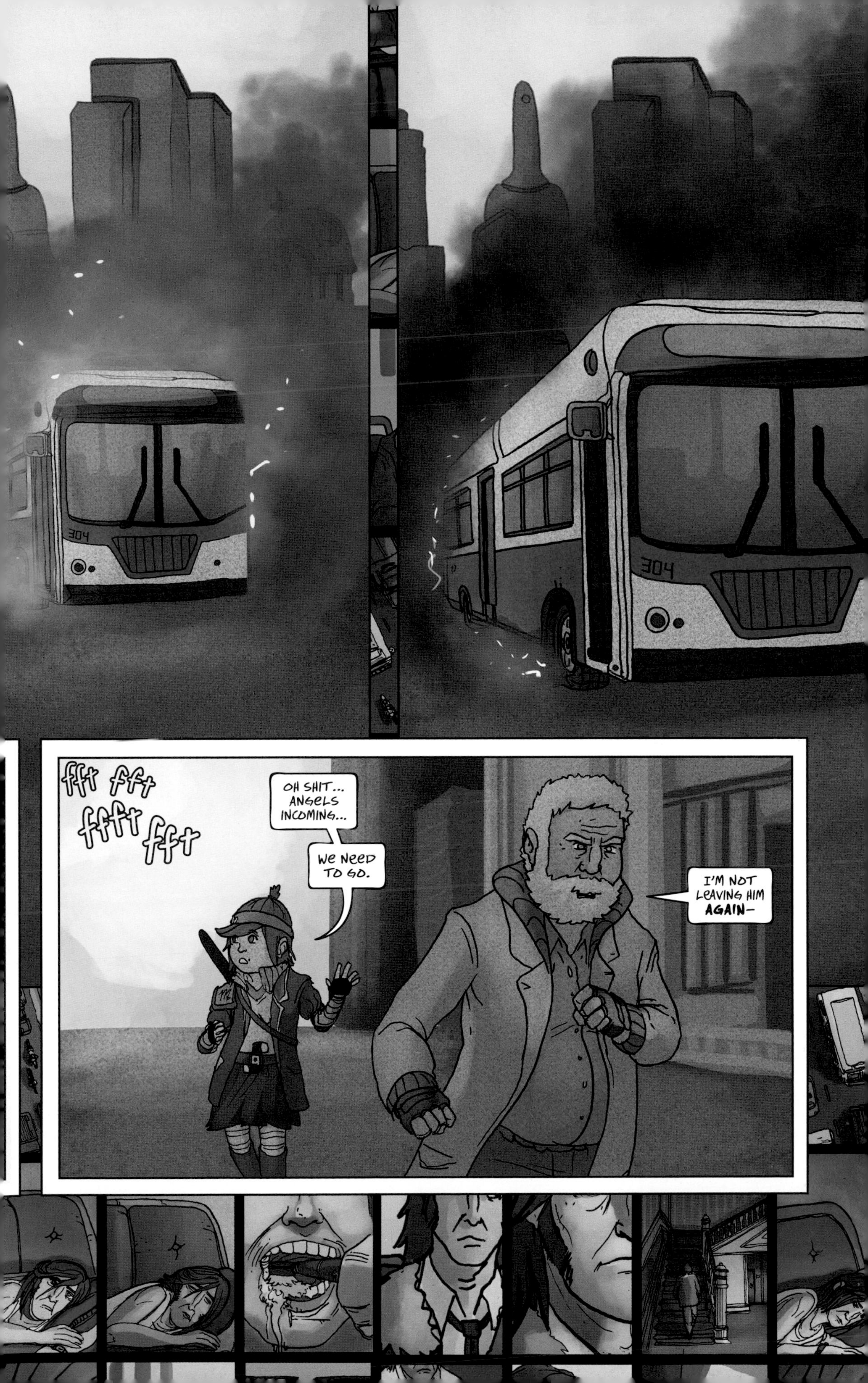
304
304
fft fft
ffft fft
OH SHIT... ANGELS INCOMING...
WE NEED TO GO.
I'M NOT LEAVING HIM AGAIN-

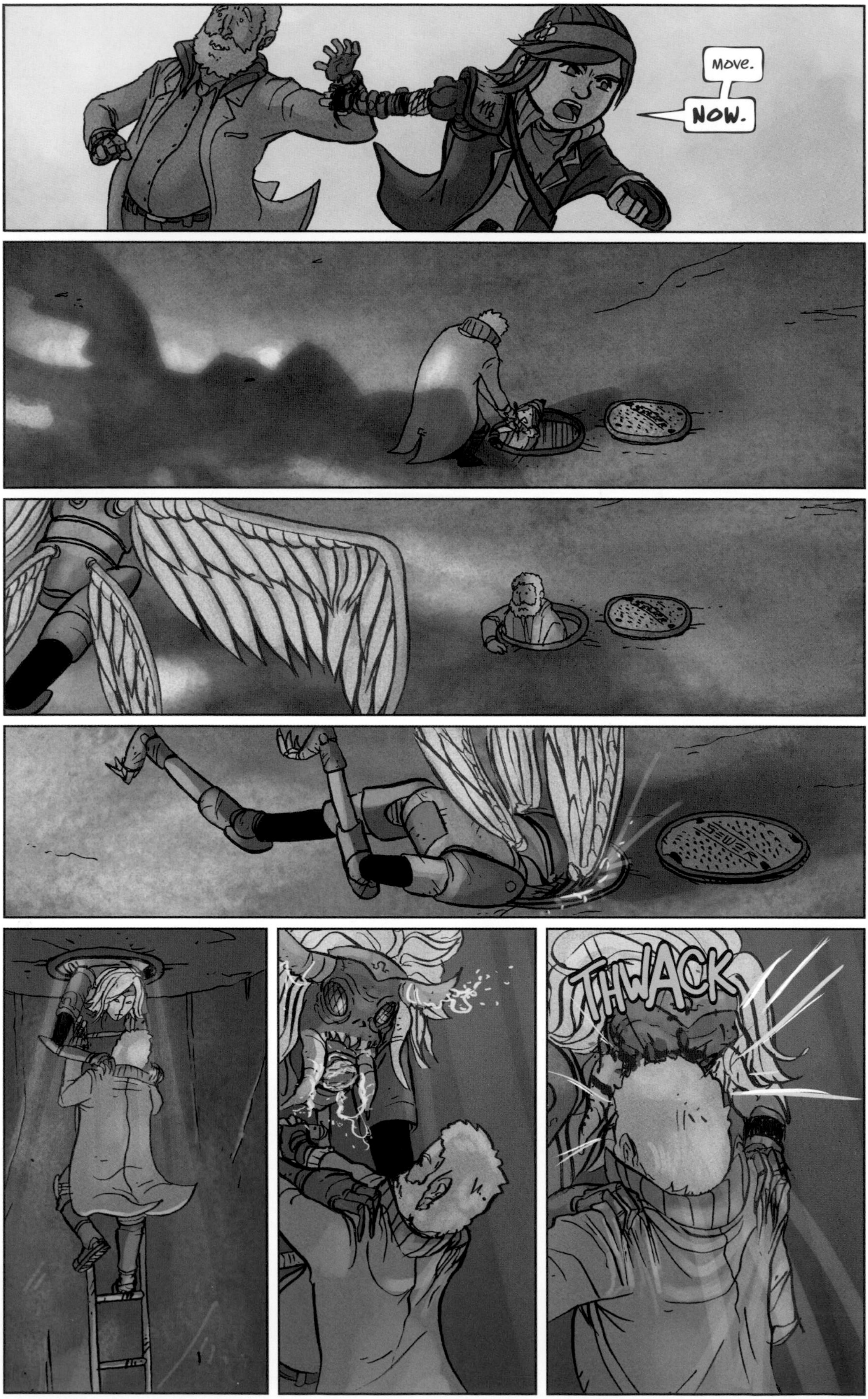
Move.
NOW.
SEWER
SEWER
SEWER
THWACK

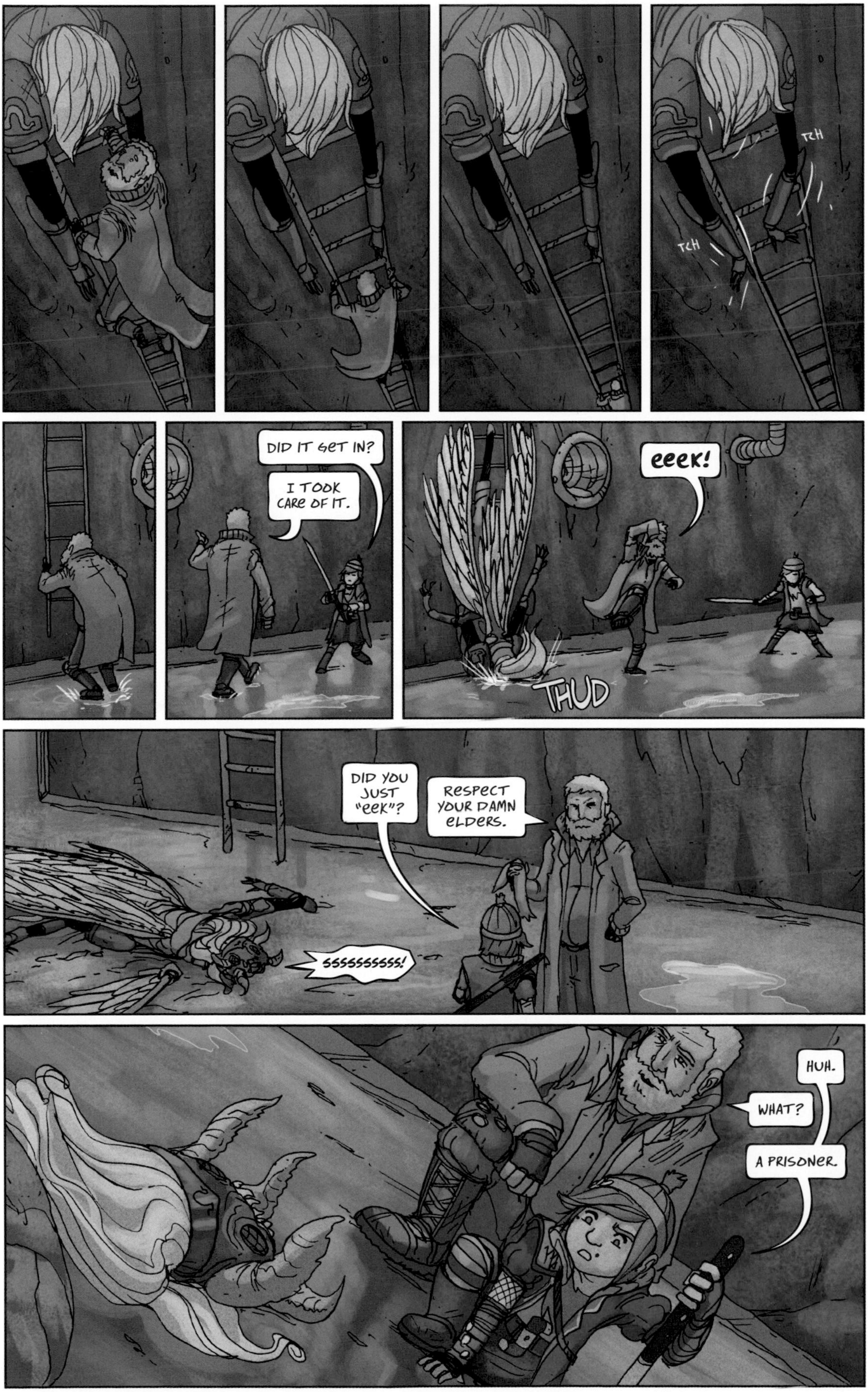
TCH
TCH
DID IT GET IN?
I TOOK CARE OF IT.
EEEK!
THUD
DID YOU JUST "EEK"?
RESPECT YOUR DAMN ELDERS.
SSSSSSSSSS!
HUH.
WHAT?
A PRISONER.

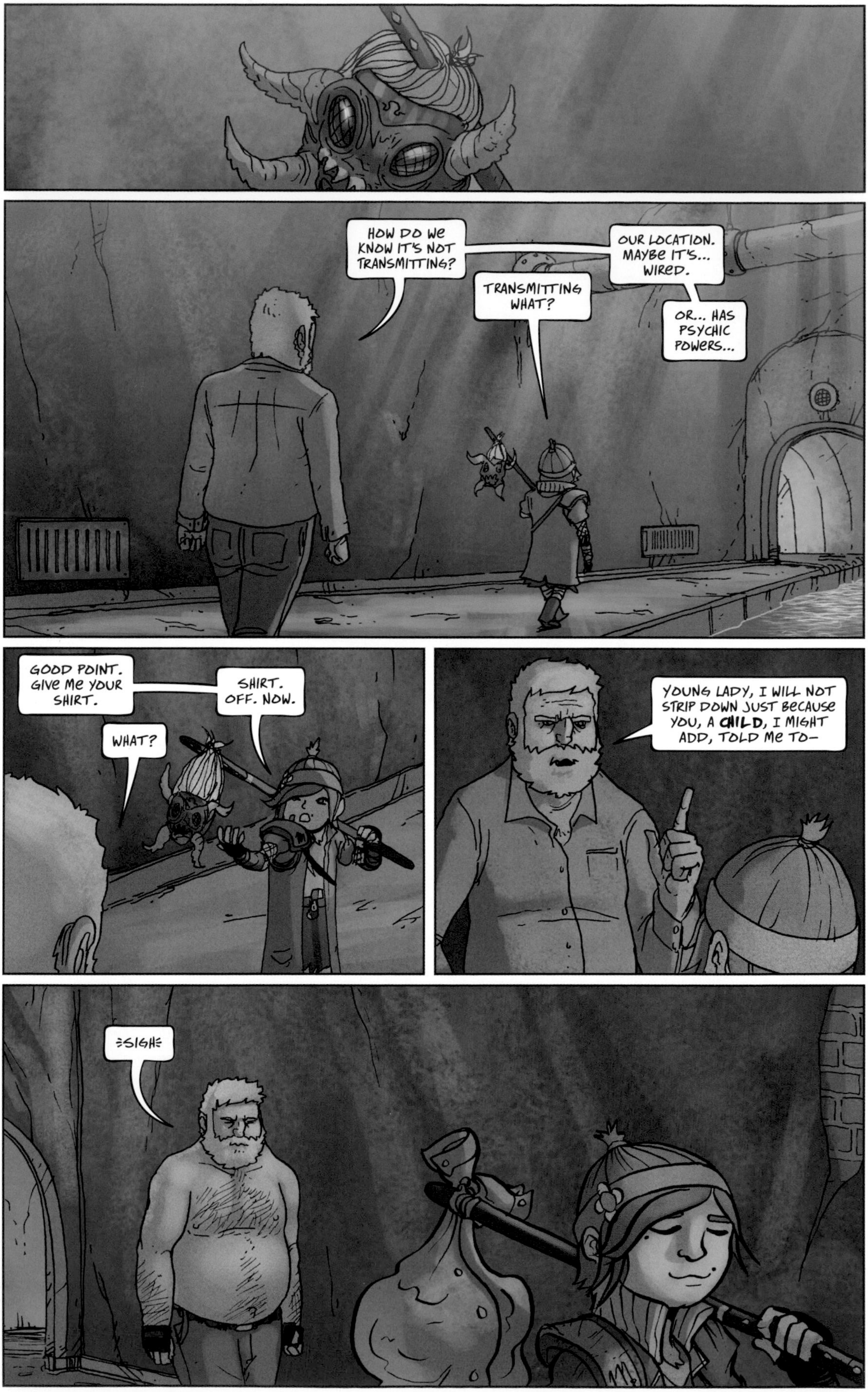
HOW DO WE KNOW IT'S NOT TRANSMITTING?
TRANSMITTING WHAT?
OUR LOCATION. MAYBE IT'S... WIRED.
OR... HAS PSYCHIC POWERS...
GOOD POINT. GIVE ME YOUR SHIRT.
WHAT?
SHIRT. OFF. NOW.
YOUNG LADY, I WILL NOT STRIP DOWN JUST BECAUSE YOU, A **CHILD**, I MIGHT ADD, TOLD ME TO—
=SIGH=

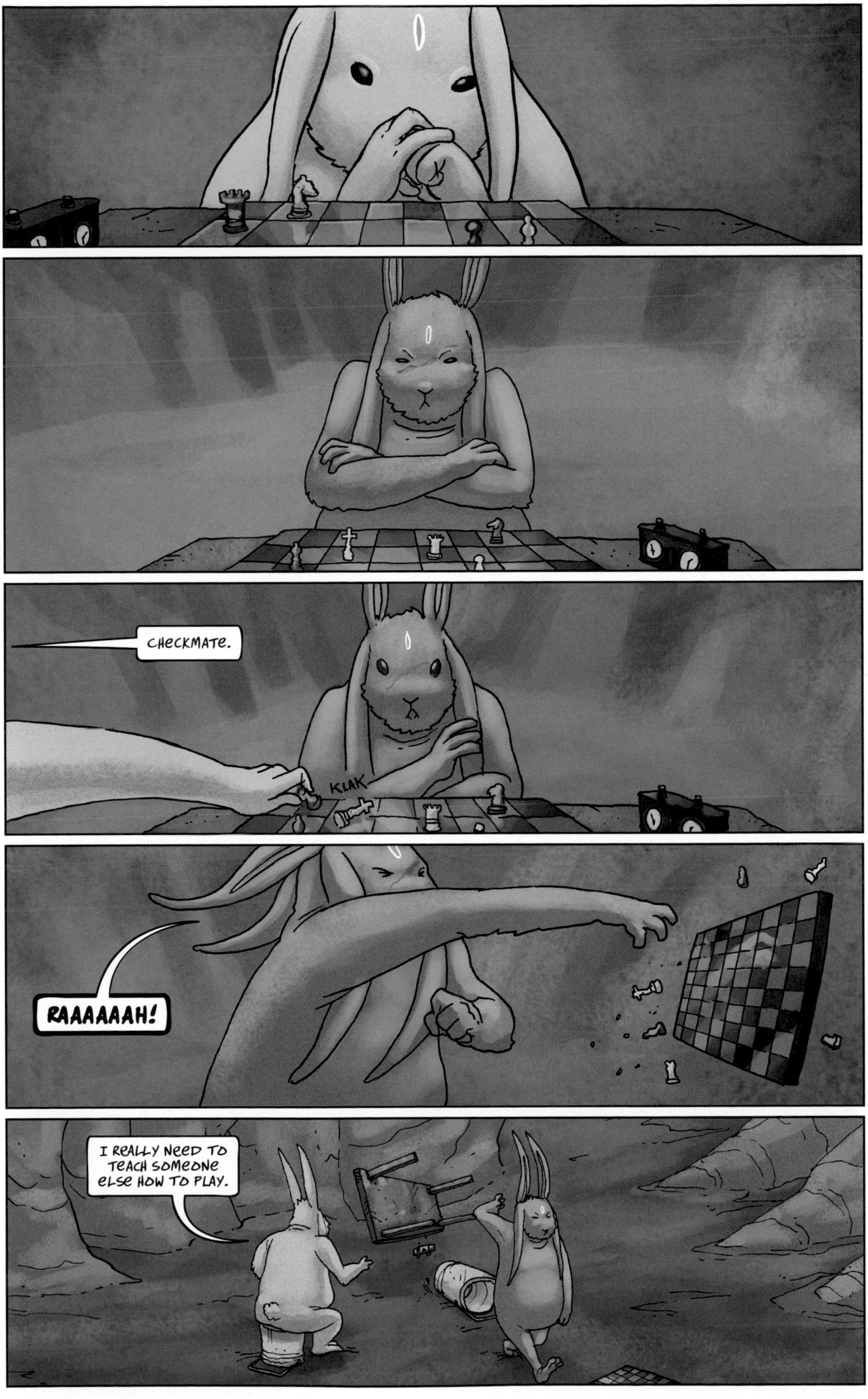
CHECKMATE.
KLAK
RAAAAAAH!
I REALLY NEED TO TEACH SOMEONE ELSE HOW TO PLAY.

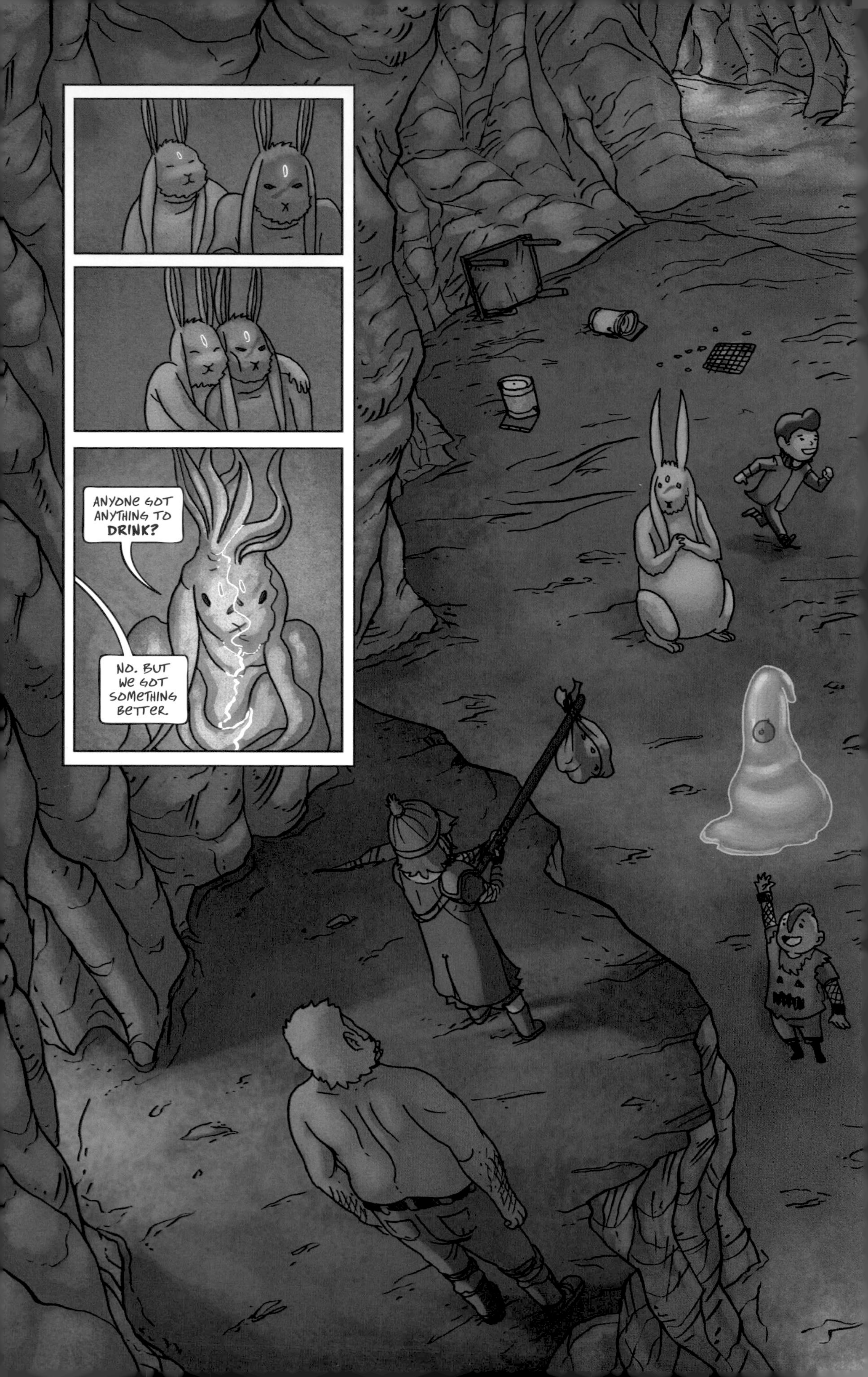
ANYONE GOT ANYTHING TO DRINK?
NO. BUT WE GOT SOMETHING BETTER.

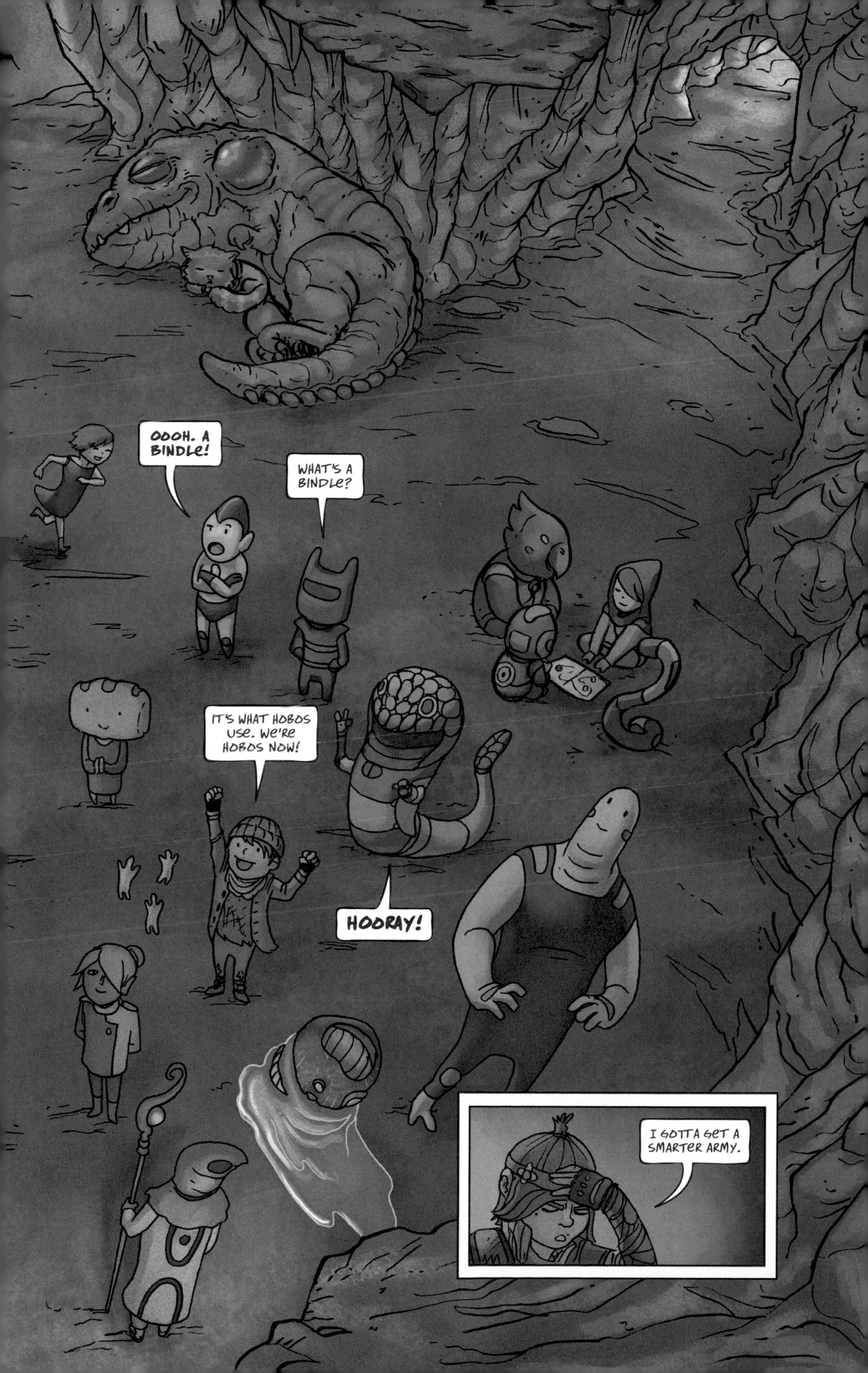
OOOH. A BINDLE!
WHAT'S A BINDLE?
IT'S WHAT HOBOS USE. WE'RE HOBOS NOW!
HOORAY!
I GOTTA GET A SMARTER ARMY.

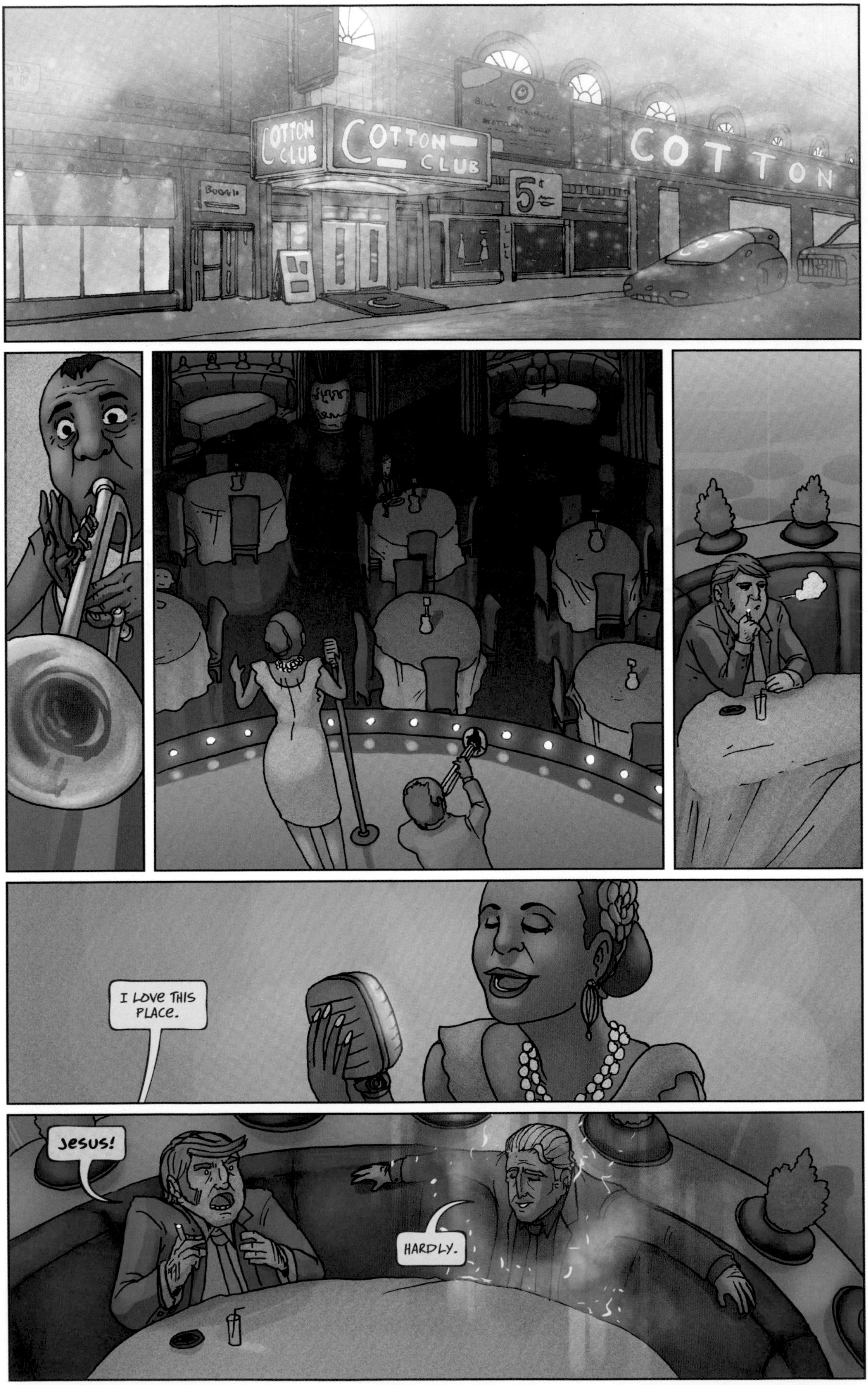
COTTON CLUB
COTTON CLUB
COTTON
I LOVE THIS PLACE.
JESUS!
HARDLY.

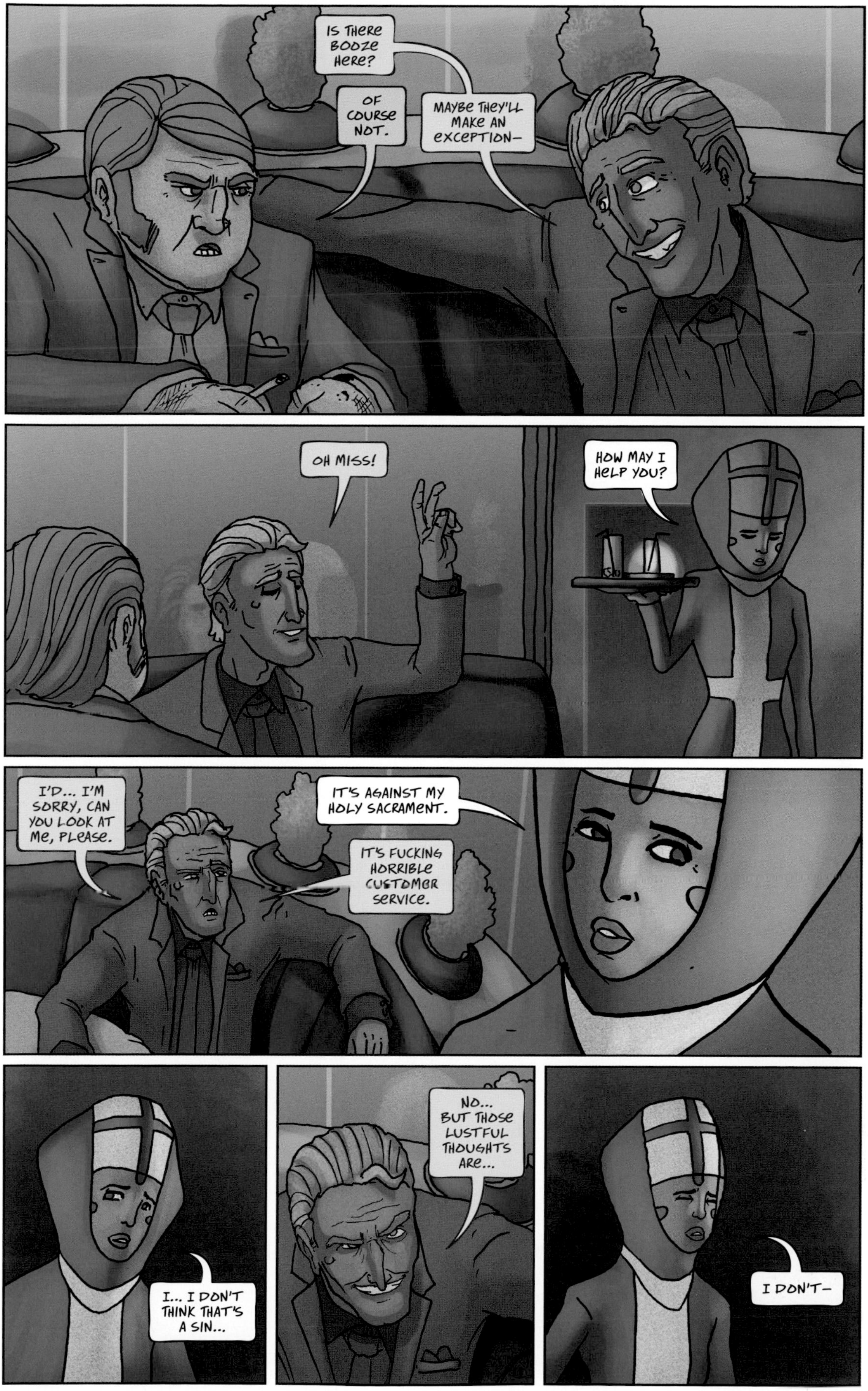
IS THERE BOOZE HERE?
OF COURSE NOT.
MAYBE THEY'LL MAKE AN EXCEPTION—
OH MISS!
HOW MAY I HELP YOU?
I'D... I'M SORRY, CAN YOU LOOK AT ME, PLEASE.
IT'S AGAINST MY HOLY SACRAMENT.
IT'S FUCKING HORRIBLE CUSTOMER SERVICE.
I... I DON'T THINK THAT'S A SIN...
NO... BUT THOSE LUSTFUL THOUGHTS ARE...
I DON'T—

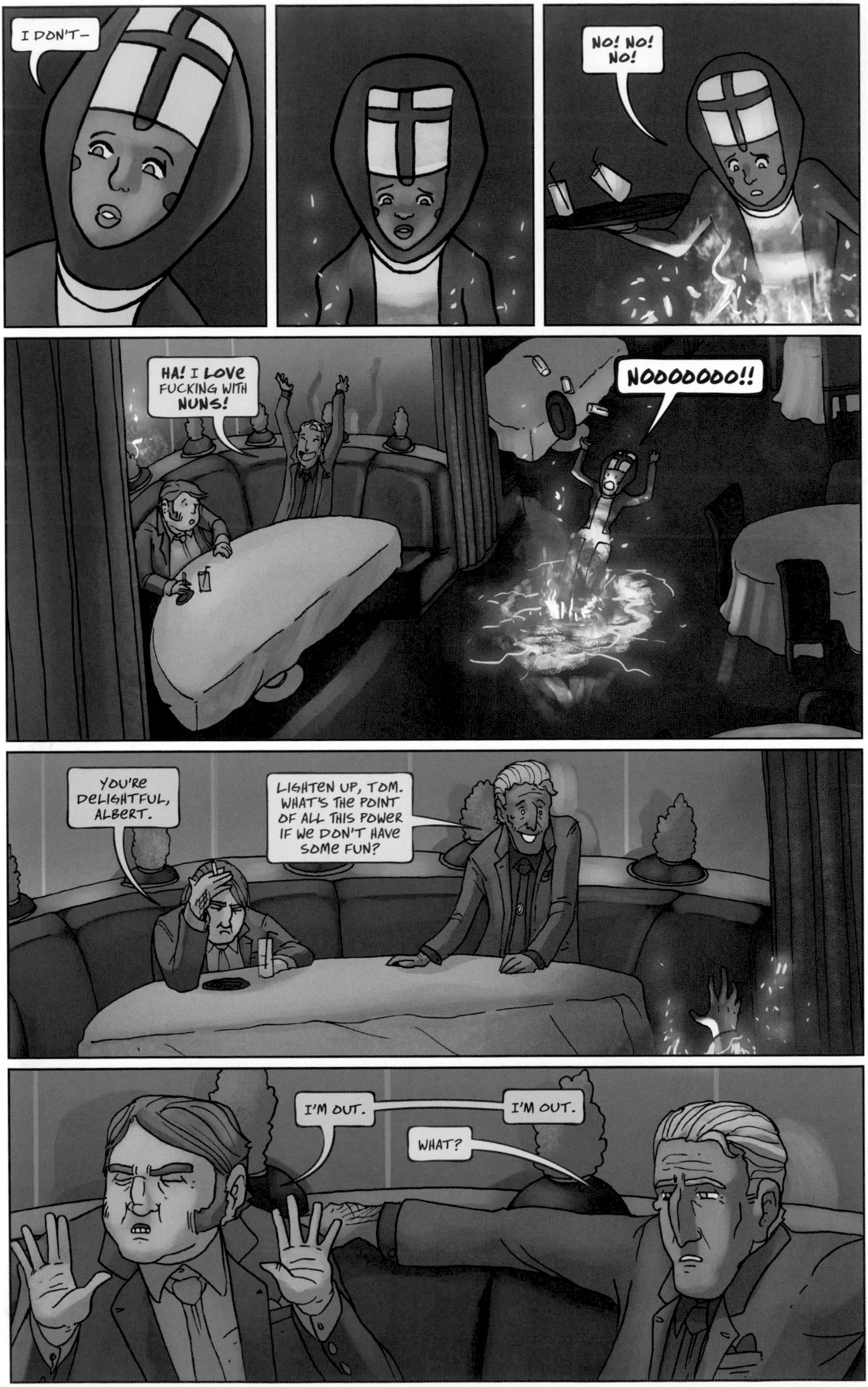
I DON'T–
NO! NO! NO!
HA! I LOVE FUCKING WITH NUNS!
NOOOOOOO!!
YOU'RE DELIGHTFUL, ALBERT.
LIGHTEN UP, TOM. WHAT'S THE POINT OF ALL THIS POWER IF WE DON'T HAVE SOME FUN?
I'M OUT.
I'M OUT.
WHAT?

YOU'RE NOT **OUT**. WE'RE ALREADY ALL IN—

THE KID IS **GONE**. I HAVE NO IDEA **WHERE** HE IS—

IF YOU THINK I'M GOING BACK TO MIDDLE MANAGEMENT BECAUSE **YOU** CAN'T DO YOUR **FUCKING JOB**—

DO IT, ALBERT. KILL ME. EAT ME. DRAG ME BACK TO YOUR HELL. WHATEVER. I DON'T CARE ANYMORE.

TOM. PLEASE. WE DON'T DIE. WE JUST GET WORSE JOBS.

LET'S DO THIS. I'LL SEND SOME MORE OF MY AGENTS TO HELP SEARCH PURGATORY, AND WE'LL FIND WHERE THE BIG GUY PUT HIM.

I...

FINE. YEAH. THAT'D BE GREAT.

TOM, HOSTILE TAKEOVERS COME WITH A PRICE. FOR US, THAT PRICE IS AGGRAVATION. WHICH, COMPARED TO OUR ETERNAL SOULS—

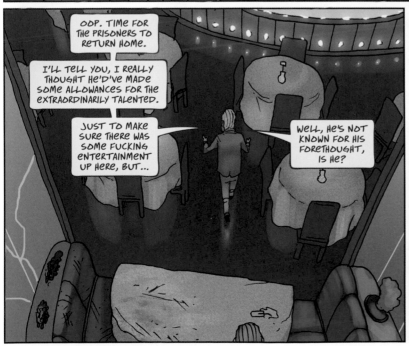

OOP. TIME FOR THE PRISONERS TO RETURN HOME.

I'LL TELL YOU, I REALLY THOUGHT HE'D'VE MADE SOME ALLOWANCES FOR THE EXTRAORDINARILY TALENTED.

JUST TO MAKE SURE THERE WAS SOME FUCKING ENTERTAINMENT UP HERE, BUT...

WELL, HE'S NOT KNOWN FOR HIS FORETHOUGHT, IS HE?

COME ALONG, MILES. TIME TO GO HOME.

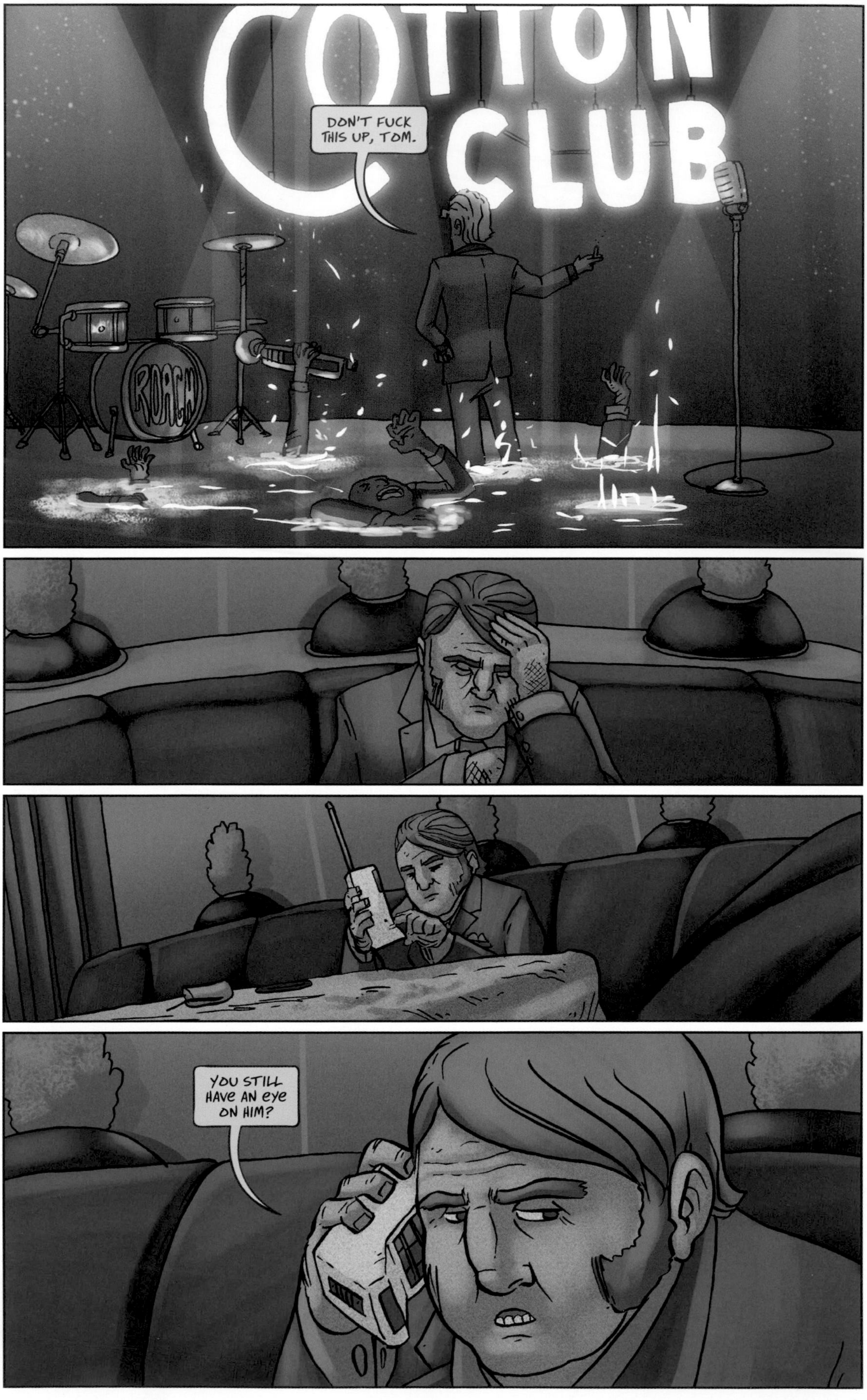
COTTON CLUB
DON'T FUCK THIS UP, TOM.
ROACH
YOU STILL HAVE AN EYE ON HIM?

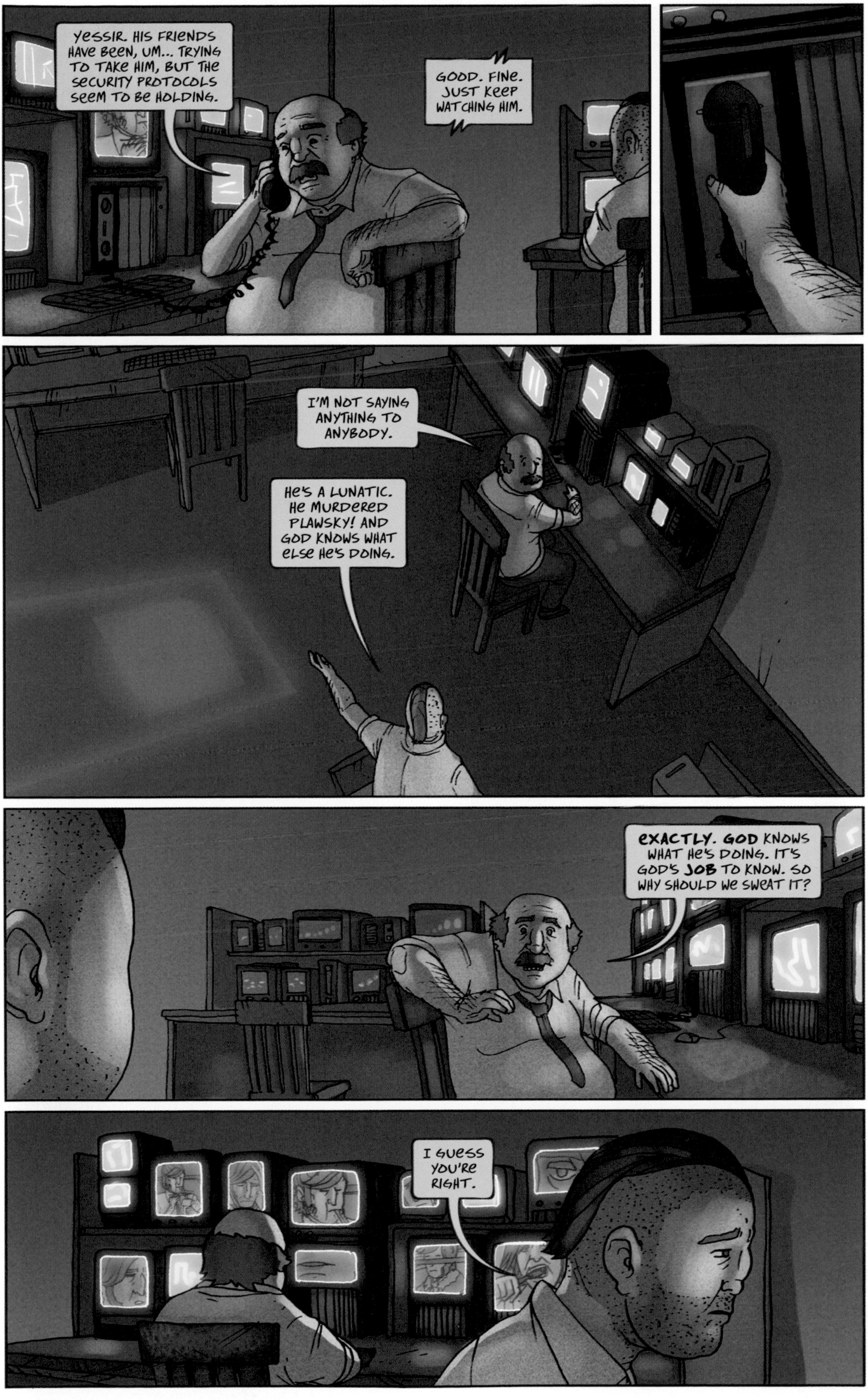
YESSIR. HIS FRIENDS HAVE BEEN, UM... TRYING TO TAKE HIM, BUT THE SECURITY PROTOCOLS SEEM TO BE HOLDING.
GOOD. FINE. JUST KEEP WATCHING HIM.
I'M NOT SAYING ANYTHING TO ANYBODY.
HE'S A LUNATIC. HE MURDERED PLAWSKY! AND GOD KNOWS WHAT ELSE HE'S DOING.
EXACTLY. GOD KNOWS WHAT HE'S DOING. IT'S GOD'S JOB TO KNOW. SO WHY SHOULD WE SWEAT IT?
I GUESS YOU'RE RIGHT.

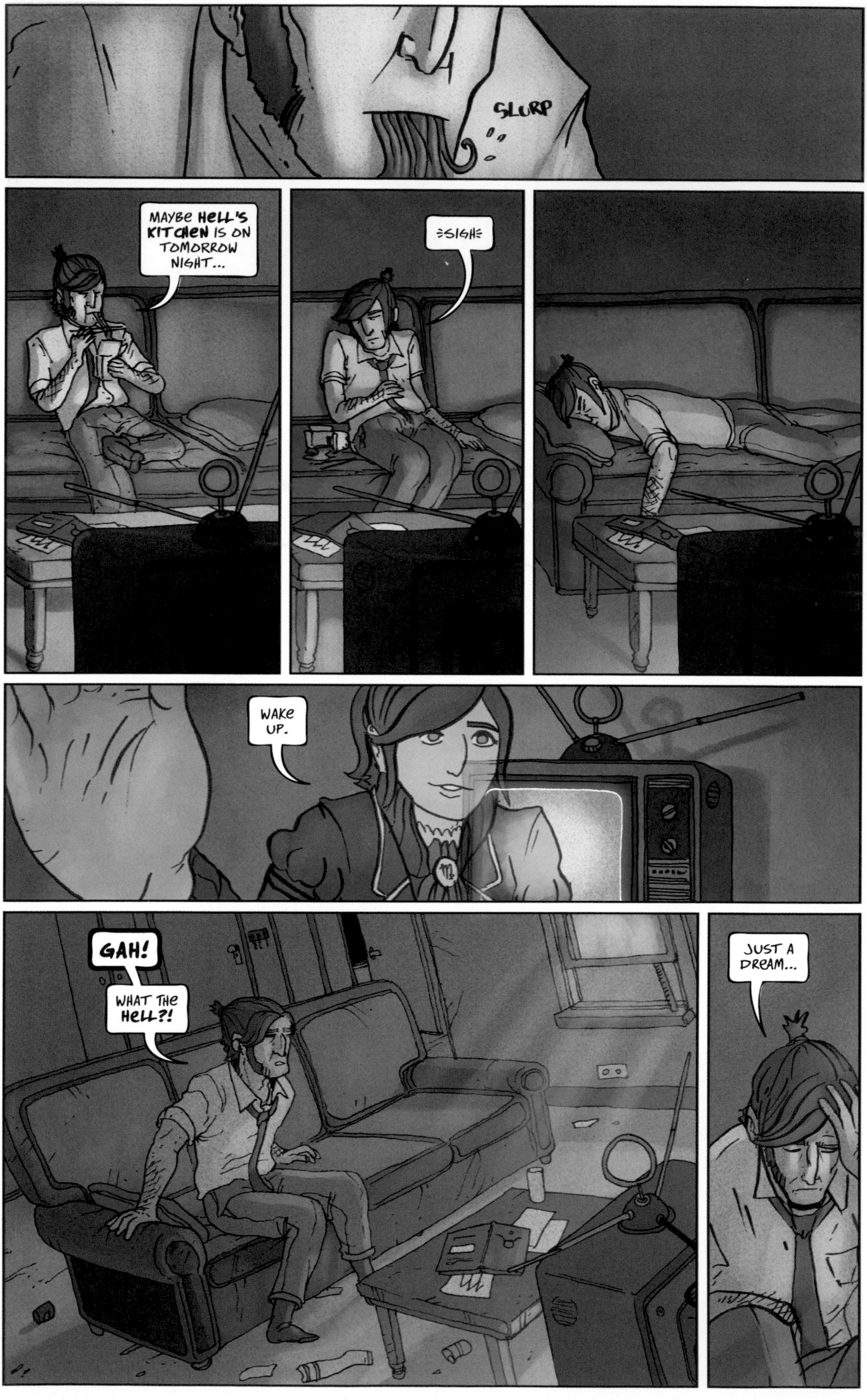
SLURP
MAYBE HELL'S KITCHEN IS ON TOMORROW NIGHT...
=SIGH=
WAKE UP.
GAH!
WHAT THE HELL?!
JUST A DREAM...

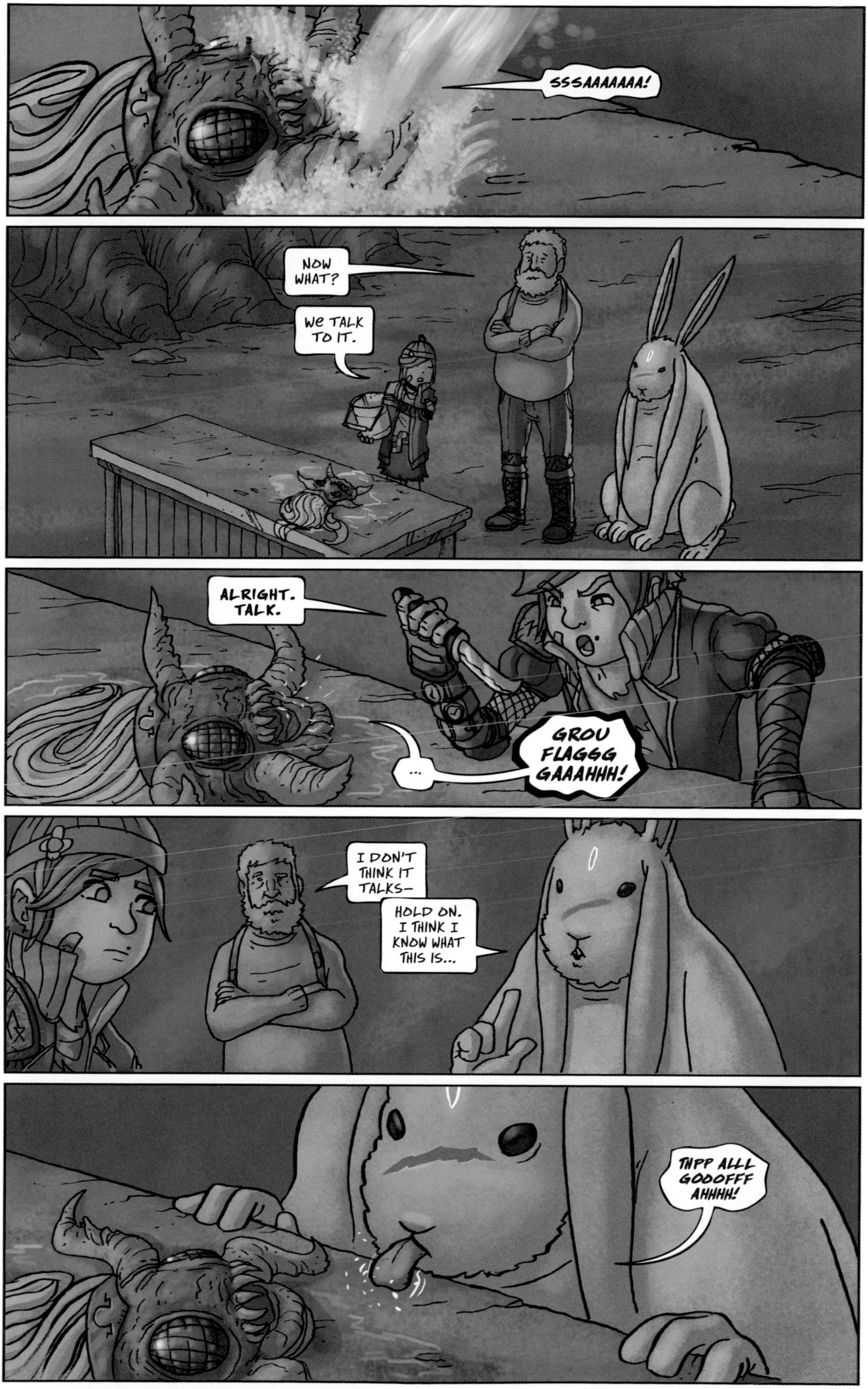
SSSAAAAAAA!
NOW WHAT?
WE TALK TO IT.
ALRIGHT. TALK.
...
GROU FLAGGG GAAAHHH!
I DON'T THINK IT TALKS–
HOLD ON. I THINK I KNOW WHAT THIS IS...
THPP ALLL GOOOFFF AHHHH!

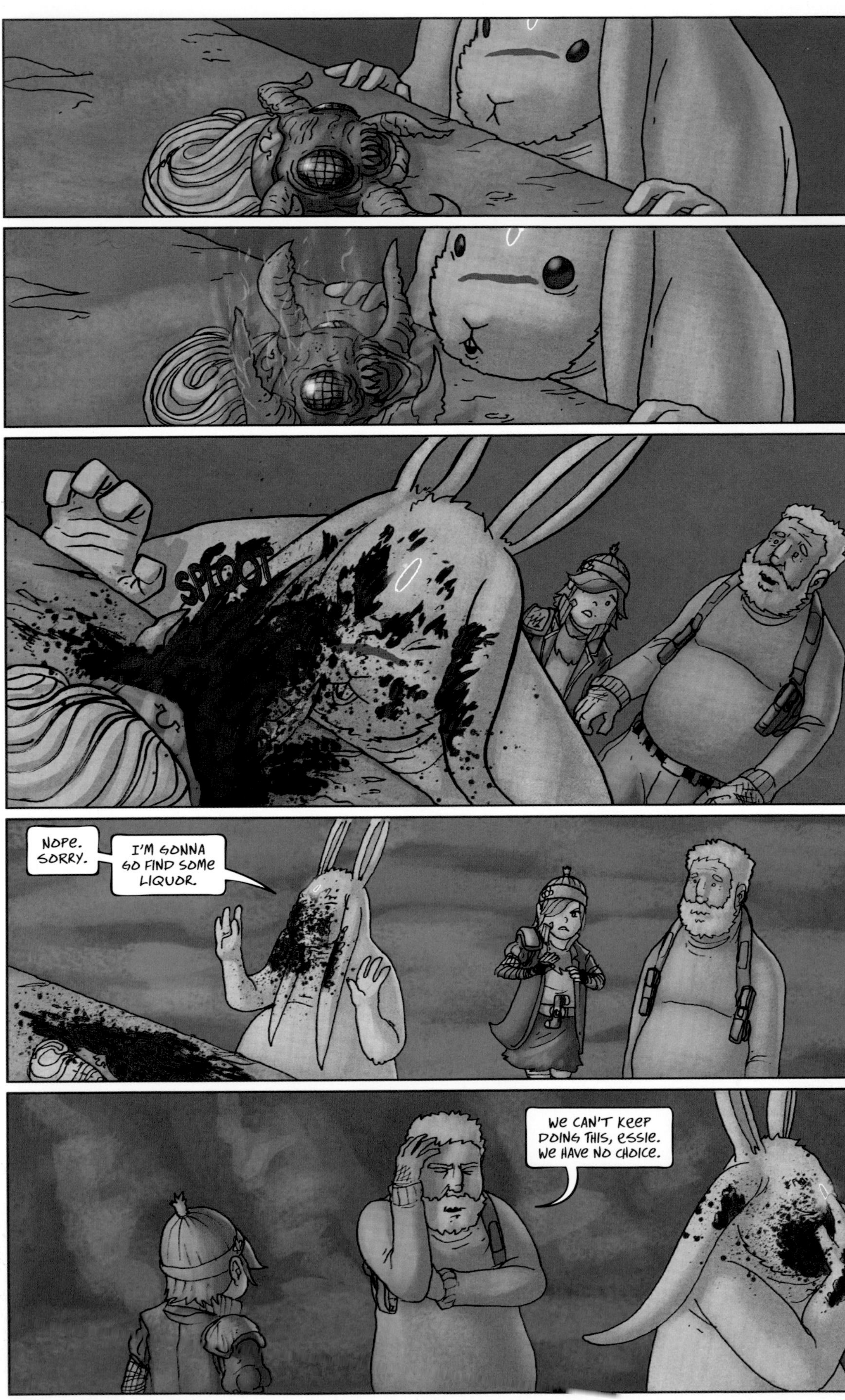
SPLOOT
NOPE. SORRY.
I'M GONNA GO FIND SOME LIQUOR.
WE CAN'T KEEP DOING THIS, ESSIE. WE HAVE NO CHOICE.

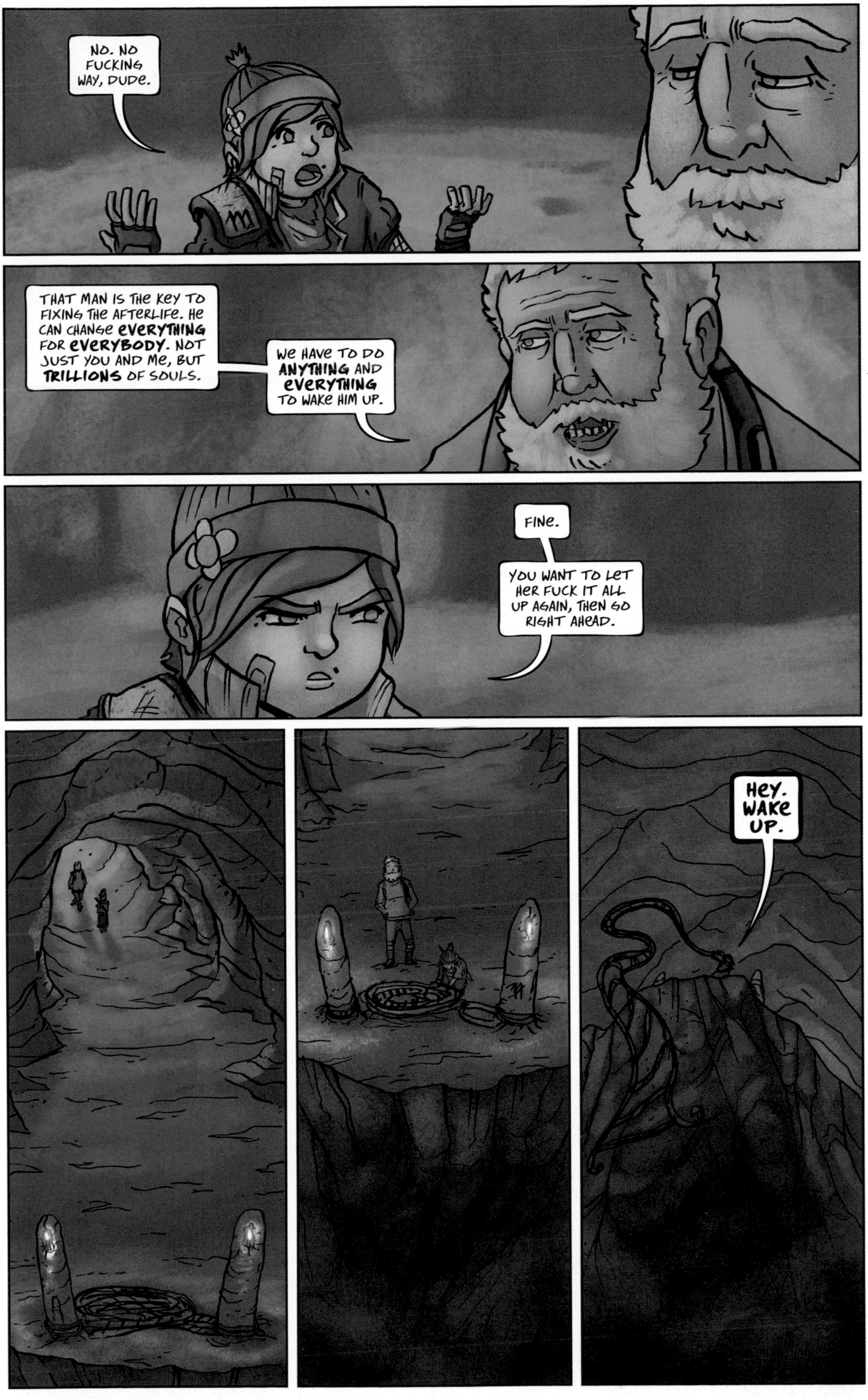
NO. NO FUCKING WAY, DUDE.
THAT MAN IS THE KEY TO FIXING THE AFTERLIFE. HE CAN CHANGE EVERYTHING FOR EVERYBODY. NOT JUST YOU AND ME, BUT TRILLIONS OF SOULS.
WE HAVE TO DO ANYTHING AND EVERYTHING TO WAKE HIM UP.
FINE.
YOU WANT TO LET HER FUCK IT ALL UP AGAIN, THEN GO RIGHT AHEAD.
HEY. WAKE UP.

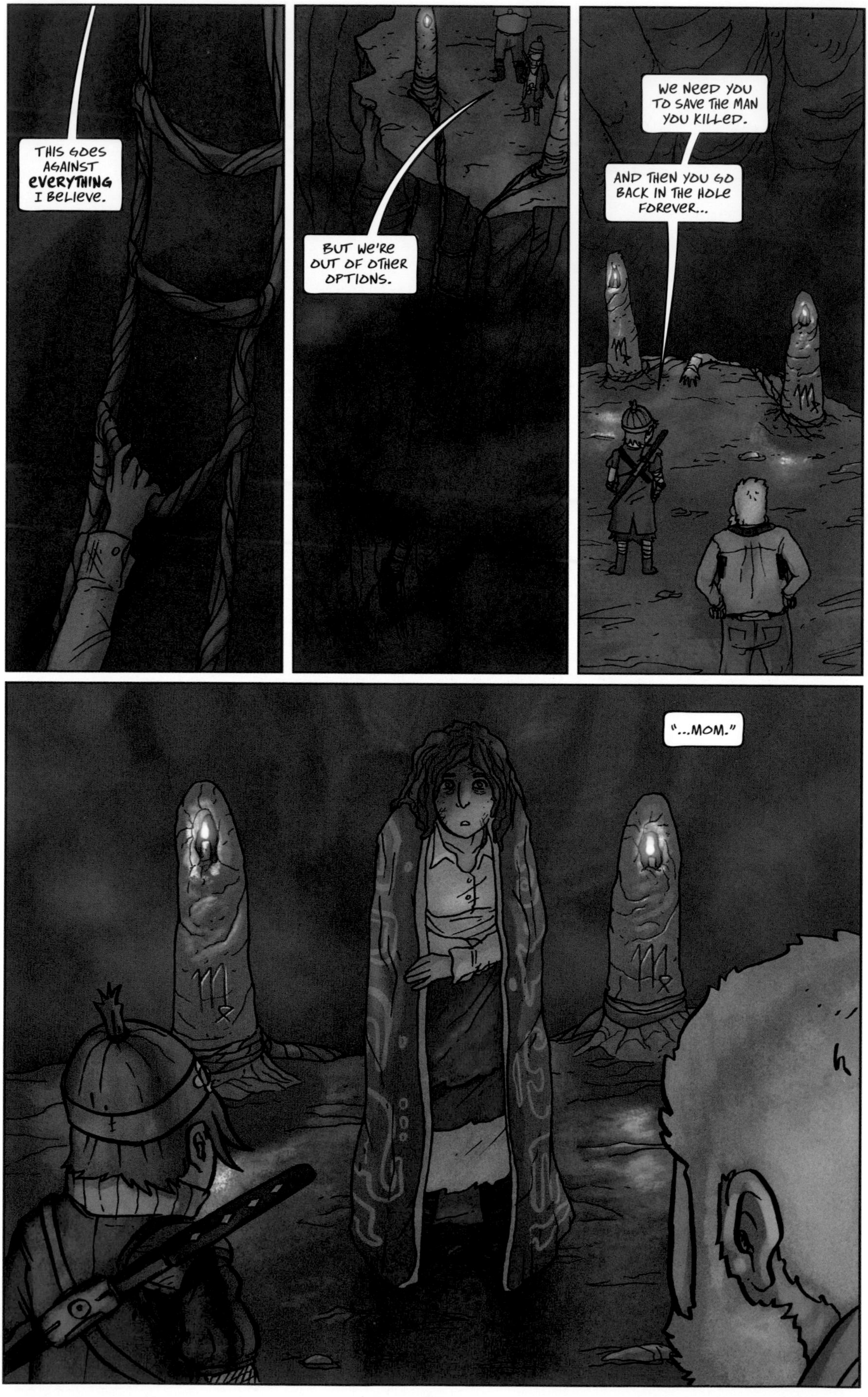
THIS GOES AGAINST EVERYTHING I BELIEVE.
BUT WE'RE OUT OF OTHER OPTIONS.
WE NEED YOU TO SAVE THE MAN YOU KILLED.
AND THEN YOU GO BACK IN THE HOLE FOREVER...
"...MOM."

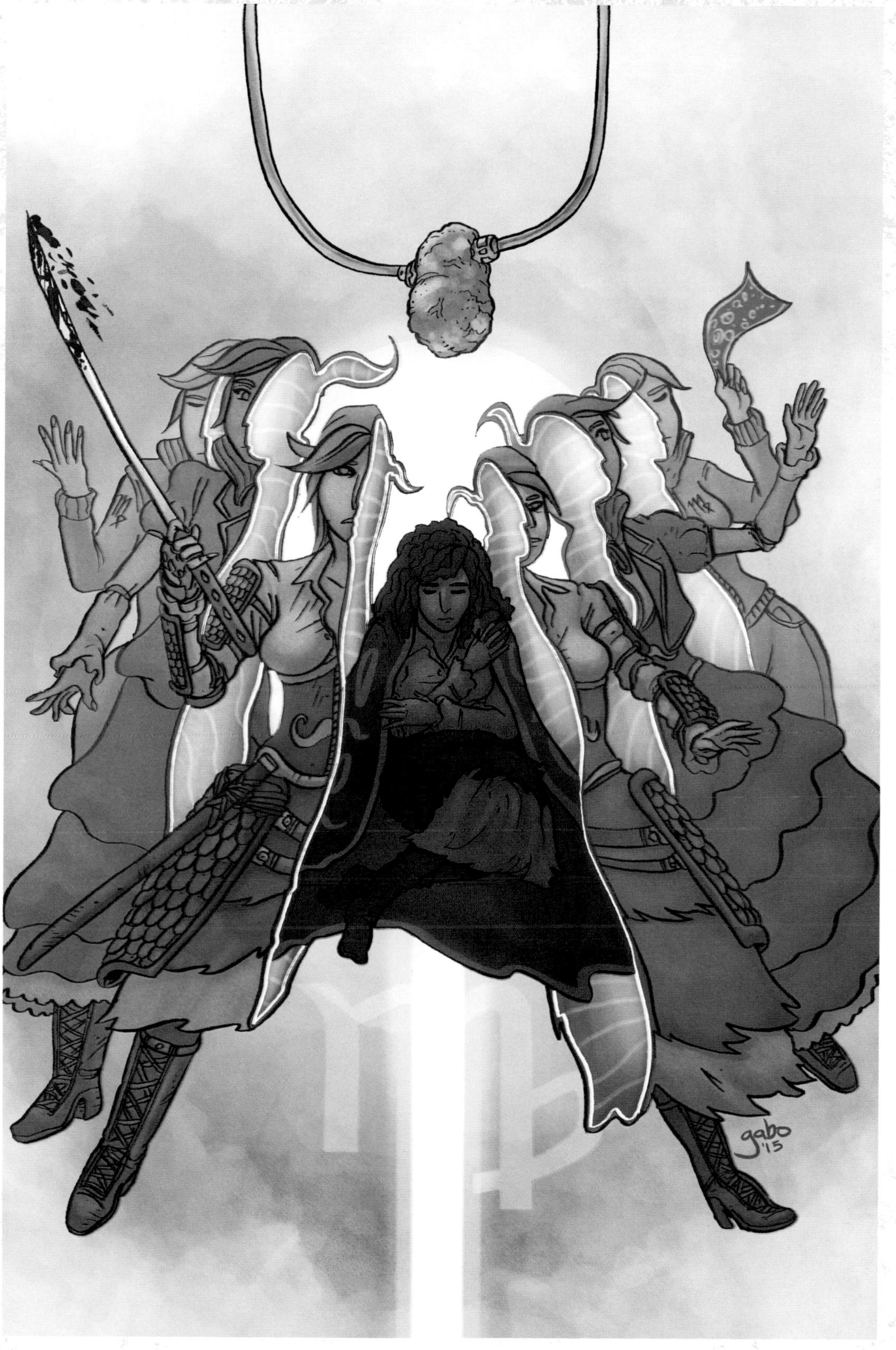

Chapter Twelve

THE LIFE
AFTER

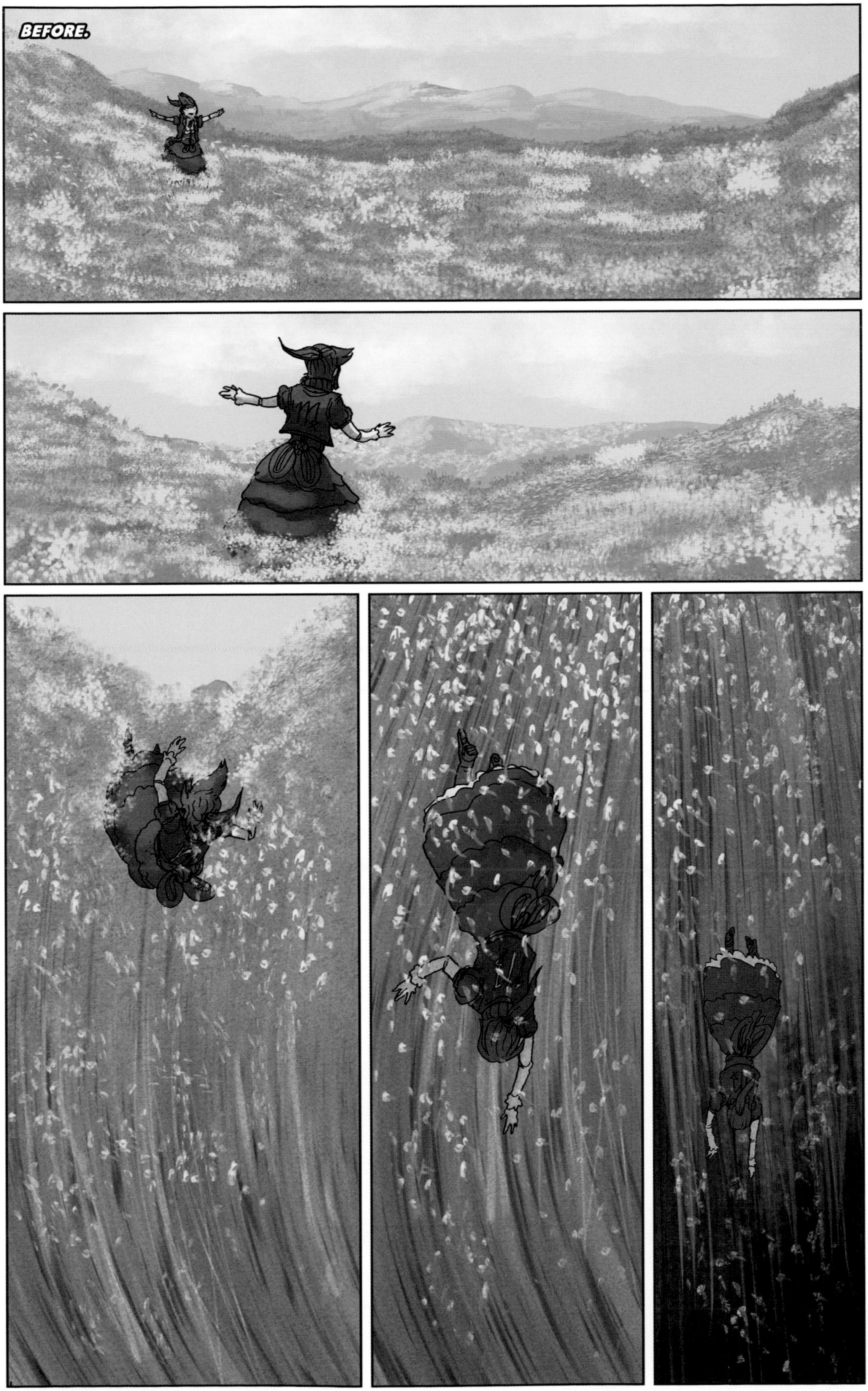
BEFORE.

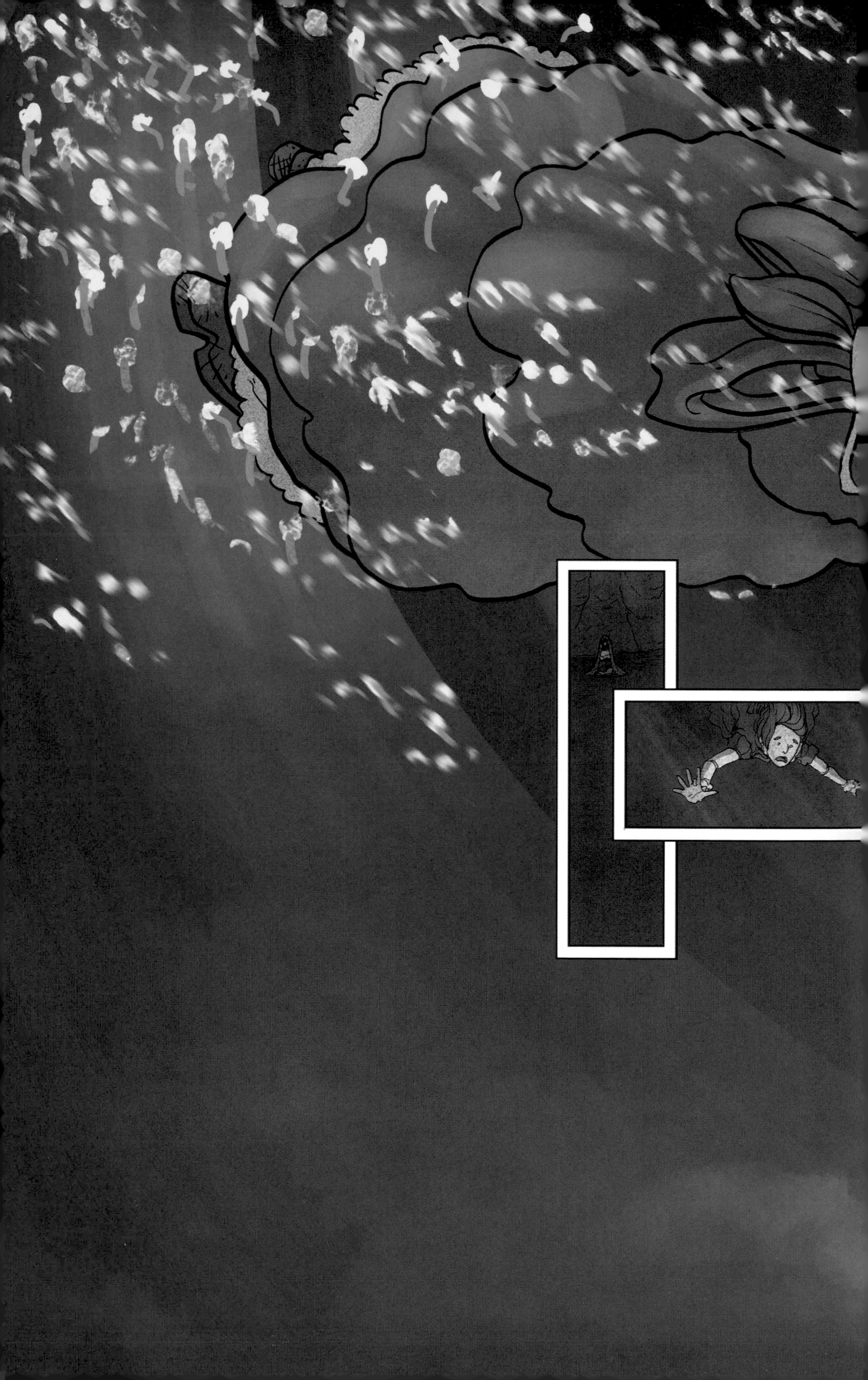

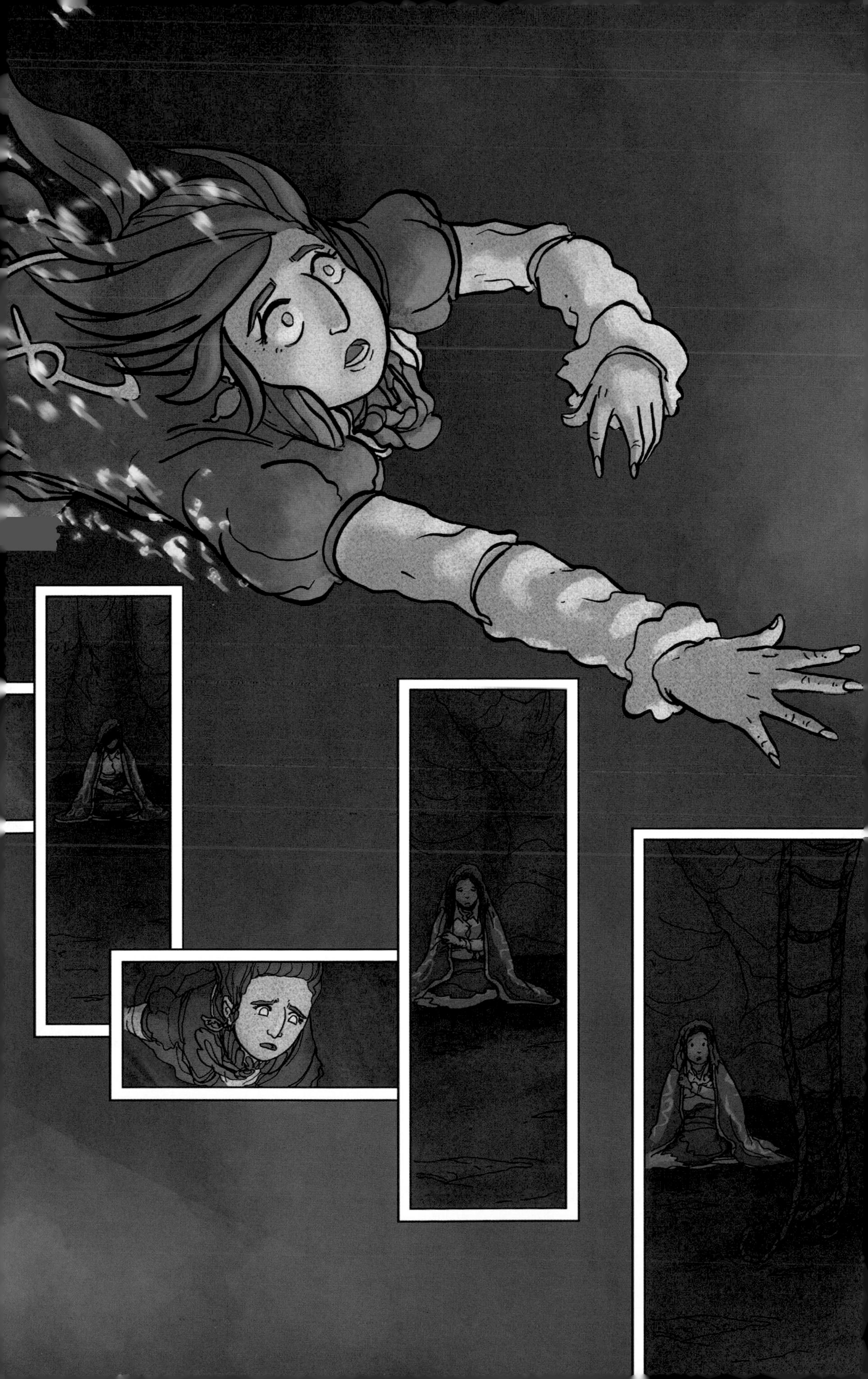

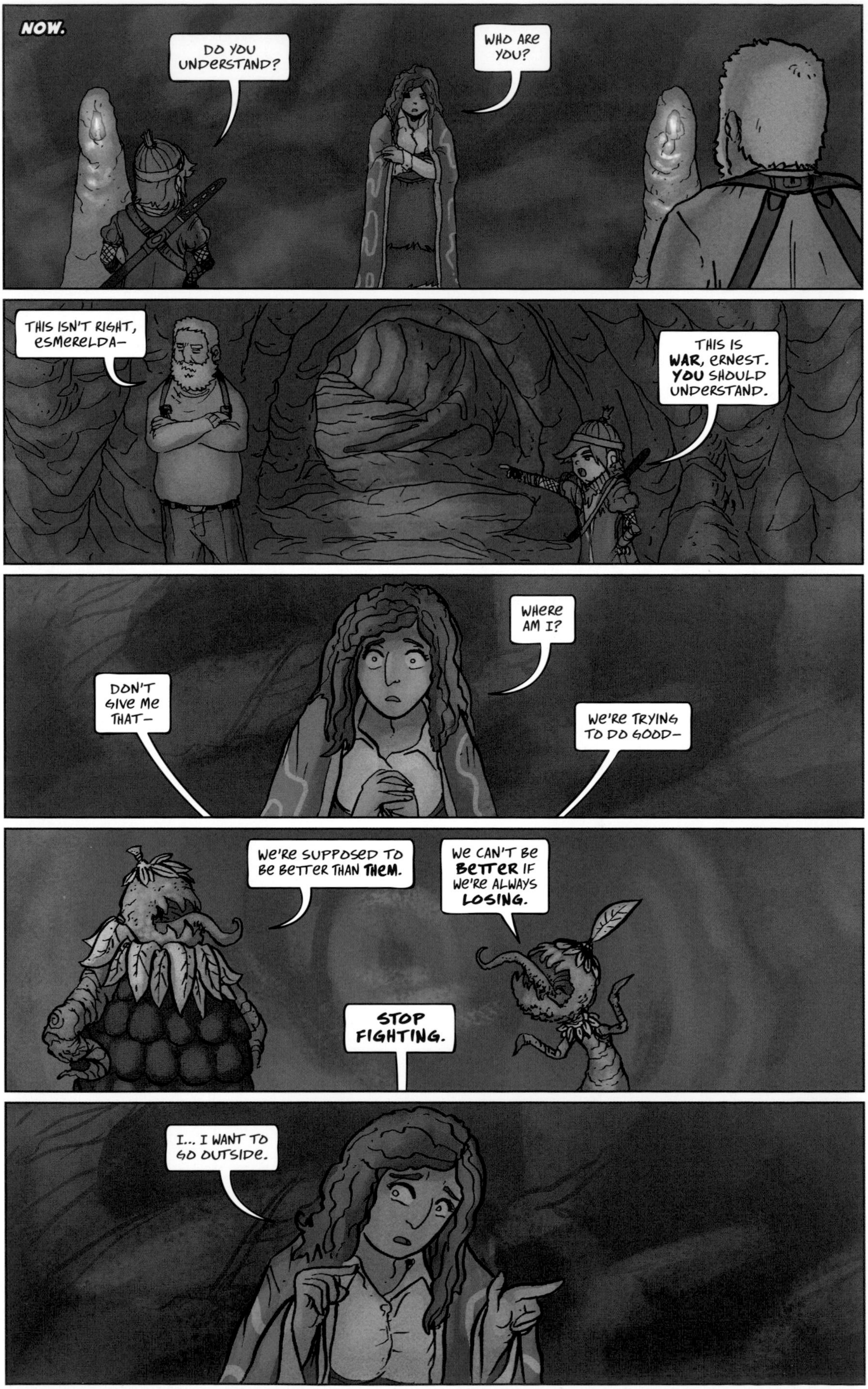
NOW.
DO YOU UNDERSTAND?
WHO ARE YOU?
THIS ISN'T RIGHT, ESMERELDA—
THIS IS WAR, ERNEST. YOU SHOULD UNDERSTAND.
WHERE AM I?
DON'T GIVE ME THAT—
WE'RE TRYING TO DO GOOD—
WE'RE SUPPOSED TO BE BETTER THAN THEM.
WE CAN'T BE BETTER IF WE'RE ALWAYS LOSING.
STOP FIGHTING.
I... I WANT TO GO OUTSIDE.

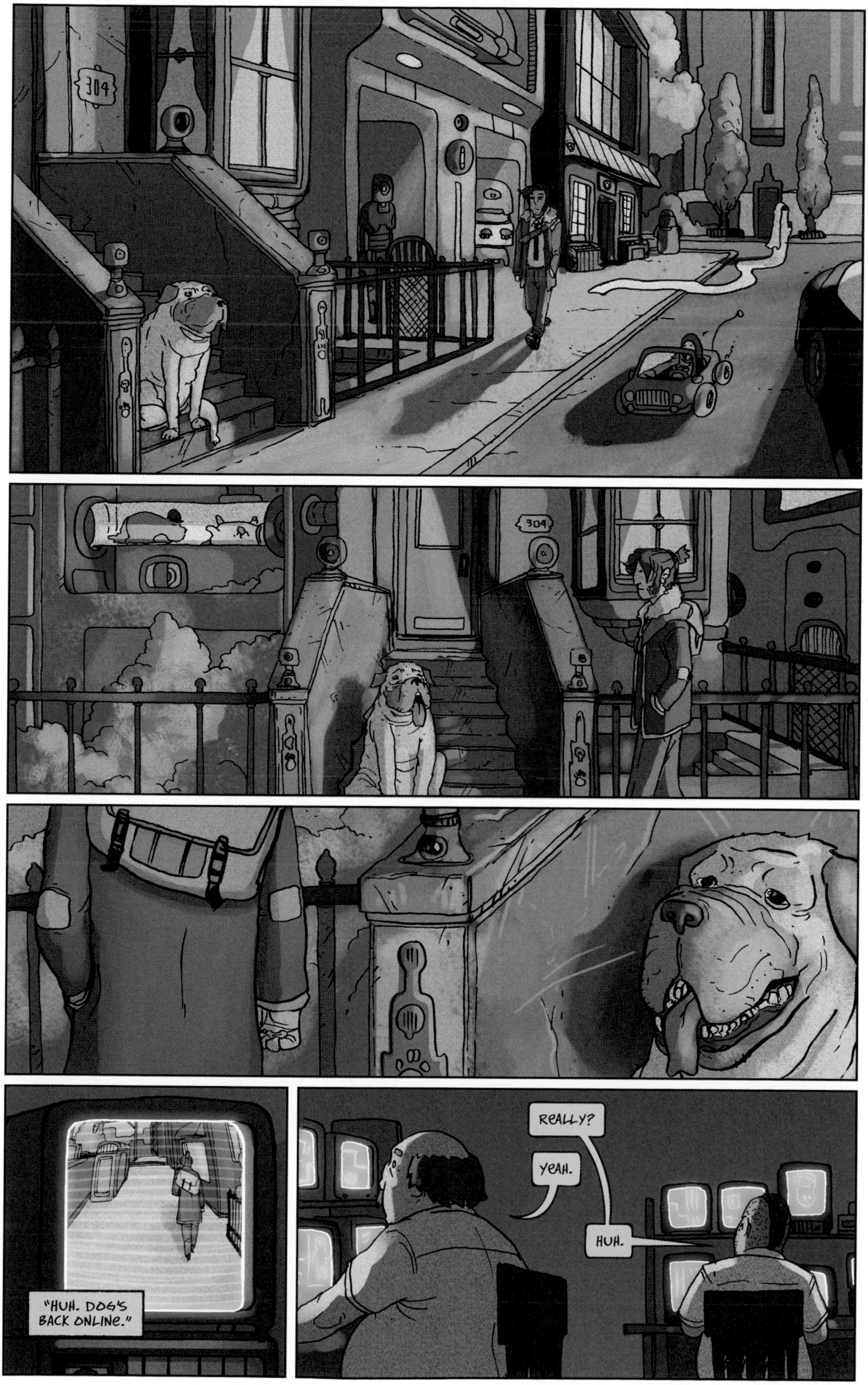

304
304
"HUH. DOG'S BACK ONLINE."
REALLY?
YEAH.
HUH.

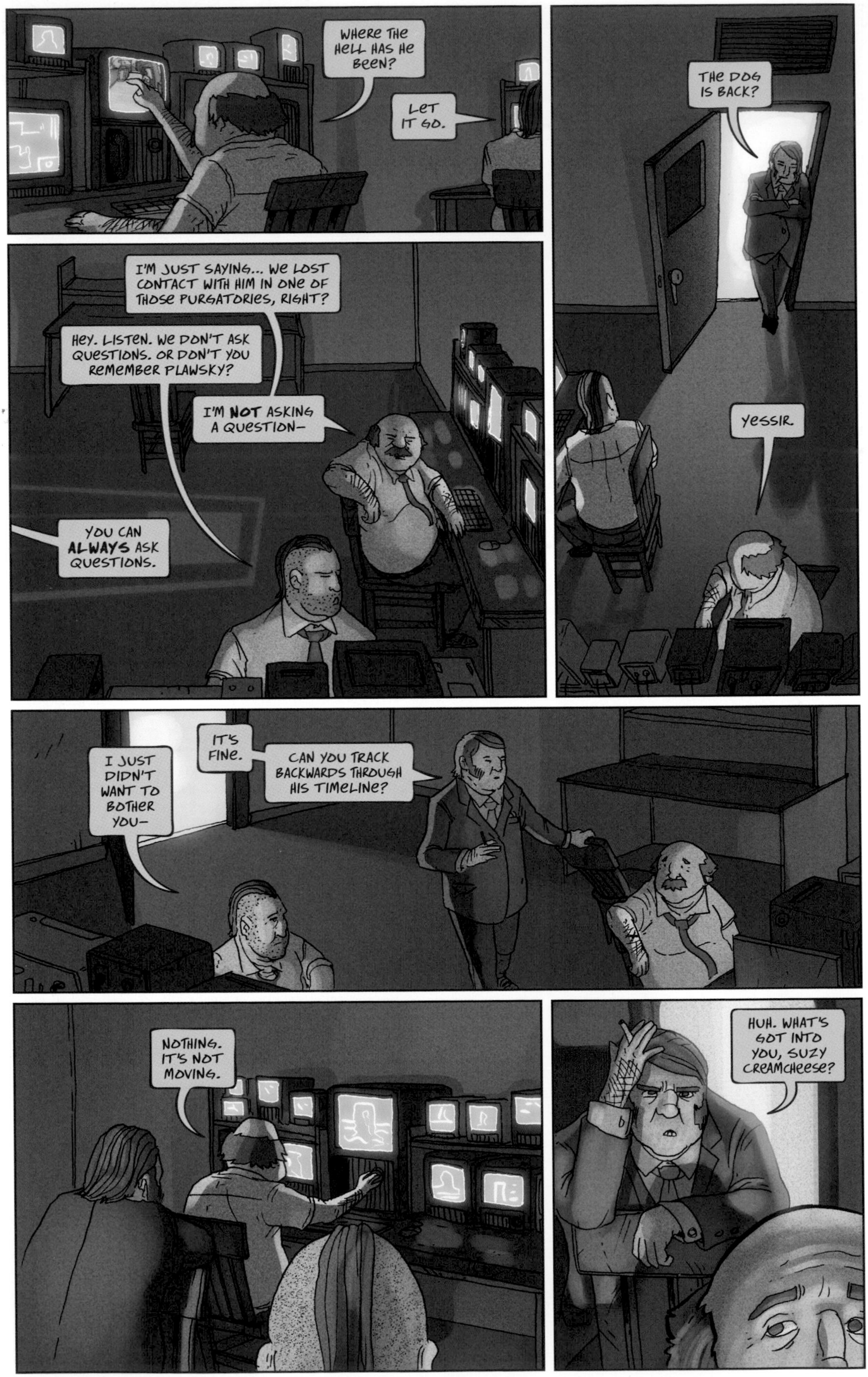
WHERE THE HELL HAS HE BEEN?
LET IT GO.
THE DOG IS BACK?
I'M JUST SAYING... WE LOST CONTACT WITH HIM IN ONE OF THOSE PURGATORIES, RIGHT?
HEY. LISTEN. WE DON'T ASK QUESTIONS. OR DON'T YOU REMEMBER PLAWSKY?
I'M **NOT** ASKING A QUESTION—
YOU CAN **ALWAYS** ASK QUESTIONS.
YESSIR.
I JUST DIDN'T WANT TO BOTHER YOU—
IT'S FINE.
CAN YOU TRACK BACKWARDS THROUGH HIS TIMELINE?
NOTHING. IT'S NOT MOVING.
HUH. WHAT'S GOT INTO YOU, SUZY CREAMCHEESE?

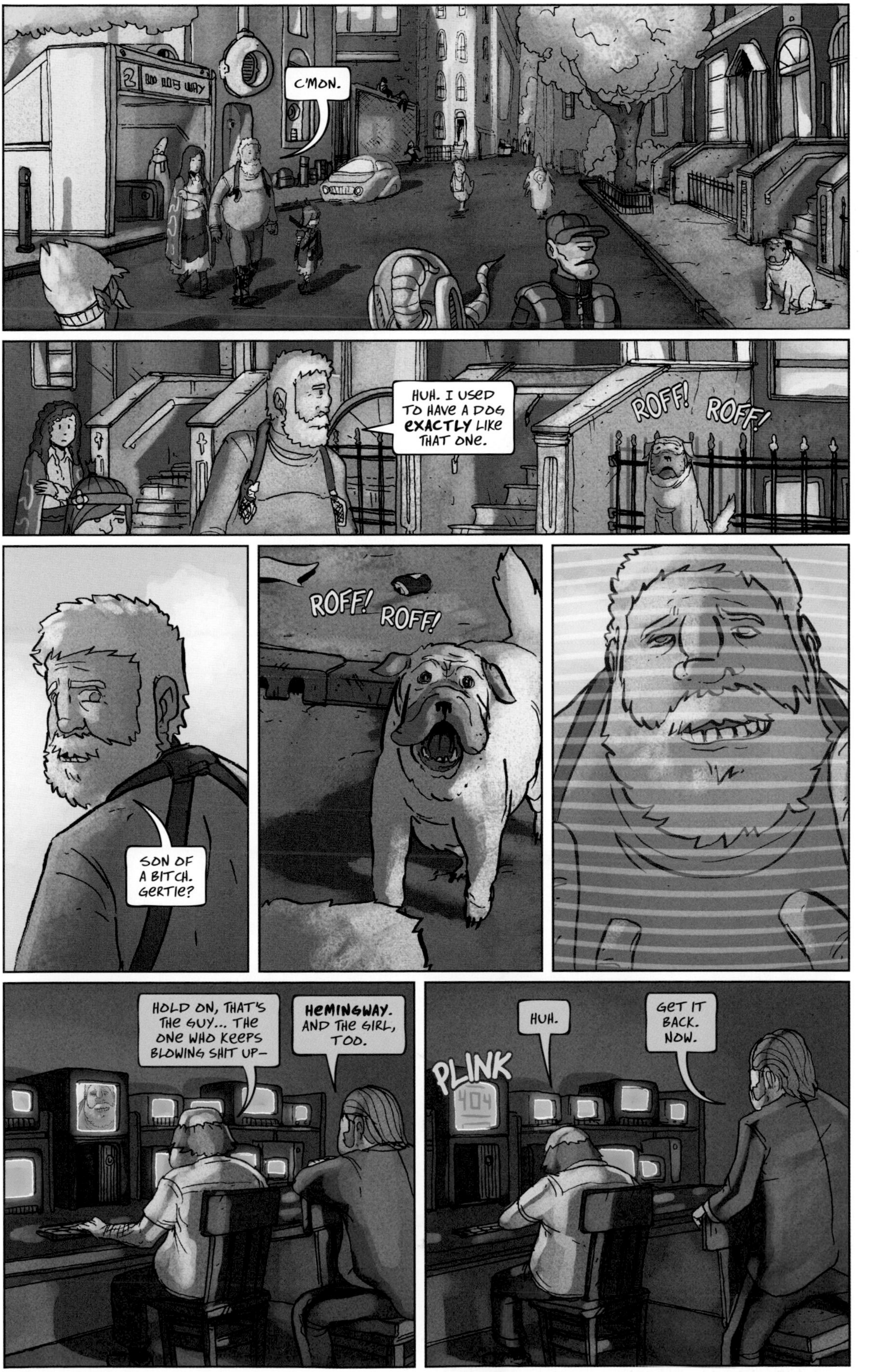
2
C'MON.
HUH. I USED TO HAVE A DOG EXACTLY LIKE THAT ONE.
ROFF! ROFF!
SON OF A BITCH. GERTIE?
ROFF! ROFF!
HOLD ON, THAT'S THE GUY... THE ONE WHO KEEPS BLOWING SHIT UP—
HEMINGWAY. AND THE GIRL, TOO.
PLINK
404
HUH.
GET IT BACK. NOW.

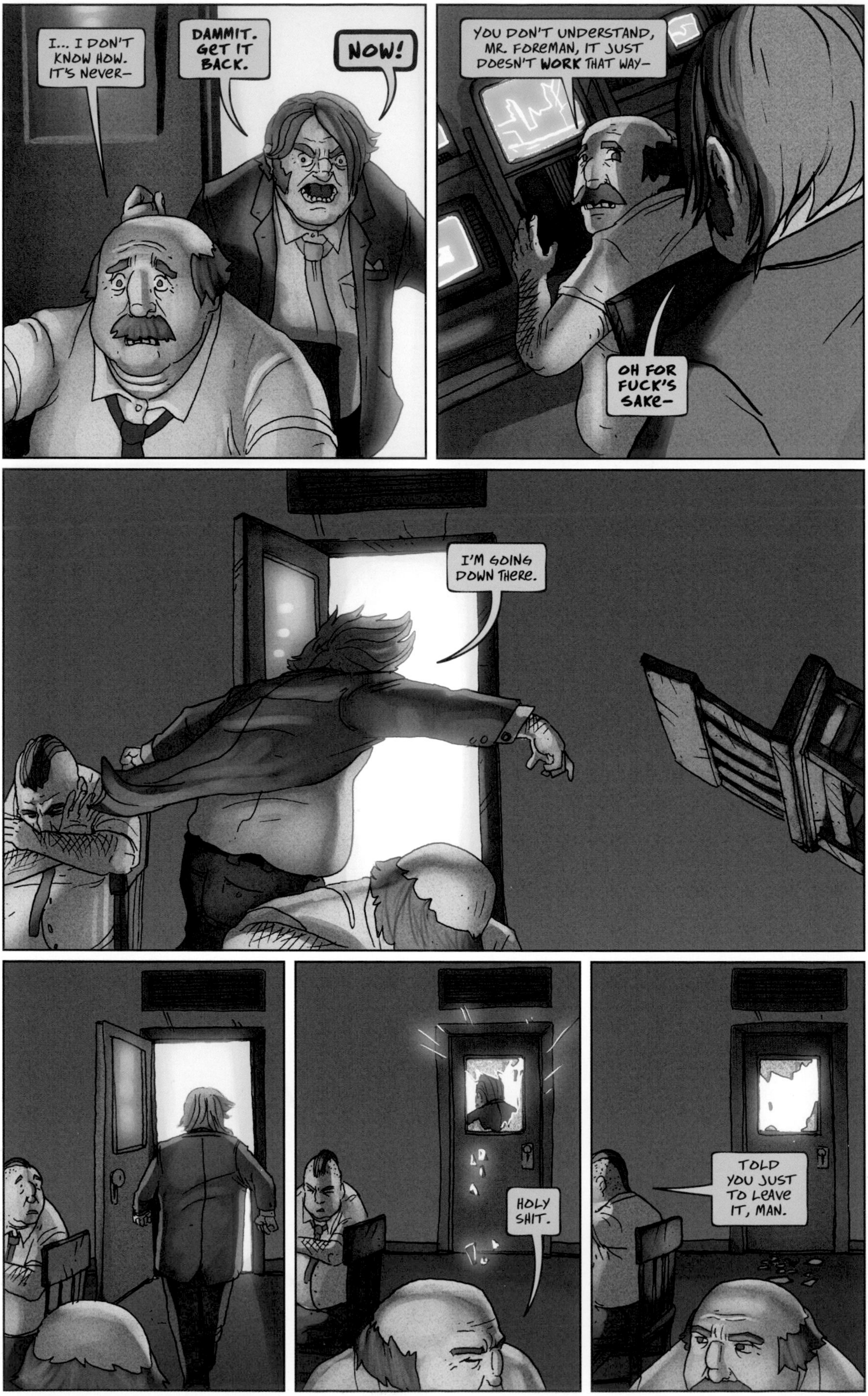
I... I DON'T KNOW HOW. IT'S NEVER—
DAMMIT. GET IT BACK.
NOW!
YOU DON'T UNDERSTAND, MR. FOREMAN, IT JUST DOESN'T WORK THAT WAY—
OH FOR FUCK'S SAKE—
I'M GOING DOWN THERE.
HOLY SHIT.
TOLD YOU JUST TO LEAVE IT, MAN.

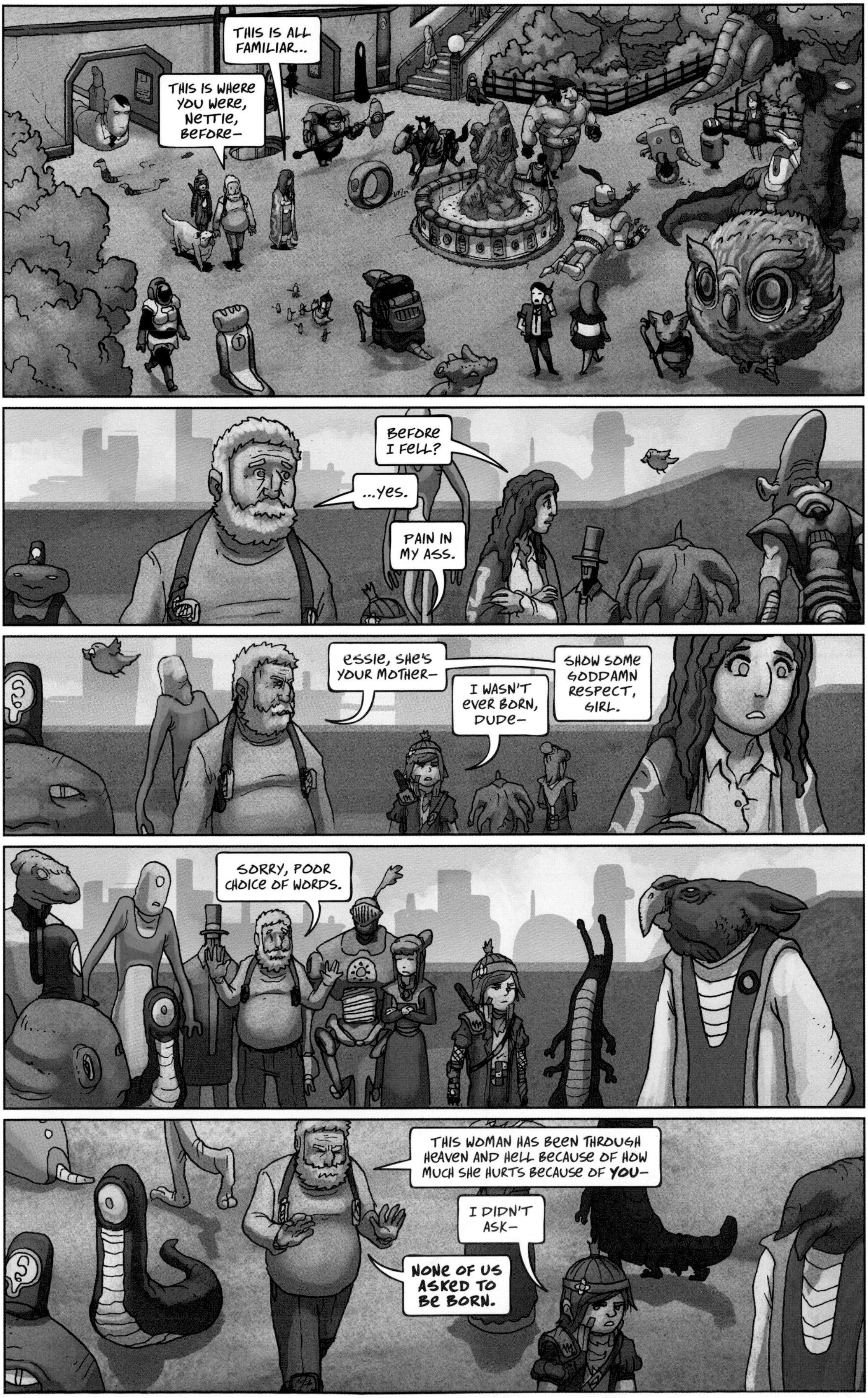
THIS IS ALL FAMILIAR...
THIS IS WHERE YOU WERE, NETTIE, BEFORE–
BEFORE I FELL?
...YES.
PAIN IN MY ASS.
ESSIE, SHE'S YOUR MOTHER–
SHOW SOME GODDAMN RESPECT, GIRL.
I WASN'T EVER BORN, DUDE–
SORRY, POOR CHOICE OF WORDS.
THIS WOMAN HAS BEEN THROUGH HEAVEN AND HELL BECAUSE OF HOW MUCH SHE HURTS BECAUSE OF **YOU**–
I DIDN'T ASK–
NONE OF US ASKED TO BE BORN.

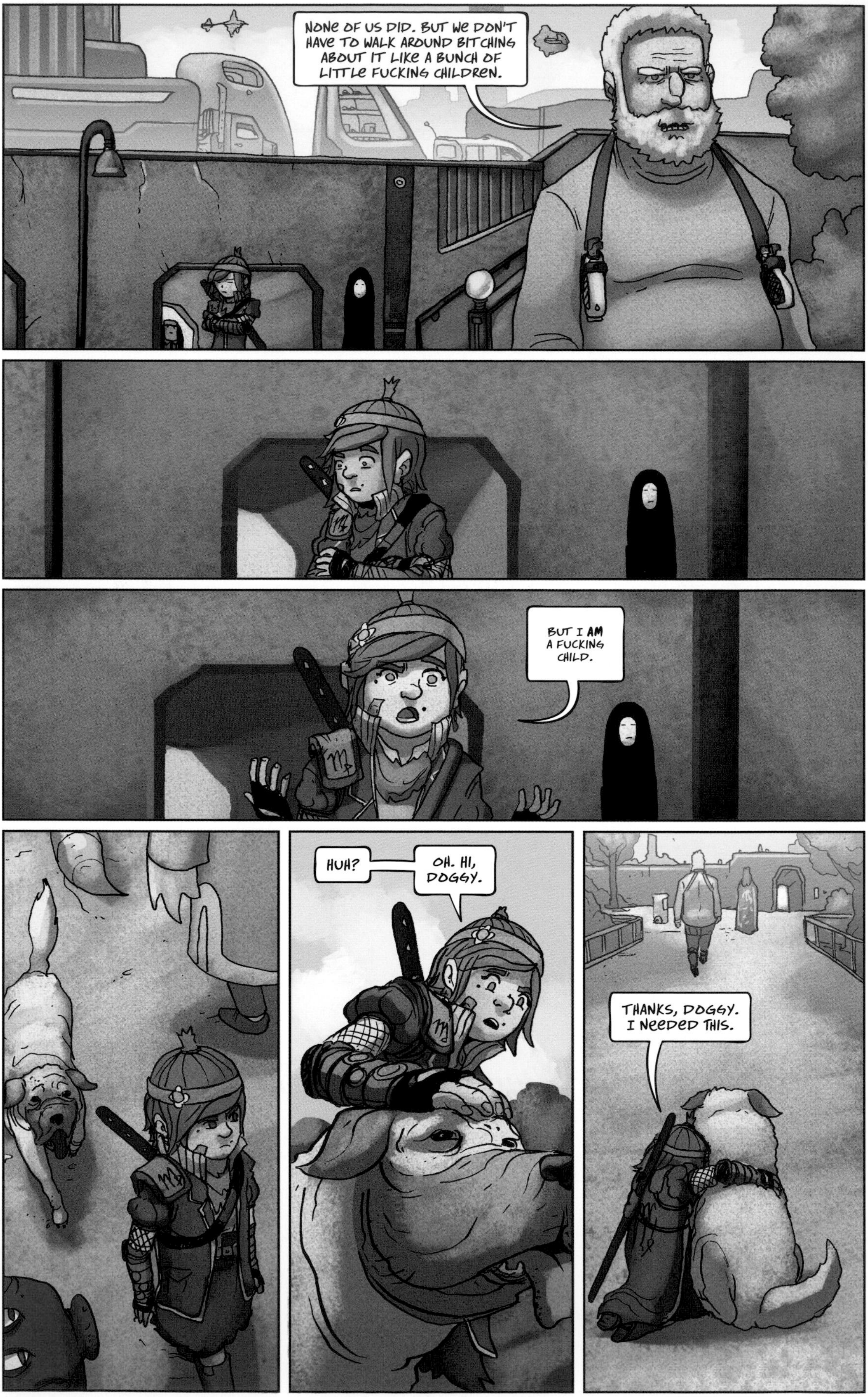

NONE OF US DID. BUT WE DON'T HAVE TO WALK AROUND BITCHING ABOUT IT LIKE A BUNCH OF LITTLE FUCKING CHILDREN.
BUT I **AM** A FUCKING CHILD.
HUH?
OH. HI, DOGGY.
THANKS, DOGGY. I NEEDED THIS.

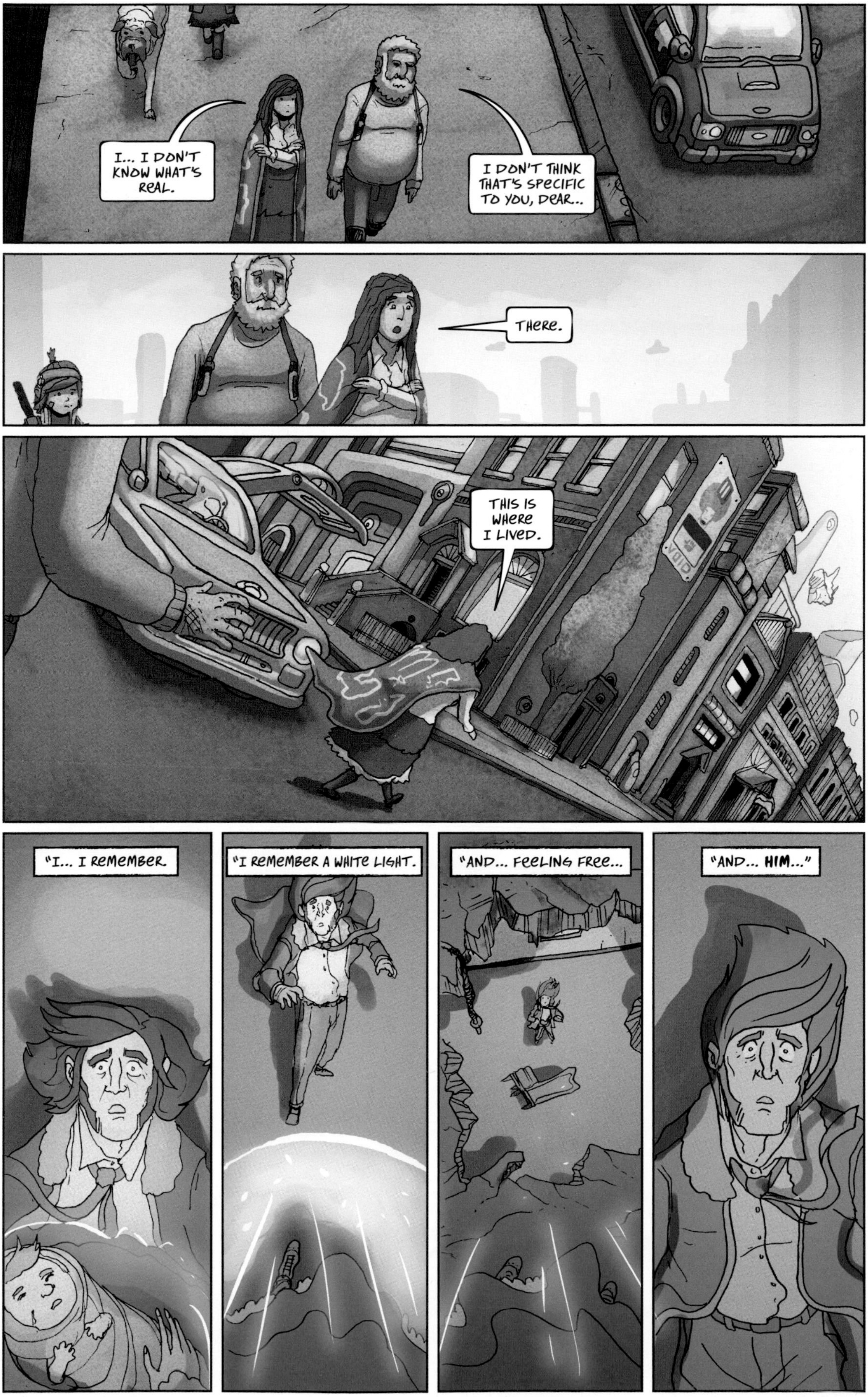

I... I DON'T KNOW WHAT'S REAL.
I DON'T THINK THAT'S SPECIFIC TO YOU, DEAR...
THERE.
THIS IS WHERE I LIVED.
"I... I REMEMBER.
"I REMEMBER A WHITE LIGHT.
"AND... FEELING FREE...
"AND... HIM..."

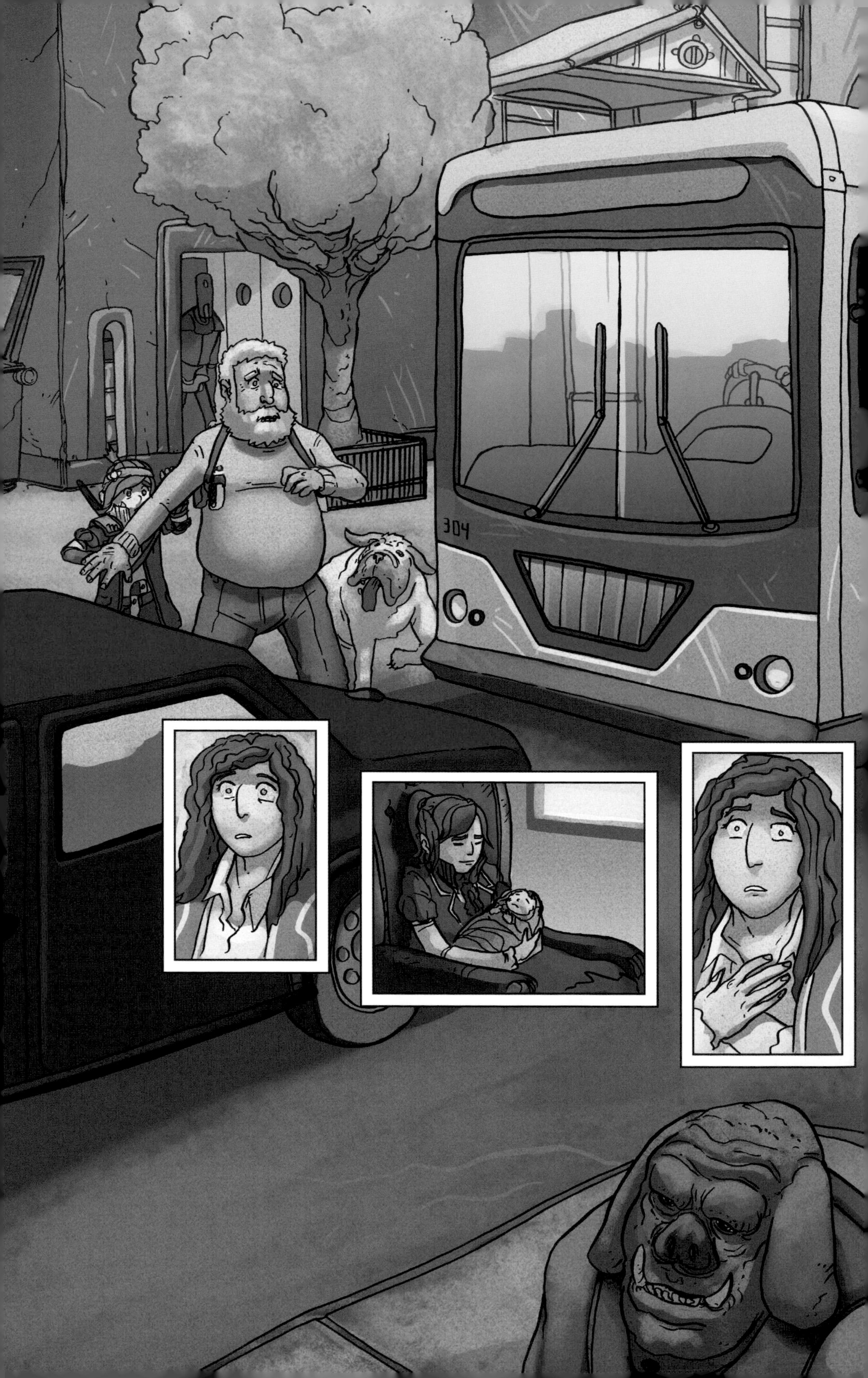
304

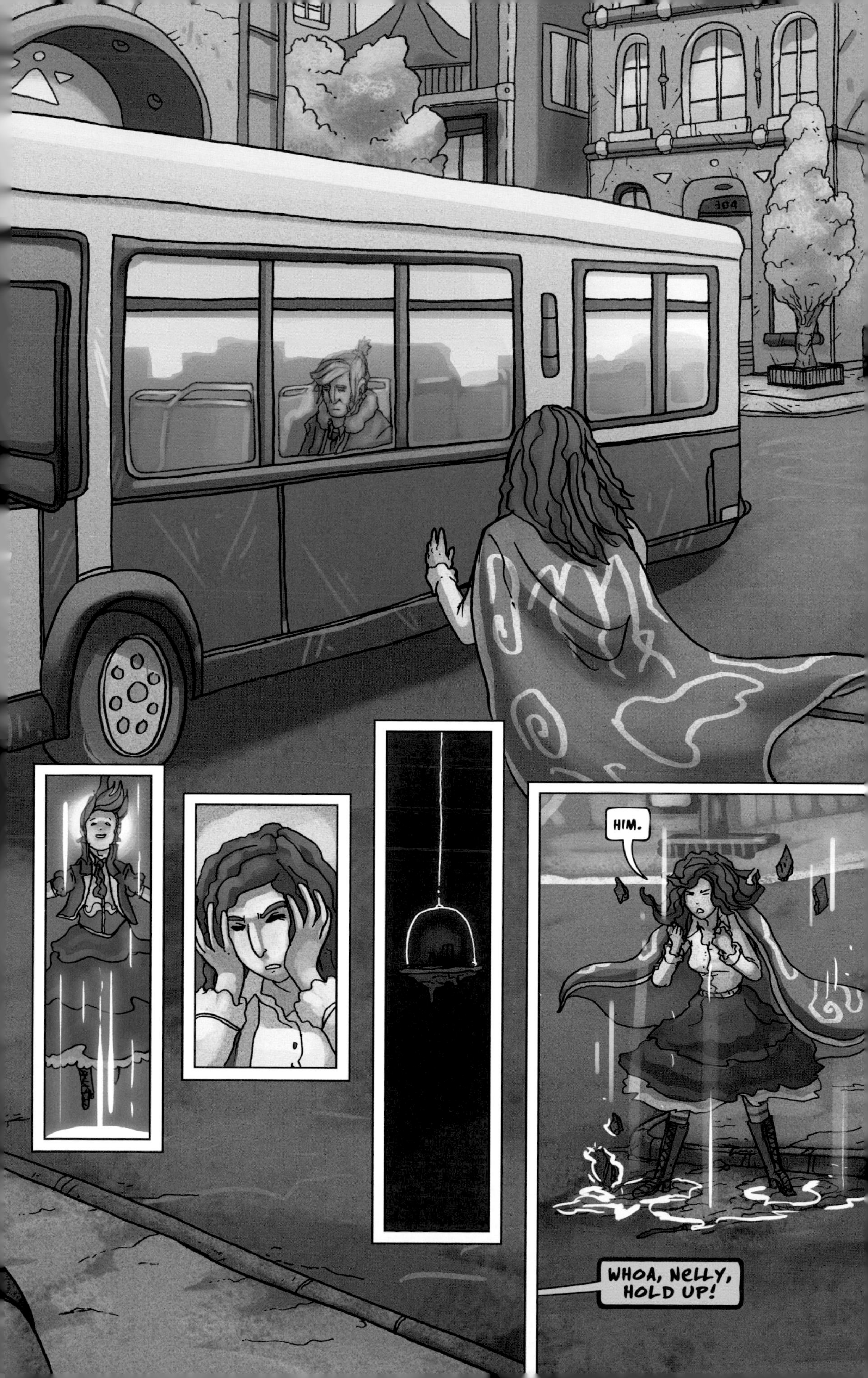

HIM.
WHOA, NELLY, HOLD UP!

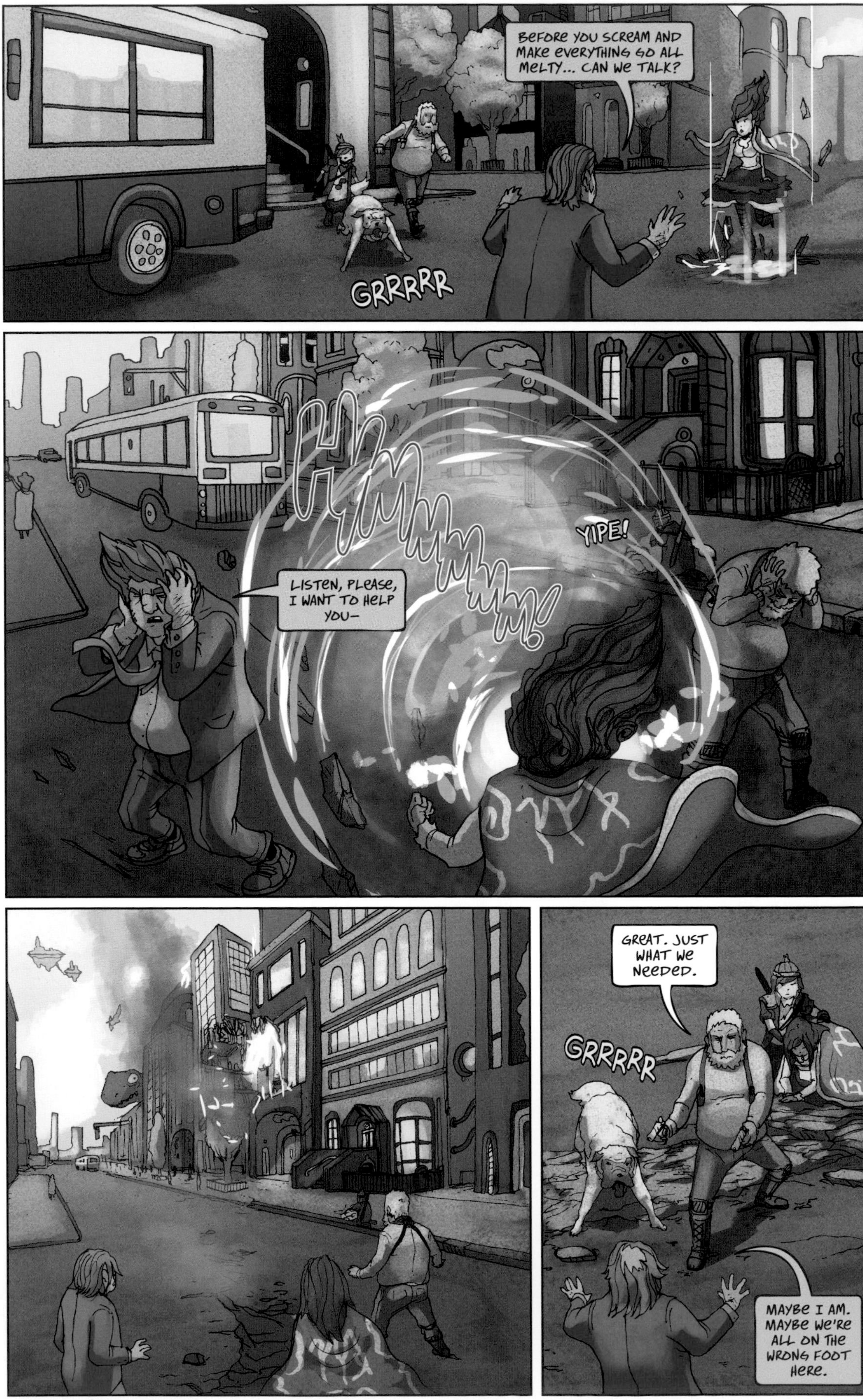
BEFORE YOU SCREAM AND MAKE EVERYTHING GO ALL MELTY... CAN WE TALK?
GRRRRR
LISTEN, PLEASE, I WANT TO HELP YOU—
YIPE!
GREAT. JUST WHAT WE NEEDED.
GRRRRR
MAYBE I AM. MAYBE WE'RE ALL ON THE WRONG FOOT HERE.

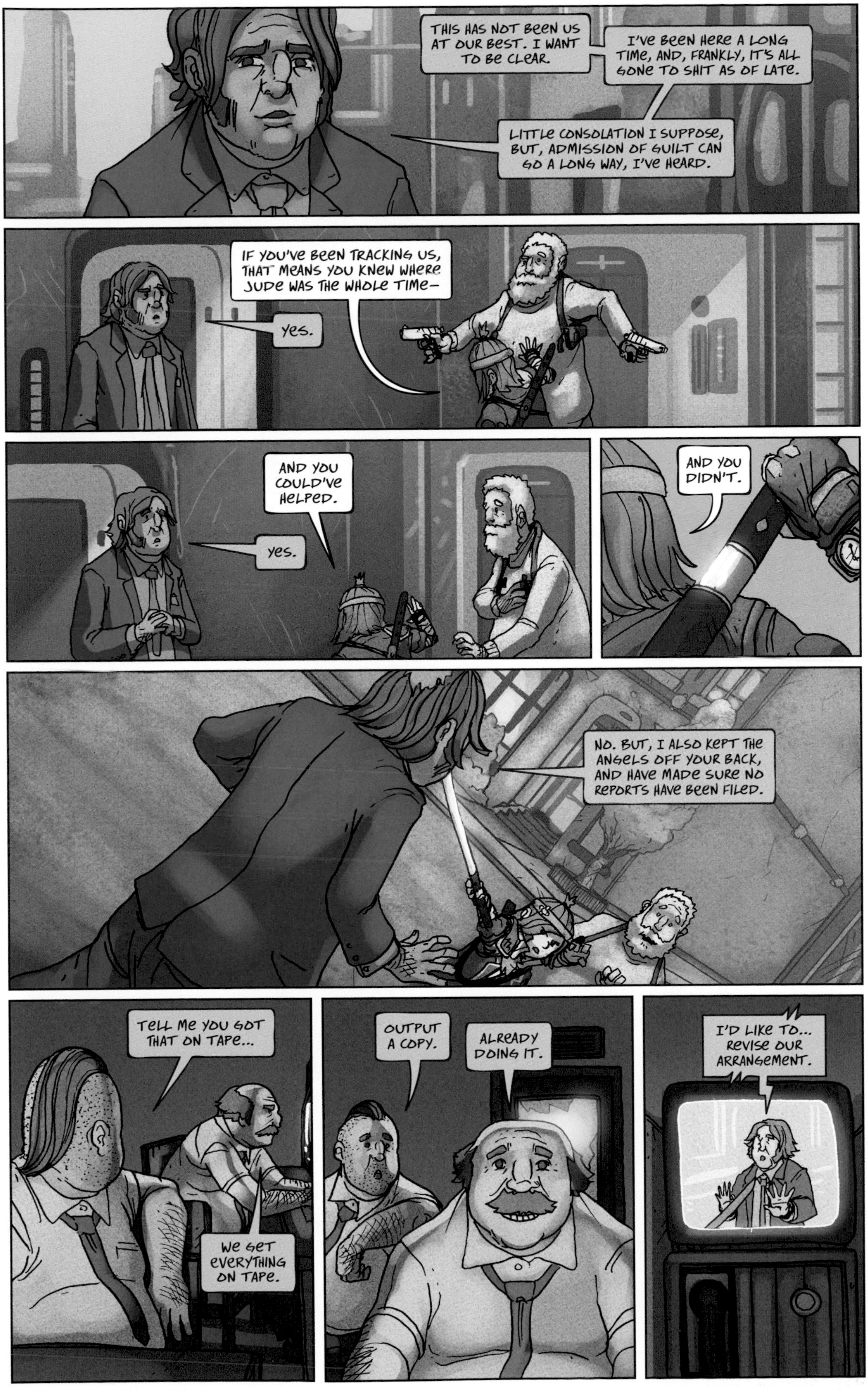
THIS HAS NOT BEEN US AT OUR BEST. I WANT TO BE CLEAR.
I'VE BEEN HERE A LONG TIME, AND, FRANKLY, IT'S ALL GONE TO SHIT AS OF LATE.
LITTLE CONSOLATION I SUPPOSE, BUT, ADMISSION OF GUILT CAN GO A LONG WAY, I'VE HEARD.
IF YOU'VE BEEN TRACKING US, THAT MEANS YOU KNEW WHERE JUDE WAS THE WHOLE TIME—
YES.
AND YOU COULD'VE HELPED.
YES.
AND YOU DIDN'T.
NO. BUT, I ALSO KEPT THE ANGELS OFF YOUR BACK, AND HAVE MADE SURE NO REPORTS HAVE BEEN FILED.
TELL ME YOU GOT THAT ON TAPE...
WE GET EVERYTHING ON TAPE.
OUTPUT A COPY.
ALREADY DOING IT.
I'D LIKE TO... REVISE OUR ARRANGEMENT.

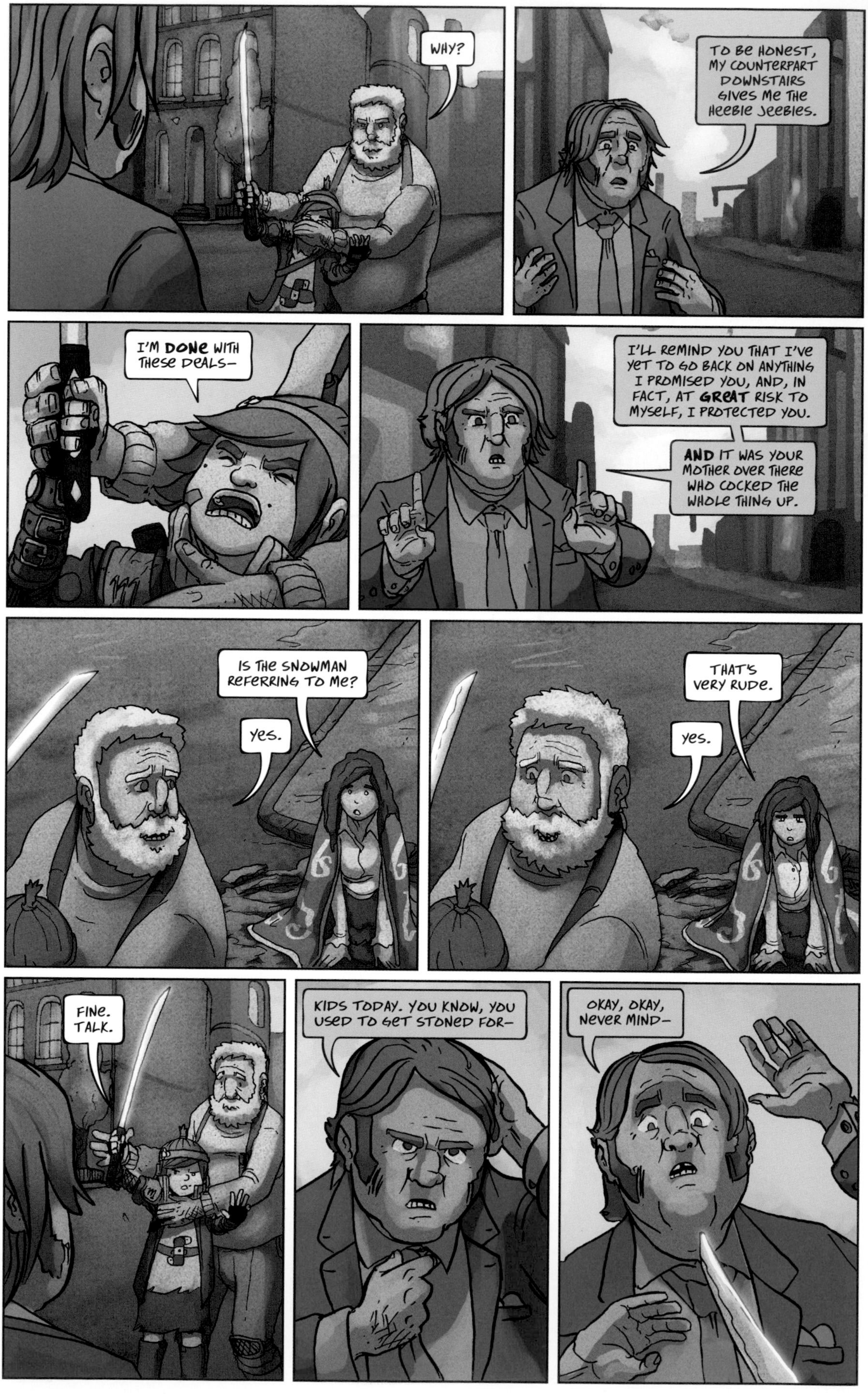
WHY?
TO BE HONEST, MY COUNTERPART DOWNSTAIRS GIVES ME THE HEEBIE JEEBIES.
I'M DONE WITH THESE DEALS–
I'LL REMIND YOU THAT I'VE YET TO GO BACK ON ANYTHING I PROMISED YOU, AND, IN FACT, AT GREAT RISK TO MYSELF, I PROTECTED YOU.
AND IT WAS YOUR MOTHER OVER THERE WHO COCKED THE WHOLE THING UP.
IS THE SNOWMAN REFERRING TO ME?
YES.
THAT'S VERY RUDE.
YES.
FINE. TALK.
KIDS TODAY. YOU KNOW, YOU USED TO GET STONED FOR–
OKAY, OKAY, NEVER MIND–

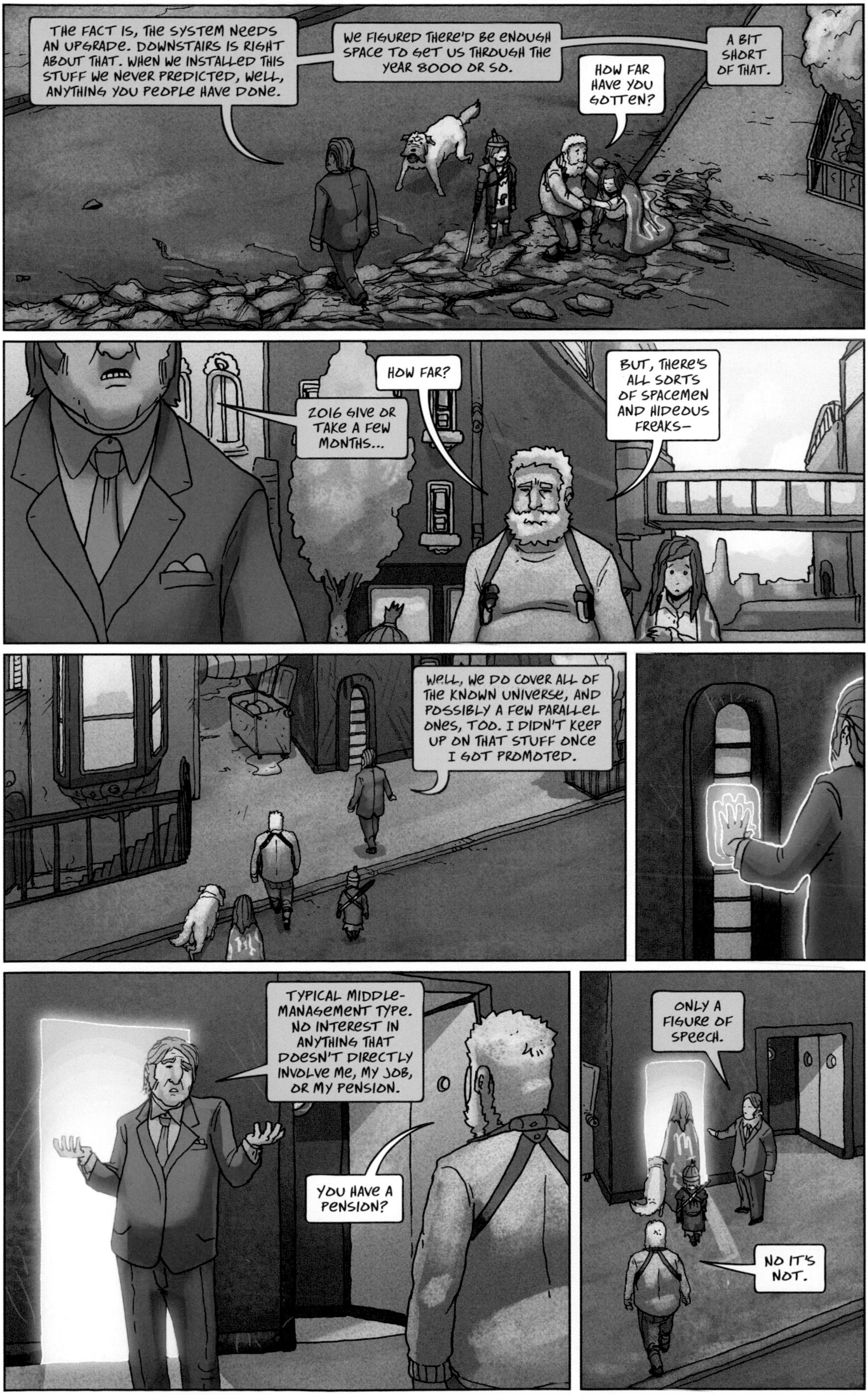
THE FACT IS, THE SYSTEM NEEDS AN UPGRADE. DOWNSTAIRS IS RIGHT ABOUT THAT. WHEN WE INSTALLED THIS STUFF WE NEVER PREDICTED, WELL, ANYTHING YOU PEOPLE HAVE DONE.
WE FIGURED THERE'D BE ENOUGH SPACE TO GET US THROUGH THE YEAR 8000 OR SO.
A BIT SHORT OF THAT.
HOW FAR HAVE YOU GOTTEN?
2016 GIVE OR TAKE A FEW MONTHS...
HOW FAR?
BUT, THERE'S ALL SORTS OF SPACEMEN AND HIDEOUS FREAKS—
WELL, WE DO COVER ALL OF THE KNOWN UNIVERSE, AND POSSIBLY A FEW PARALLEL ONES, TOO. I DIDN'T KEEP UP ON THAT STUFF ONCE I GOT PROMOTED.
TYPICAL MIDDLE-MANAGEMENT TYPE. NO INTEREST IN ANYTHING THAT DOESN'T DIRECTLY INVOLVE ME, MY JOB, OR MY PENSION.
YOU HAVE A PENSION?
ONLY A FIGURE OF SPEECH.
NO IT'S NOT.

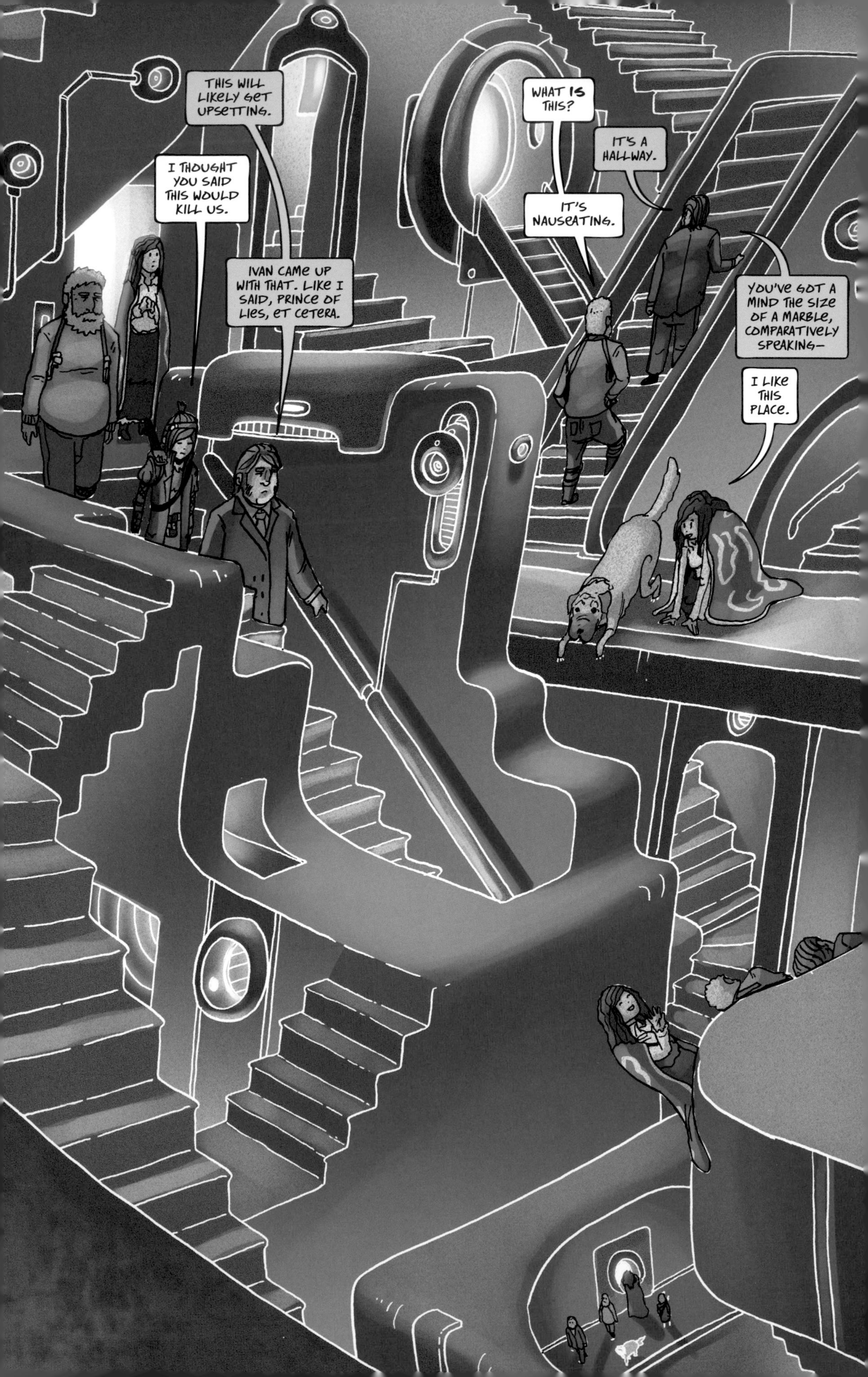

THIS WILL LIKELY GET UPSETTING.
I THOUGHT YOU SAID THIS WOULD KILL US.
IVAN CAME UP WITH THAT. LIKE I SAID, PRINCE OF LIES, ET CETERA.
WHAT IS THIS?
IT'S A HALLWAY.
IT'S NAUSEATING.
YOU'VE GOT A MIND THE SIZE OF A MARBLE, COMPARATIVELY SPEAKING—
I LIKE THIS PLACE.

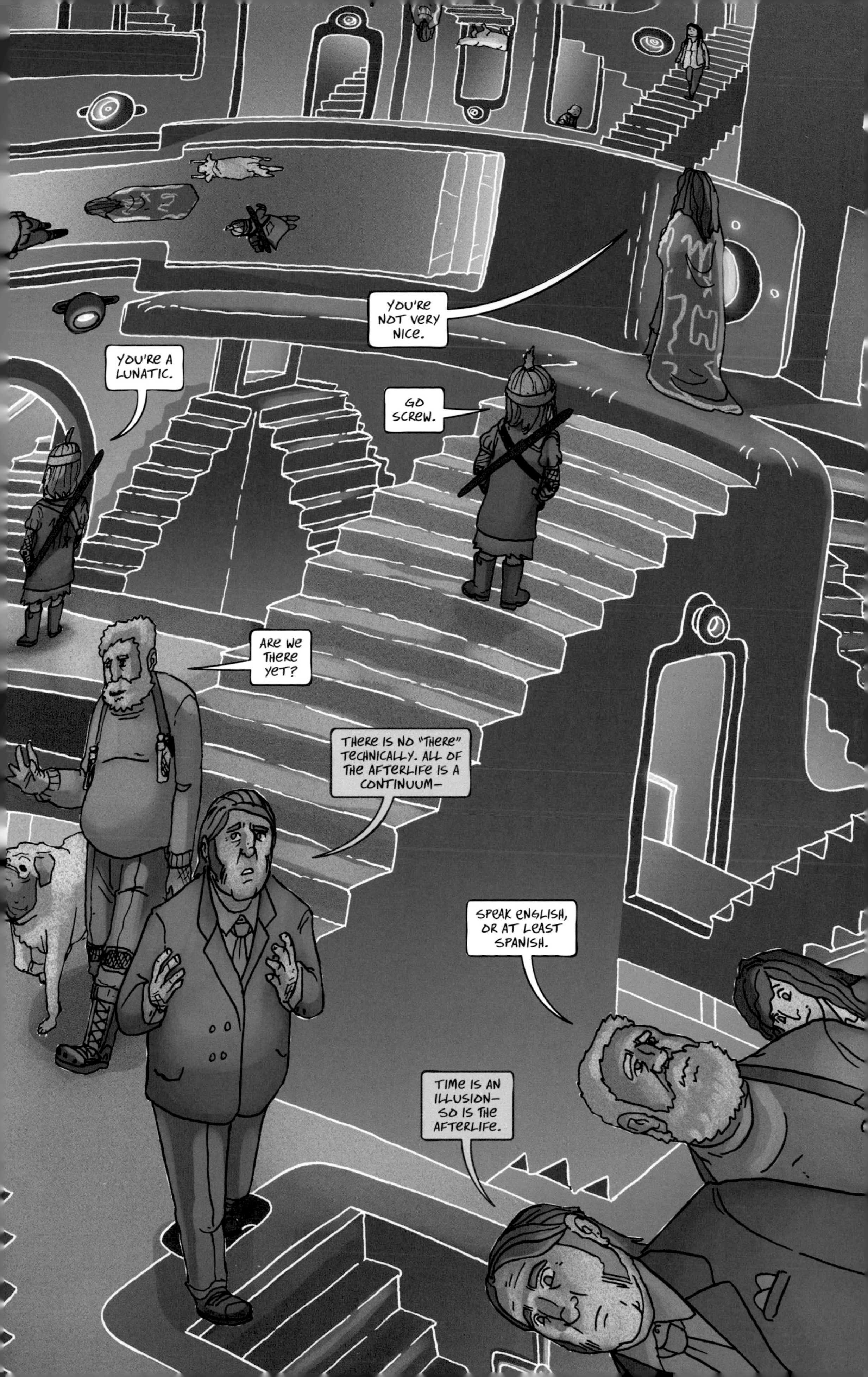
YOU'RE NOT VERY NICE.
YOU'RE A LUNATIC.
GO SCREW.
ARE WE THERE YET?
THERE IS NO "THERE" TECHNICALLY. ALL OF THE AFTERLIFE IS A CONTINUUM—
SPEAK ENGLISH, OR AT LEAST SPANISH.
TIME IS AN ILLUSION— SO IS THE AFTERLIFE.

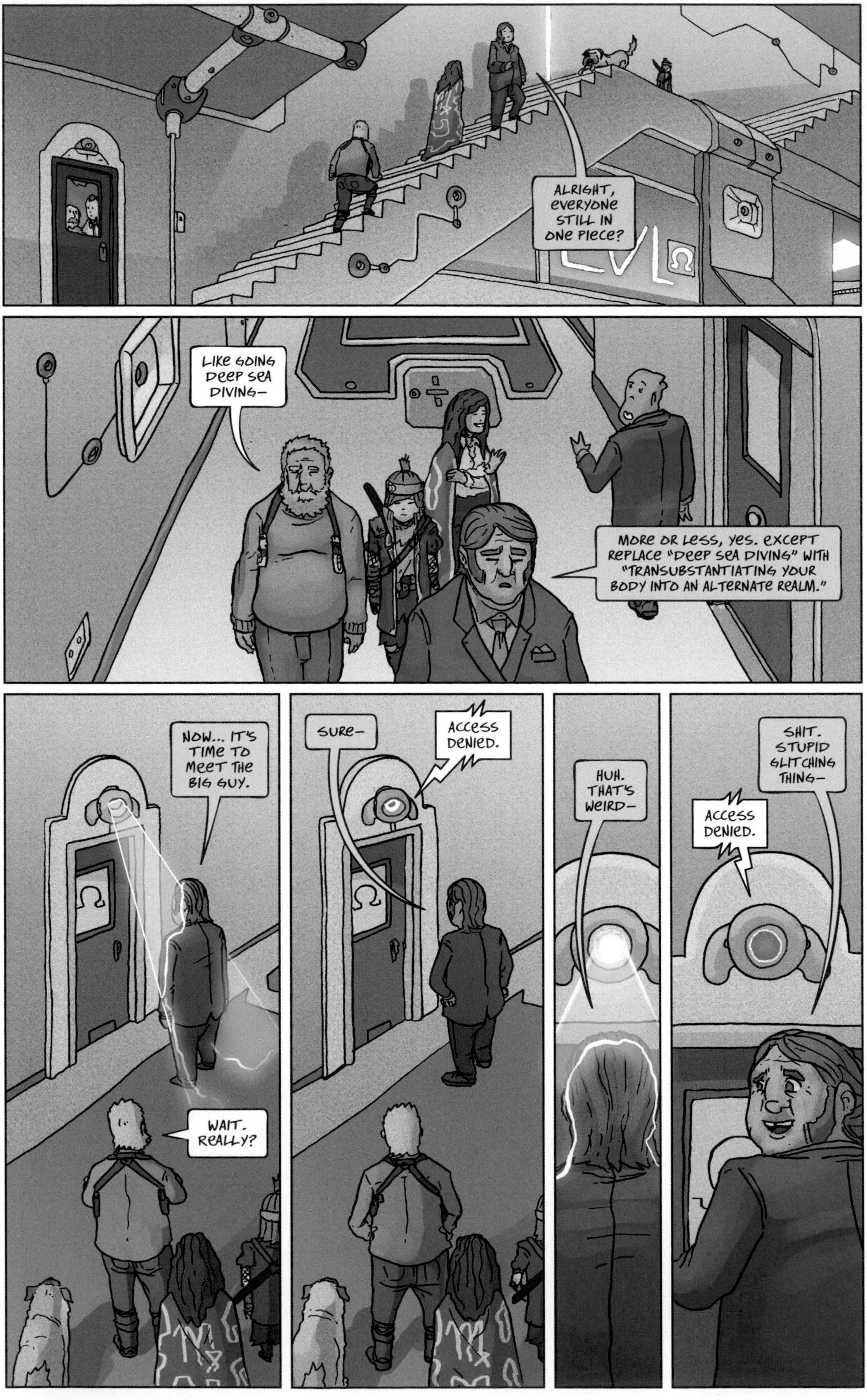
ALRIGHT, EVERYONE STILL IN ONE PIECE?
LVL Ω
LIKE GOING DEEP SEA DIVING—
MORE OR LESS, YES. EXCEPT REPLACE "DEEP SEA DIVING" WITH "TRANSUBSTANTIATING YOUR BODY INTO AN ALTERNATE REALM."
NOW... IT'S TIME TO MEET THE BIG GUY.
WAIT. REALLY?
SURE—
ACCESS DENIED.
HUH. THAT'S WEIRD—
SHIT. STUPID GLITCHING THING—
ACCESS DENIED.

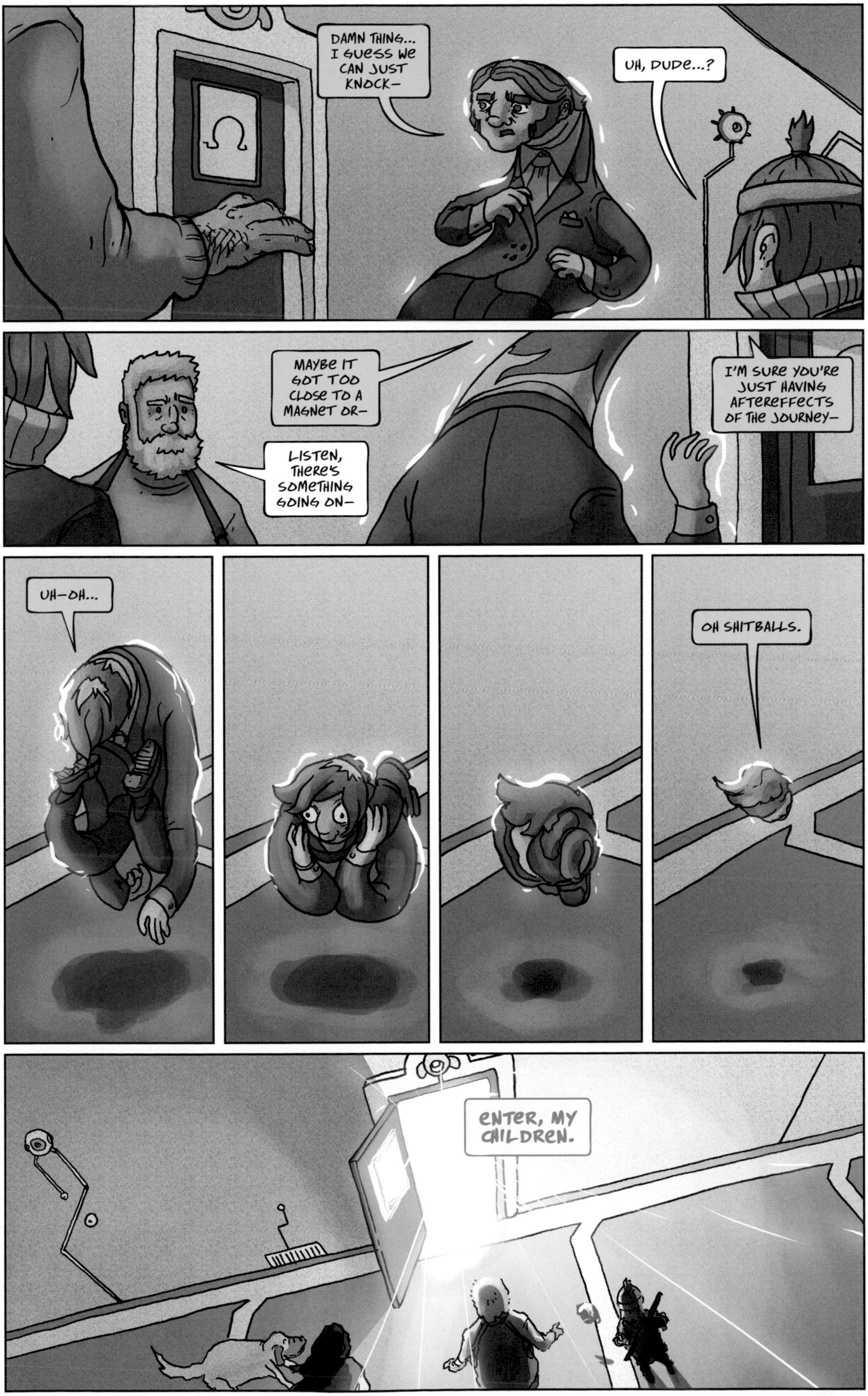
DAMN THING... I GUESS WE CAN JUST KNOCK—
UH, DUDE...?
MAYBE IT GOT TOO CLOSE TO A MAGNET OR—
LISTEN, THERE'S SOMETHING GOING ON—
I'M SURE YOU'RE JUST HAVING AFTEREFFECTS OF THE JOURNEY—
UH-OH...
OH SHITBALLS.
ENTER, MY CHILDREN.

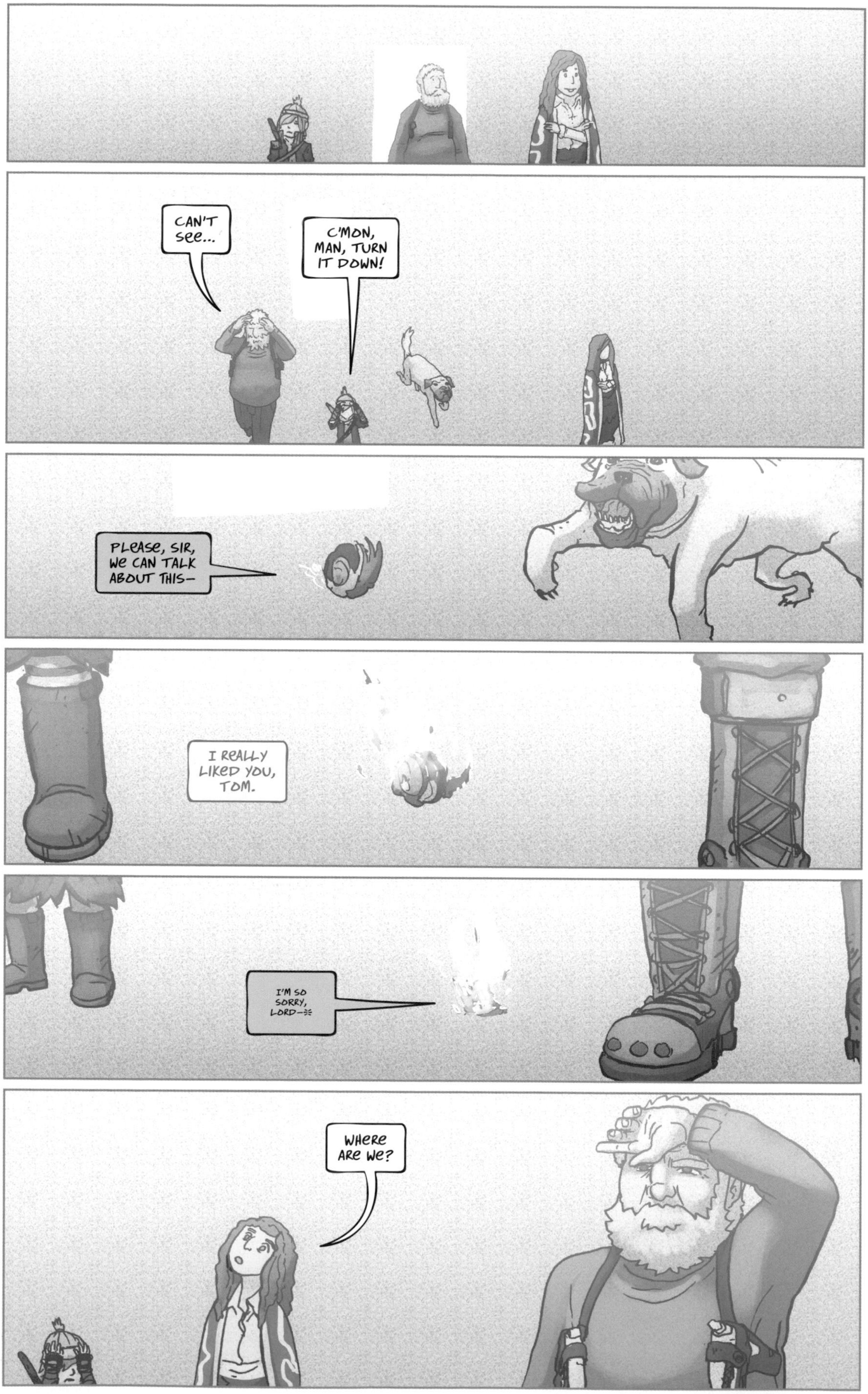
CAN'T SEE...
C'MON, MAN, TURN IT DOWN!
PLEASE, SIR, WE CAN TALK ABOUT THIS—
I REALLY LIKED YOU, TOM.
I'M SO SORRY, LORD—
WHERE ARE WE?

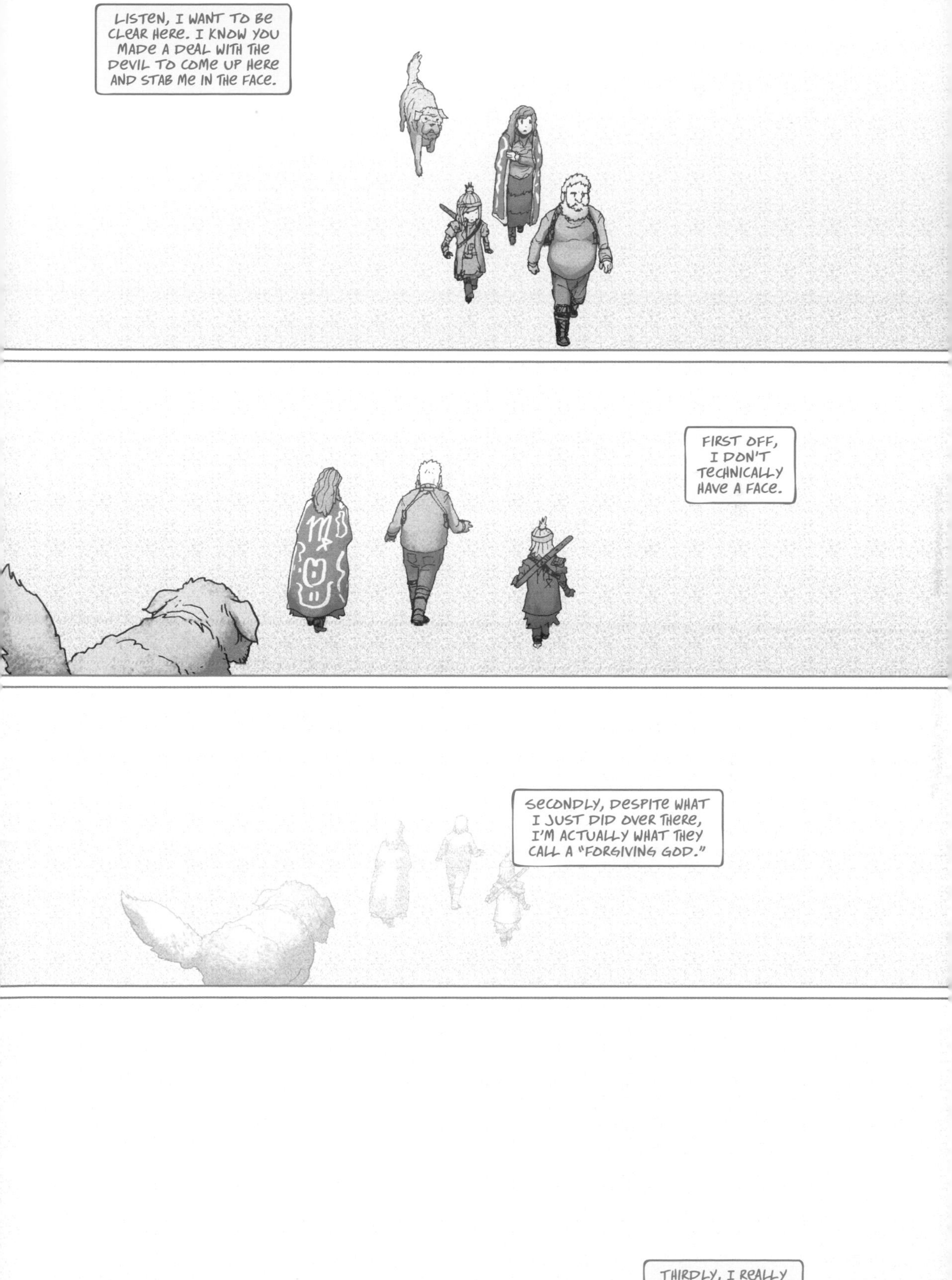
LISTEN, I WANT TO BE CLEAR HERE. I KNOW YOU MADE A DEAL WITH THE DEVIL TO COME UP HERE AND STAB ME IN THE FACE.
FIRST OFF, I DON'T TECHNICALLY HAVE A FACE.
SECONDLY, DESPITE WHAT I JUST DID OVER THERE, I'M ACTUALLY WHAT THEY CALL A "FORGIVING GOD."
THIRDLY, I REALLY ENJOYED THAT BOOK ABOUT THE FISH.

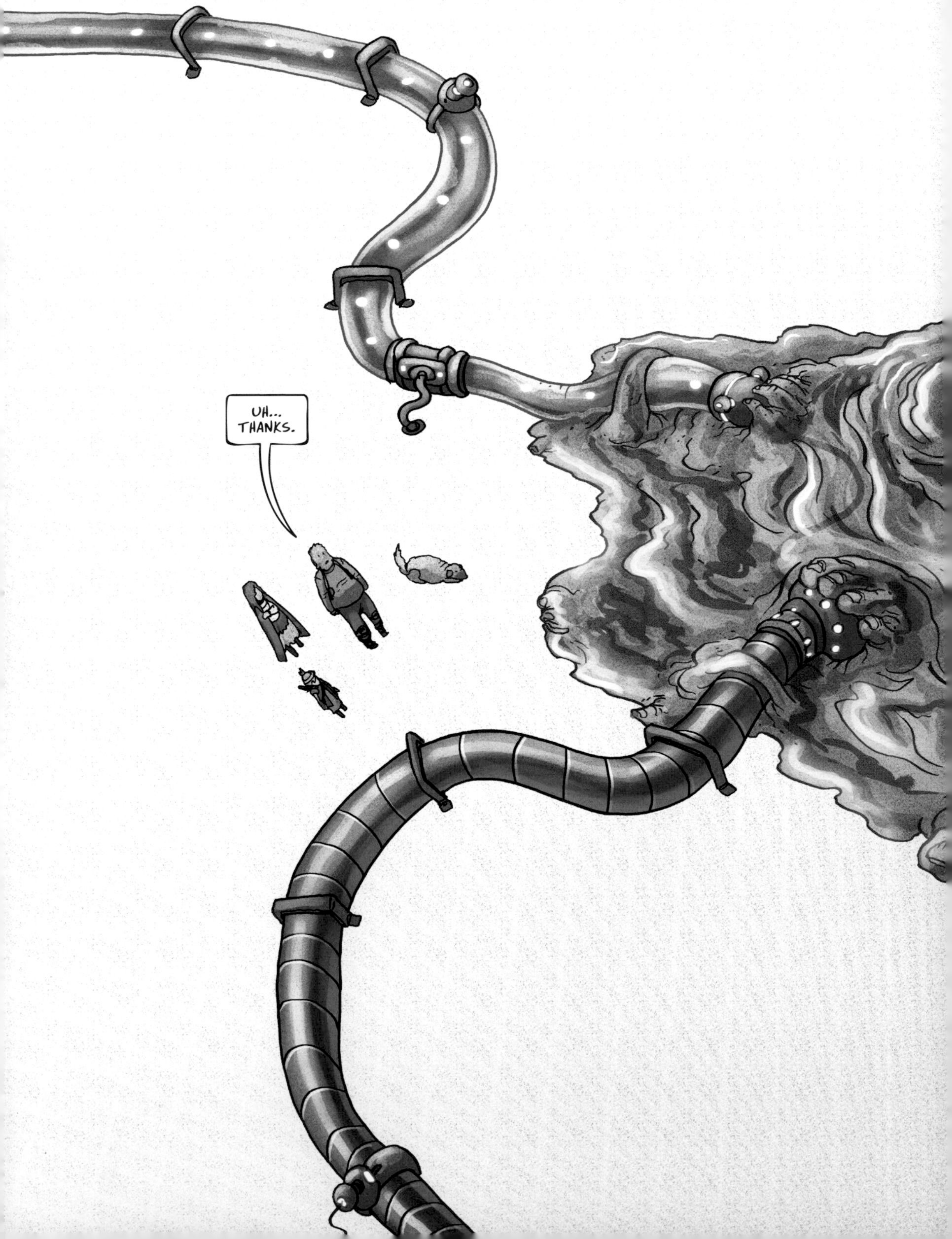
UH... THANKS.

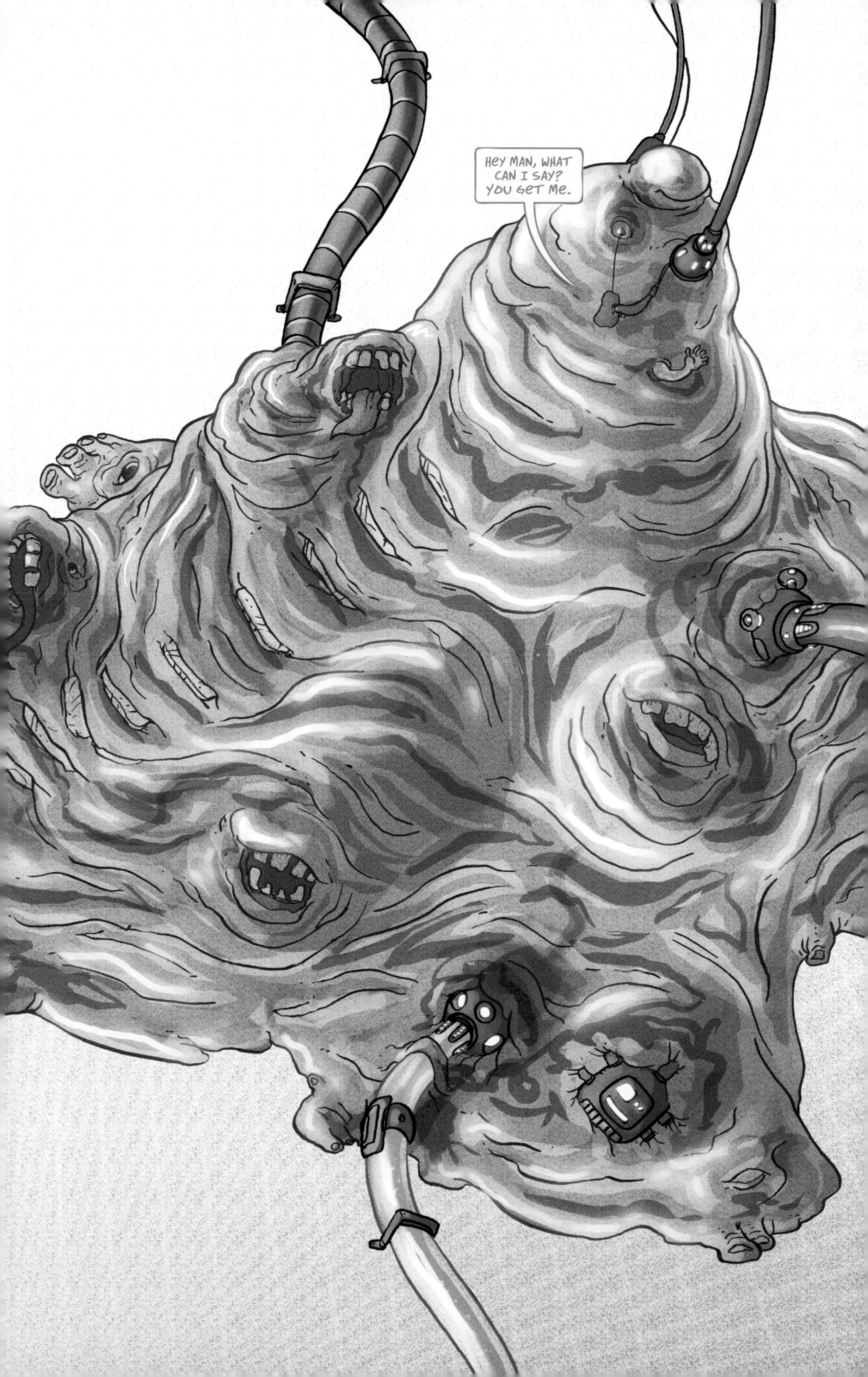
HEY MAN, WHAT CAN I SAY? YOU GET ME.

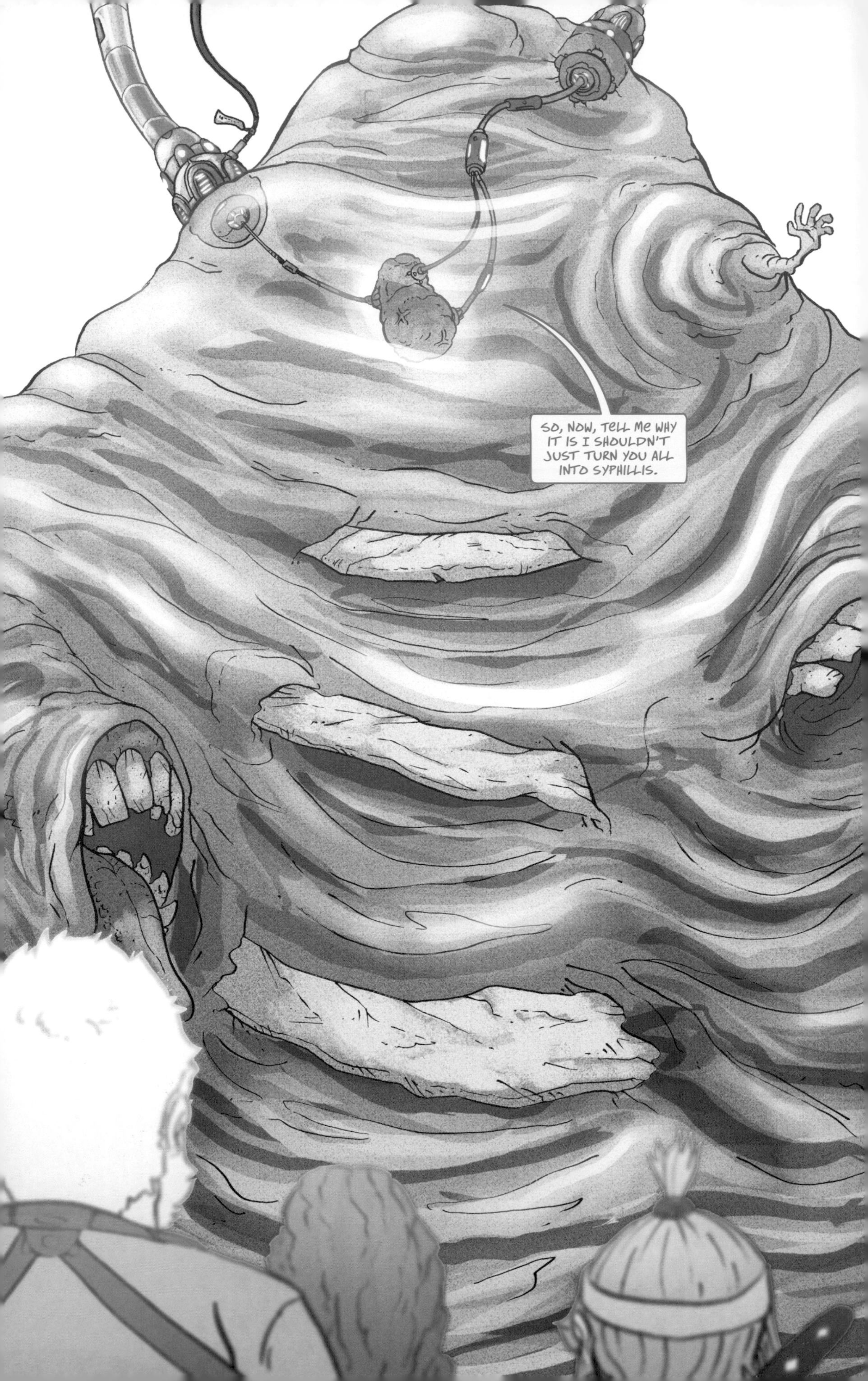
SO, NOW, TELL ME WHY IT IS I SHOULDN'T JUST TURN YOU ALL INTO SYPHILLIS.

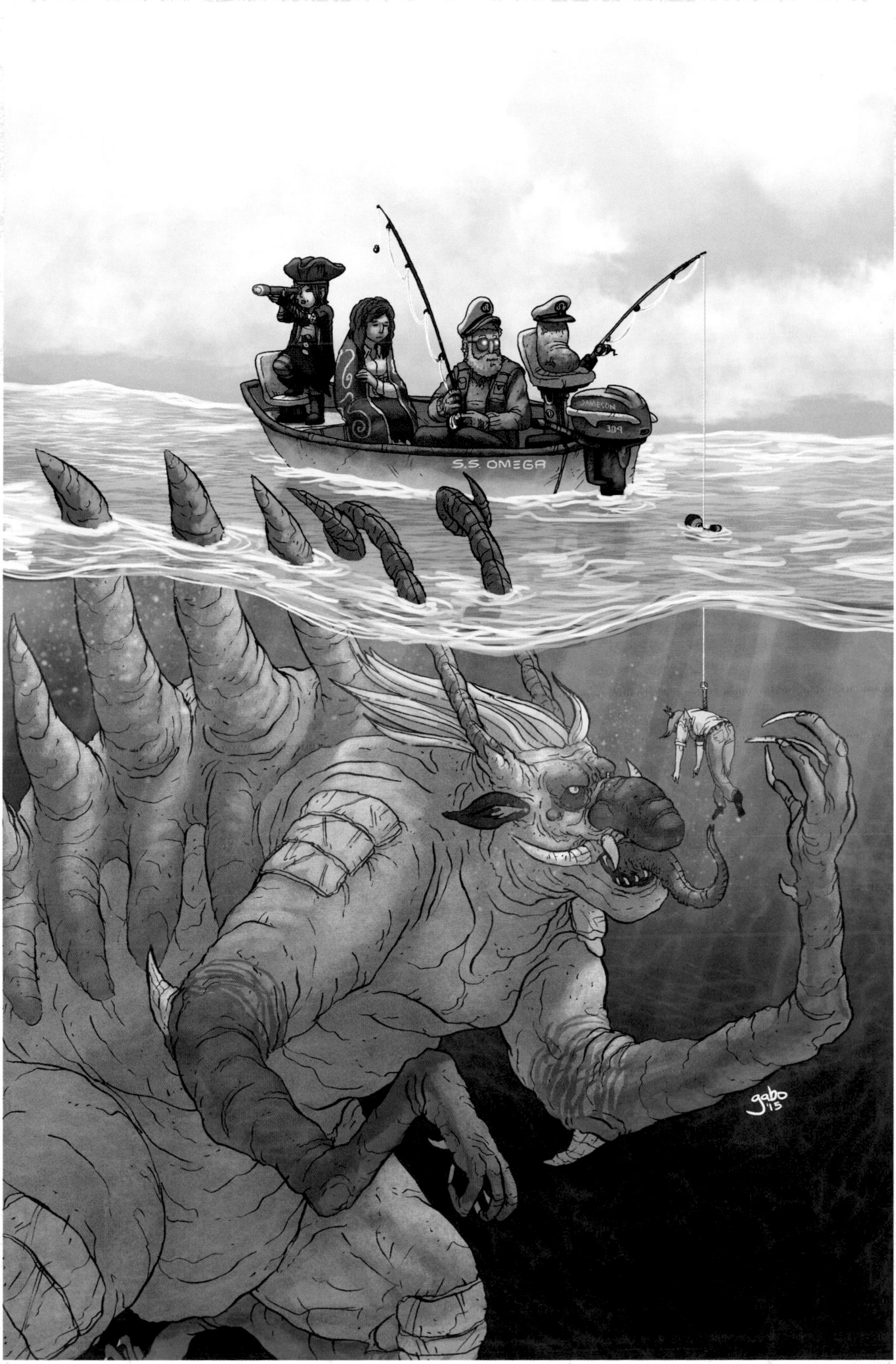
S.S. OMEGA
JAMESON
309
gabo '15

Chapter Thirteen

THE LIFE
AFTER

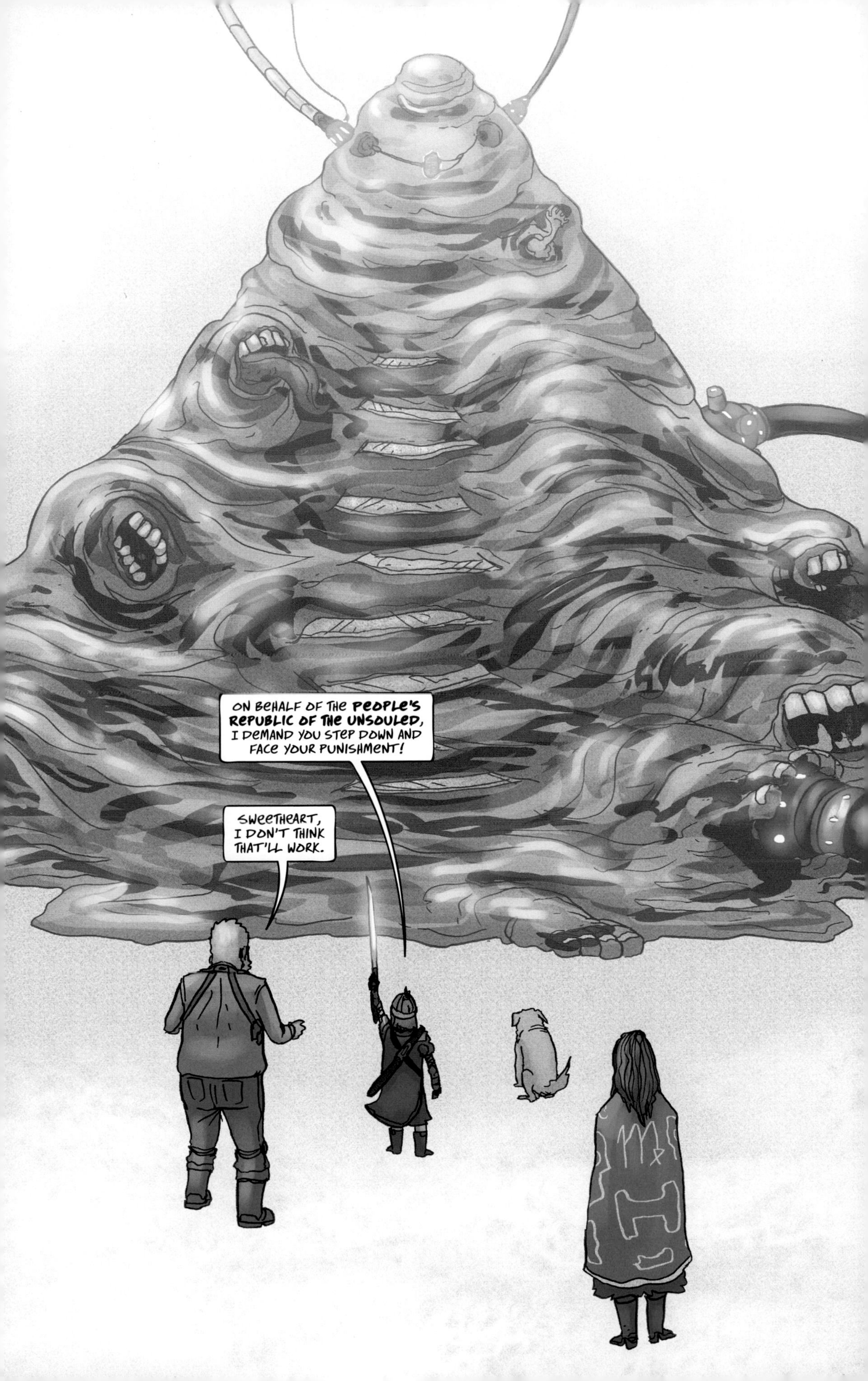
ON BEHALF OF THE **PEOPLE'S REPUBLIC OF THE UNSOULED**, I DEMAND YOU STEP DOWN AND FACE YOUR PUNISHMENT!
SWEETHEART, I DON'T THINK THAT'LL WORK.

HE CREATED THE UNIVERSE, BUILT A GIGANTIC OLIGARCHY OUT OF THE COSMOS, AND, BY THE WAY, JUST FOLDED A MAN'S EXISTENCE ENTIRELY IN HALF.

I'M PRETTY SURE HE'S NOT SCARED OF A SWORD.

I'LL TELL YOU, THOSE SENTENCES OF YOURS. THEY JUST GO ON AND ON FOREVER AMAZING.

OH. THANKS.

I MEAN, YOU JUST MADE ME THIS WAY, BUT STILL...

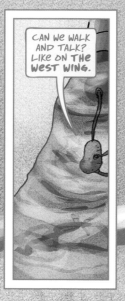

CAN WE WALK AND TALK? LIKE ON THE WEST WING.

NO. NO LADIES. JUST HIM.

WHY? SOME SORT OF GENDERIST BULLSHIT?

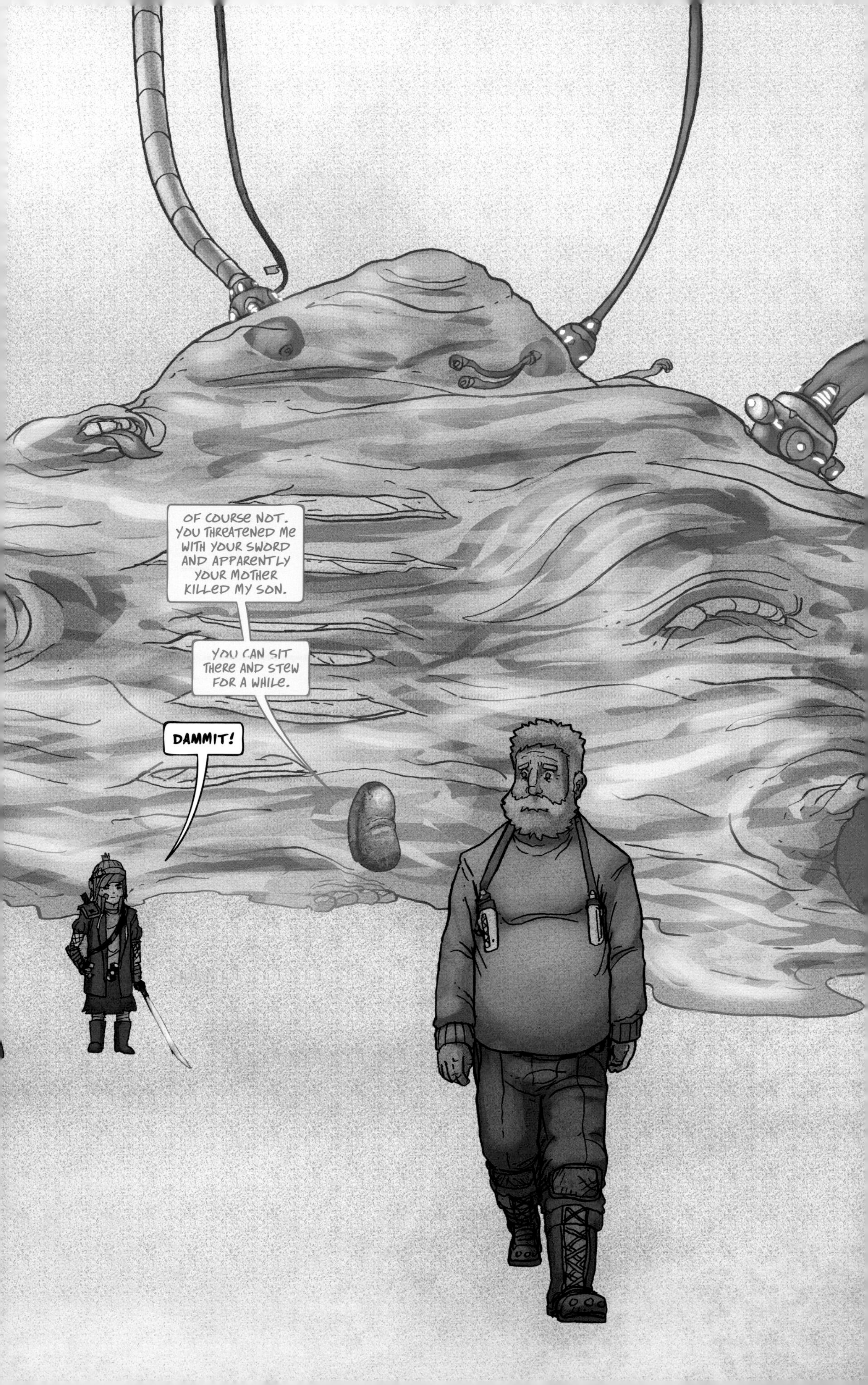
OF COURSE NOT. YOU THREATENED ME WITH YOUR SWORD AND APPARENTLY YOUR MOTHER KILLED MY SON.
YOU CAN SIT THERE AND STEW FOR A WHILE.
DAMMIT!

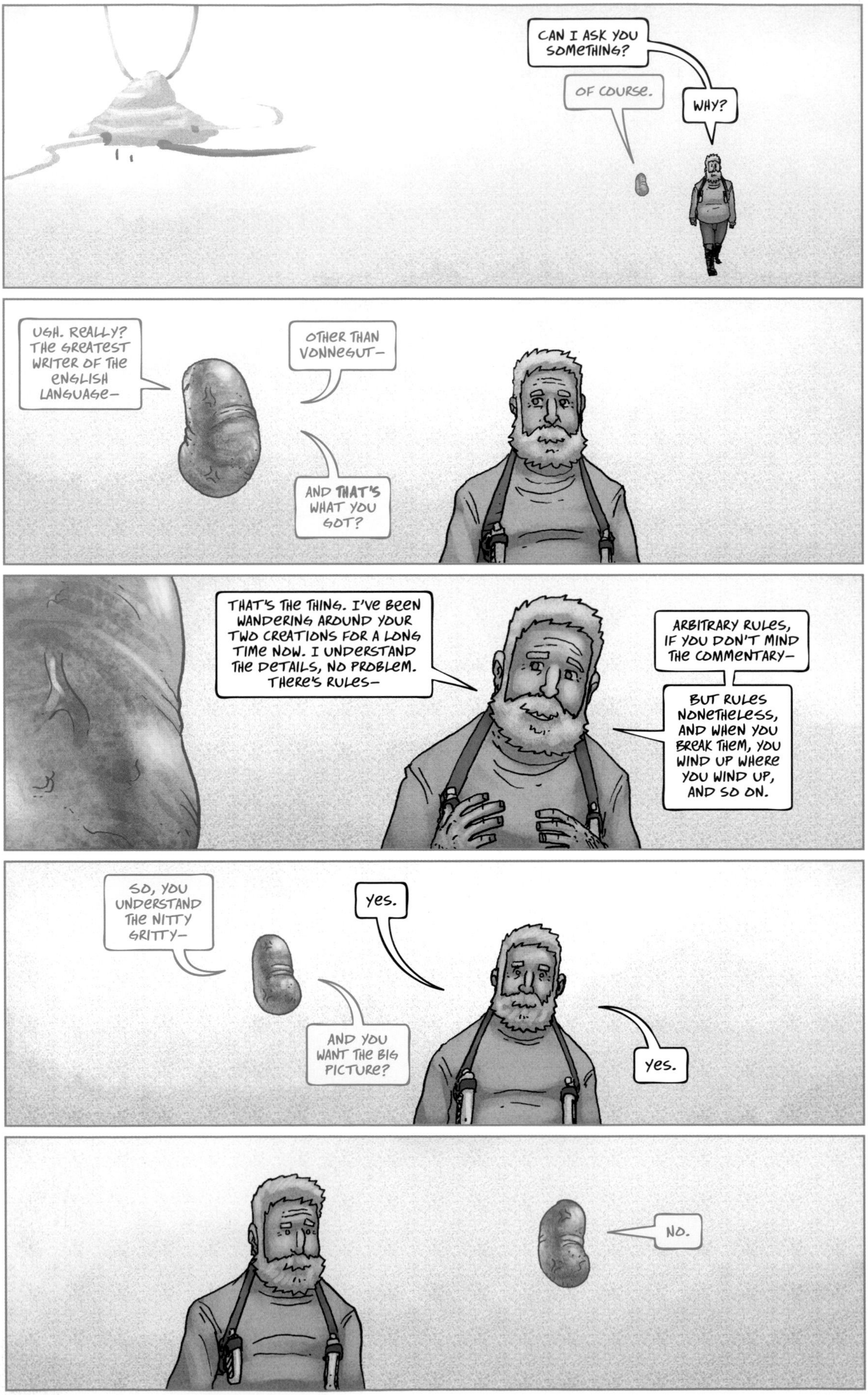
CAN I ASK YOU SOMETHING?
OF COURSE.
WHY?
UGH. REALLY? THE GREATEST WRITER OF THE ENGLISH LANGUAGE—
OTHER THAN VONNEGUT—
AND THAT'S WHAT YOU GOT?
THAT'S THE THING. I'VE BEEN WANDERING AROUND YOUR TWO CREATIONS FOR A LONG TIME NOW. I UNDERSTAND THE DETAILS, NO PROBLEM. THERE'S RULES—
ARBITRARY RULES, IF YOU DON'T MIND THE COMMENTARY—
BUT RULES NONETHELESS, AND WHEN YOU BREAK THEM, YOU WIND UP WHERE YOU WIND UP, AND SO ON.
SO, YOU UNDERSTAND THE NITTY GRITTY—
YES.
AND YOU WANT THE BIG PICTURE?
YES.
NO.

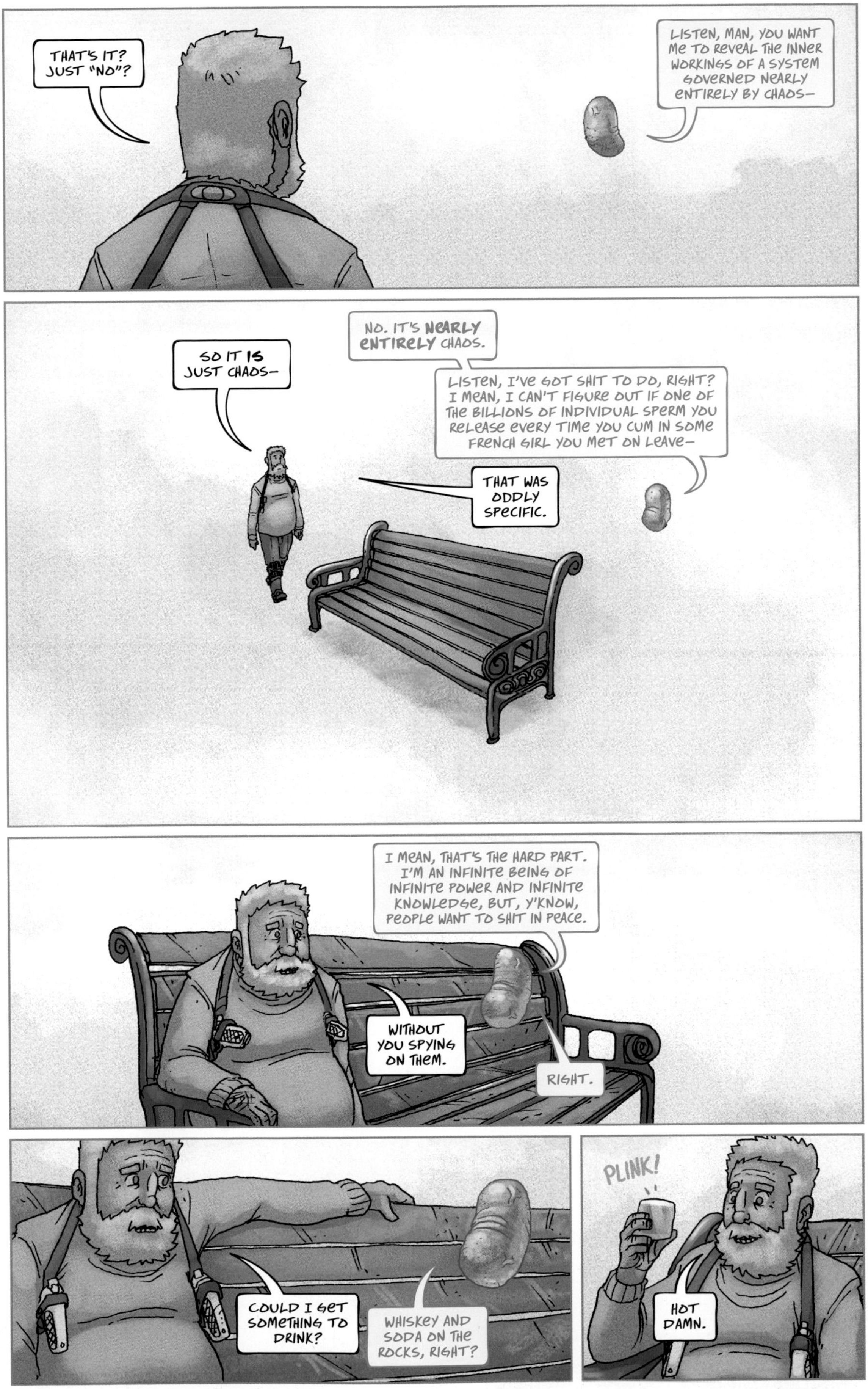
THAT'S IT? JUST "NO"?
LISTEN, MAN, YOU WANT ME TO REVEAL THE INNER WORKINGS OF A SYSTEM GOVERNED NEARLY ENTIRELY BY CHAOS—
SO IT IS JUST CHAOS—
NO. IT'S NEARLY ENTIRELY CHAOS.
LISTEN, I'VE GOT SHIT TO DO, RIGHT? I MEAN, I CAN'T FIGURE OUT IF ONE OF THE BILLIONS OF INDIVIDUAL SPERM YOU RELEASE EVERY TIME YOU CUM IN SOME FRENCH GIRL YOU MET ON LEAVE—
THAT WAS ODDLY SPECIFIC.
I MEAN, THAT'S THE HARD PART. I'M AN INFINITE BEING OF INFINITE POWER AND INFINITE KNOWLEDGE, BUT, Y'KNOW, PEOPLE WANT TO SHIT IN PEACE.
WITHOUT YOU SPYING ON THEM.
RIGHT.
COULD I GET SOMETHING TO DRINK?
WHISKEY AND SODA ON THE ROCKS, RIGHT?
PLINK!
HOT DAMN.

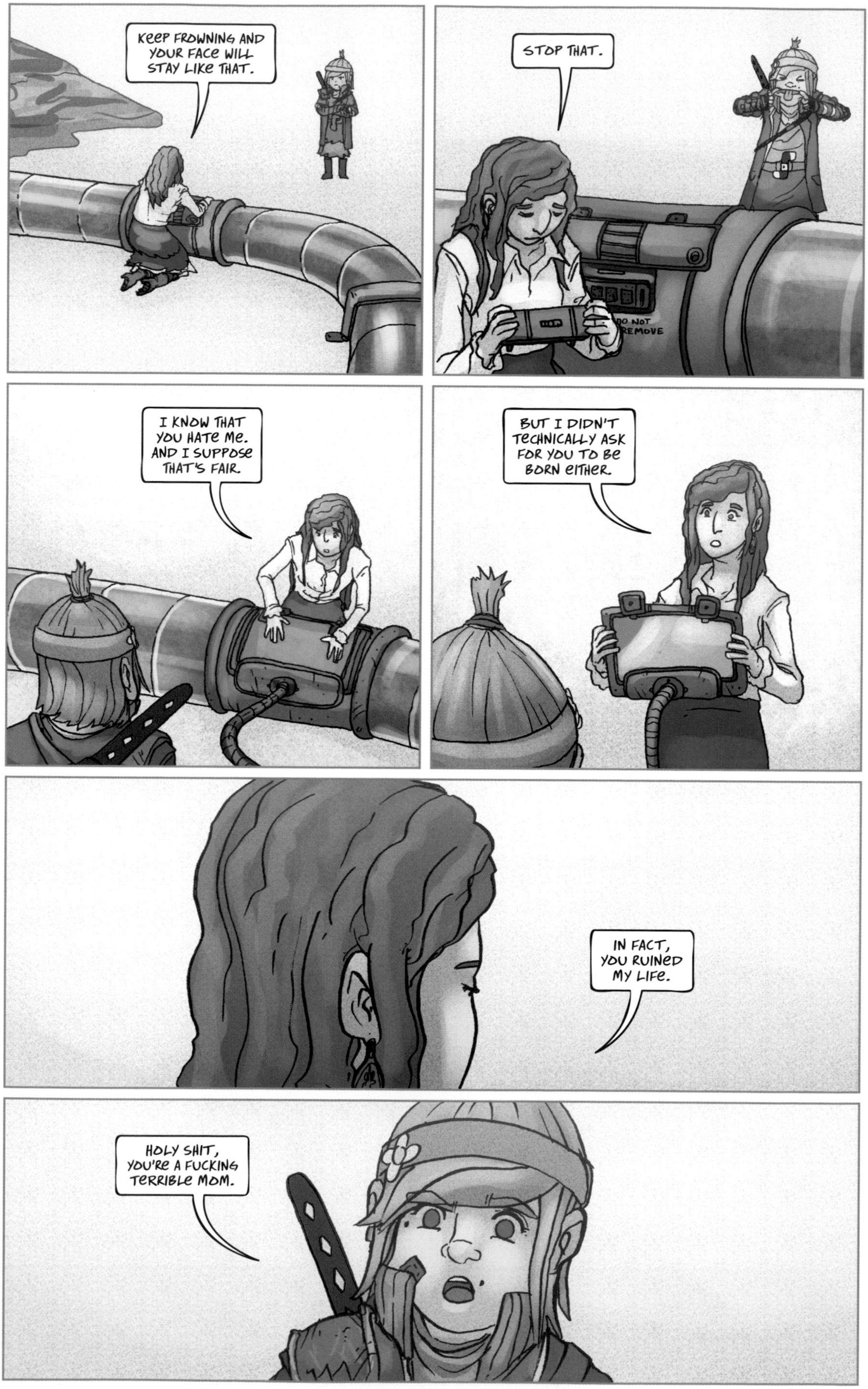
KEEP FROWNING AND YOUR FACE WILL STAY LIKE THAT.
STOP THAT.
DO NOT REMOVE
I KNOW THAT YOU HATE ME. AND I SUPPOSE THAT'S FAIR.
BUT I DIDN'T TECHNICALLY ASK FOR YOU TO BE BORN EITHER.
IN FACT, YOU RUINED MY LIFE.
HOLY SHIT, YOU'RE A FUCKING TERRIBLE MOM.

I KNOW. I'M SORRY.

APOLOGIES ARE **BULLSHIT**.

THE MAN WHO IMPREGNATED ME AND ABANDONED ME? **HE** WAS SORRY.

THE MEN WHO FUCKED ME SO THAT I COULD PAY RENT? **THEY** SHOULD BE SORRY.

THE MONSTERS WHO RAPED ME AND BEAT ME AND LEFT ME TO DIE, KILLING YOU IN THE PROCESS? **THEY** DEFINITELY DIDN'T FEEL SORRY.

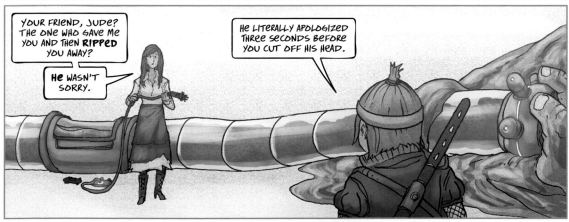

YOUR FRIEND, JUDE? THE ONE WHO GAVE ME YOU AND THEN **RIPPED** YOU AWAY?

HE WASN'T SORRY.

HE LITERALLY APOLOGIZED THREE SECONDS BEFORE YOU CUT OFF HIS HEAD.

APOLOGIES ARE BULLSHIT.

NOW HELP ME TRY TO DESTROY GOD'S SHIT PILE.

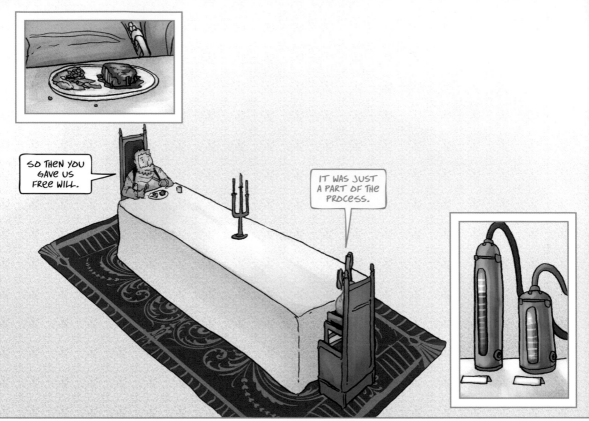

SO THEN YOU GAVE US FREE WILL.

IT WAS JUST A PART OF THE PROCESS.

I CAN'T WATCH EVERYBODY, I CAN'T MAKE DECISIONS FOR EVERYBODY, AND, FRANKLY, MORALITY WAS, I THOUGHT, INBRED.

BIG BOI CHAIR

THAT'S CLEARLY ABSURD—

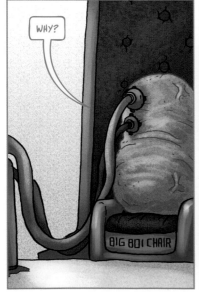

WHY?

BIG BOI CHAIR

THE SLAUGHTER OF NATIVE AMERICANS, THE AFRICAN SLAVE TRADE, WORLD WAR I **AND** 2, THE HOLOCAUST—

OUTLIERS!

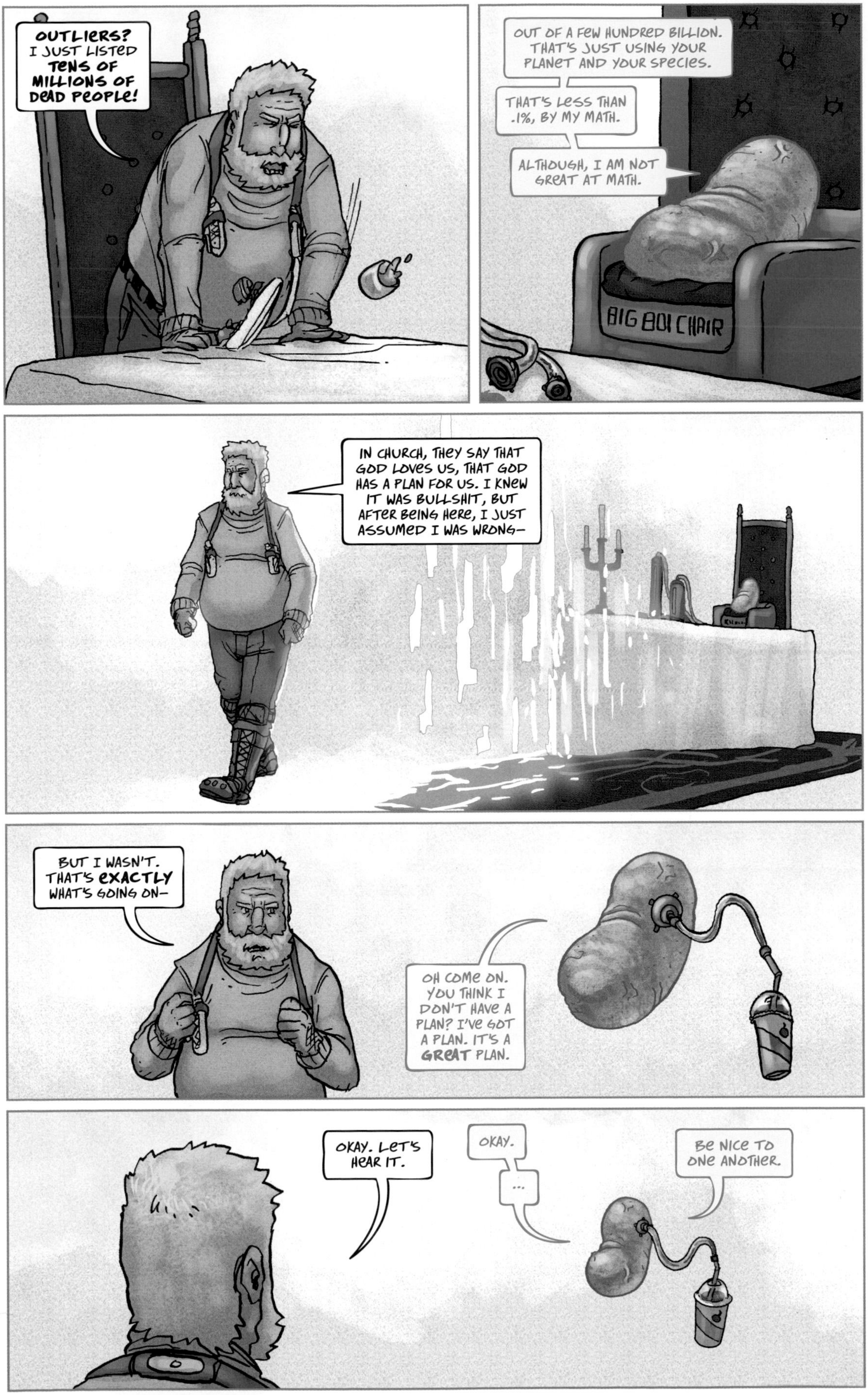
OUTLIERS? I JUST LISTED TENS OF MILLIONS OF DEAD PEOPLE!
OUT OF A FEW HUNDRED BILLION. THAT'S JUST USING YOUR PLANET AND YOUR SPECIES.
THAT'S LESS THAN .1%, BY MY MATH.
ALTHOUGH, I AM NOT GREAT AT MATH.
BIG BOI CHAIR
IN CHURCH, THEY SAY THAT GOD LOVES US, THAT GOD HAS A PLAN FOR US. I KNEW IT WAS BULLSHIT, BUT AFTER BEING HERE, I JUST ASSUMED I WAS WRONG–
BUT I WASN'T. THAT'S EXACTLY WHAT'S GOING ON–
OH COME ON. YOU THINK I DON'T HAVE A PLAN? I'VE GOT A PLAN. IT'S A GREAT PLAN.
OKAY. LET'S HEAR IT.
OKAY.
...
BE NICE TO ONE ANOTHER.

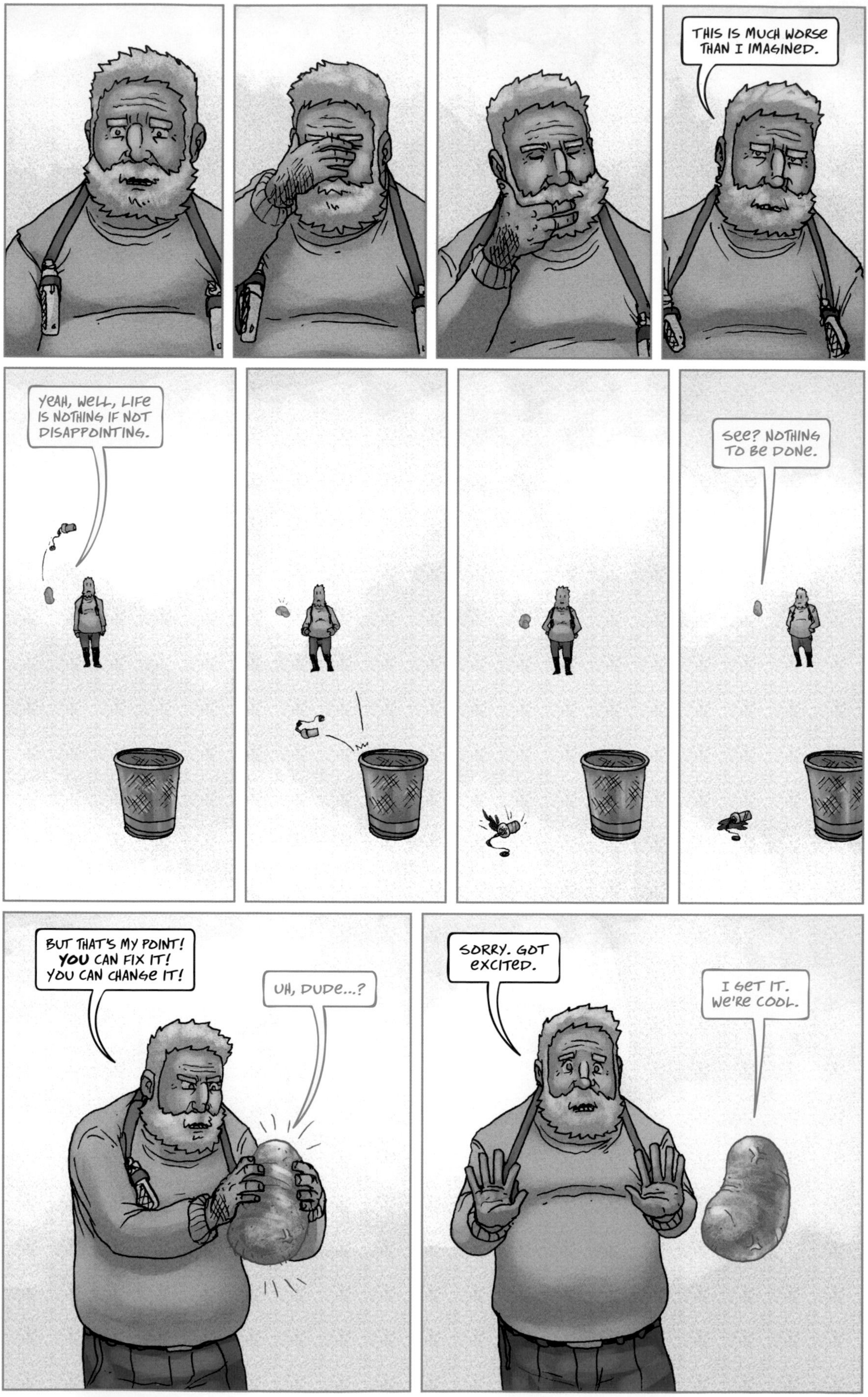
THIS IS MUCH WORSE THAN I IMAGINED.
YEAH, WELL, LIFE IS NOTHING IF NOT DISAPPOINTING.
SEE? NOTHING TO BE DONE.
BUT THAT'S MY POINT! **YOU** CAN FIX IT! YOU CAN CHANGE IT!
UH, DUDE...?
SORRY. GOT EXCITED.
I GET IT. WE'RE COOL.

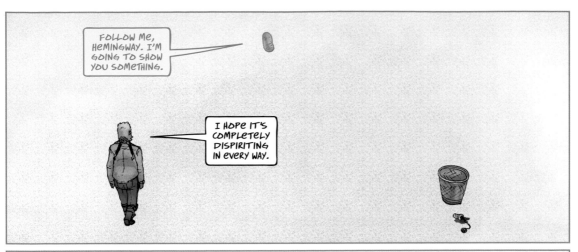

FOLLOW ME, HEMINGWAY. I'M GOING TO SHOW YOU SOMETHING.

I HOPE IT'S COMPLETELY DISPIRITING IN EVERY WAY.

HEY, FISH GOTTA SWIM, DADDY-O.

THERE'S **REALLY** NO PLAN? NO GREAT COSMIC **ANYTHING?**

WHAT DO YOU WANT ME TO SAY, ERNEST? DO YOU WANT ME TO LIE?

TO ATTEMPT TO OFFER SOME SIMPLE ANSWER THAT PACIFIES YOU AND YET OFFERS NO REAL TANGIBLE, WELL, ANYTHING?

SORT OF.

COMING RIGHT UP.

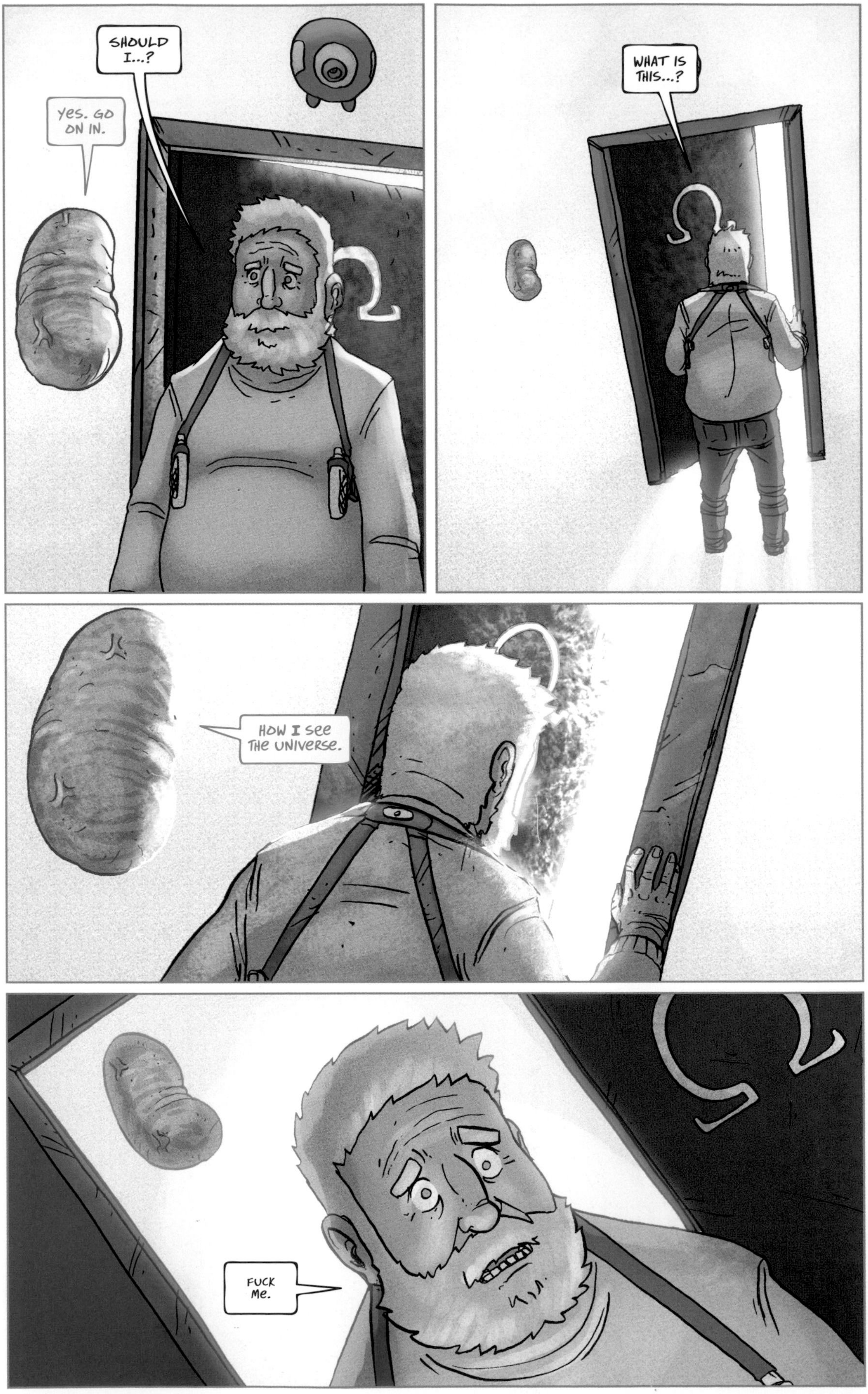
SHOULD I...?
YES. GO ON IN.
WHAT IS THIS...?
HOW I SEE THE UNIVERSE.
FUCK ME.

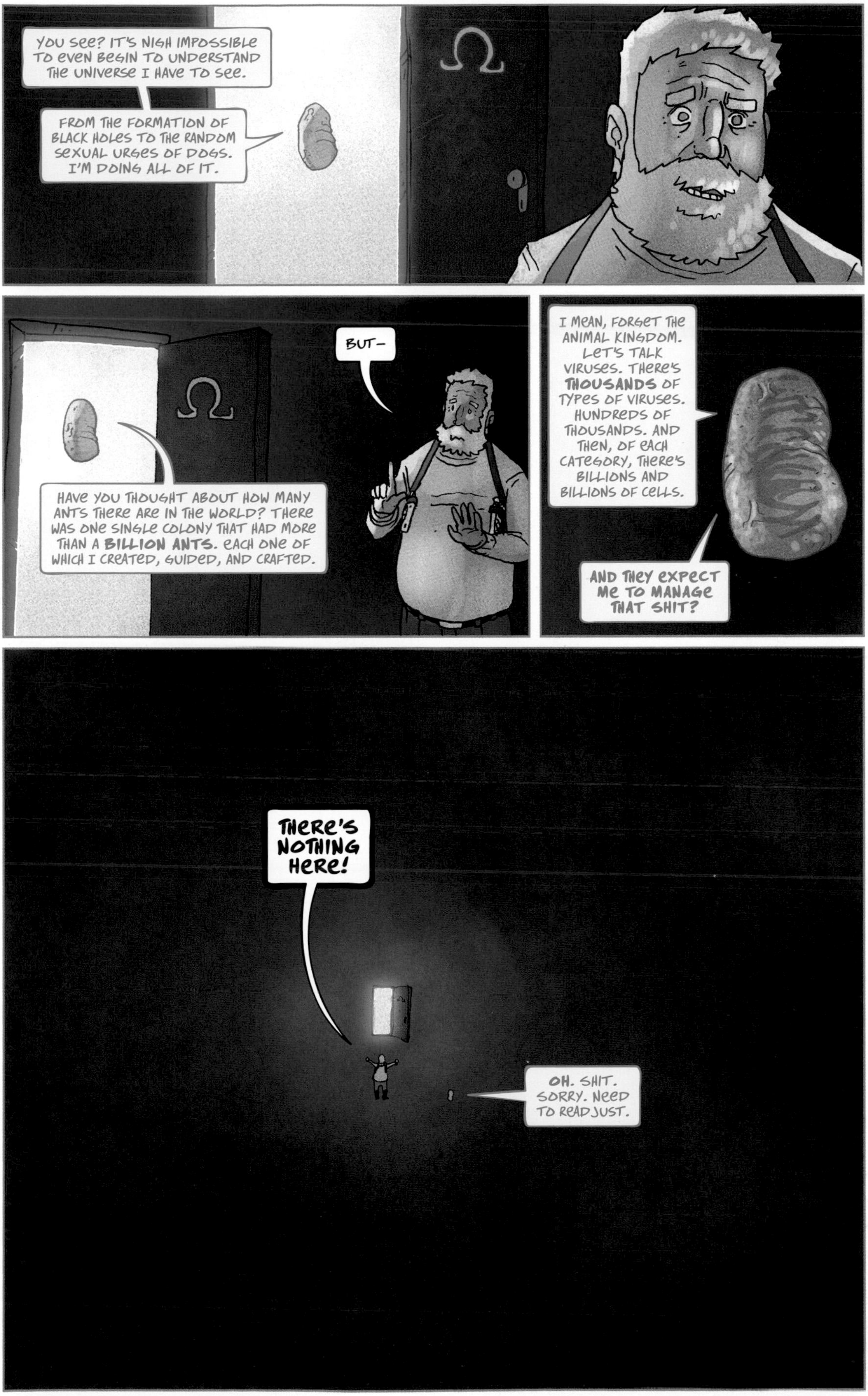
YOU SEE? IT'S NIGH IMPOSSIBLE TO EVEN BEGIN TO UNDERSTAND THE UNIVERSE I HAVE TO SEE.
FROM THE FORMATION OF BLACK HOLES TO THE RANDOM SEXUAL URGES OF DOGS. I'M DOING ALL OF IT.
HAVE YOU THOUGHT ABOUT HOW MANY ANTS THERE ARE IN THE WORLD? THERE WAS ONE SINGLE COLONY THAT HAD MORE THAN A **BILLION ANTS**. EACH ONE OF WHICH I CREATED, GUIDED, AND CRAFTED.
BUT–
I MEAN, FORGET THE ANIMAL KINGDOM. LET'S TALK VIRUSES. THERE'S **THOUSANDS** OF TYPES OF VIRUSES. HUNDREDS OF THOUSANDS. AND THEN, OF EACH CATEGORY, THERE'S BILLIONS AND BILLIONS OF CELLS.
AND THEY EXPECT ME TO MANAGE THAT SHIT?
THERE'S NOTHING HERE!
OH. SHIT. SORRY. NEED TO READJUST.

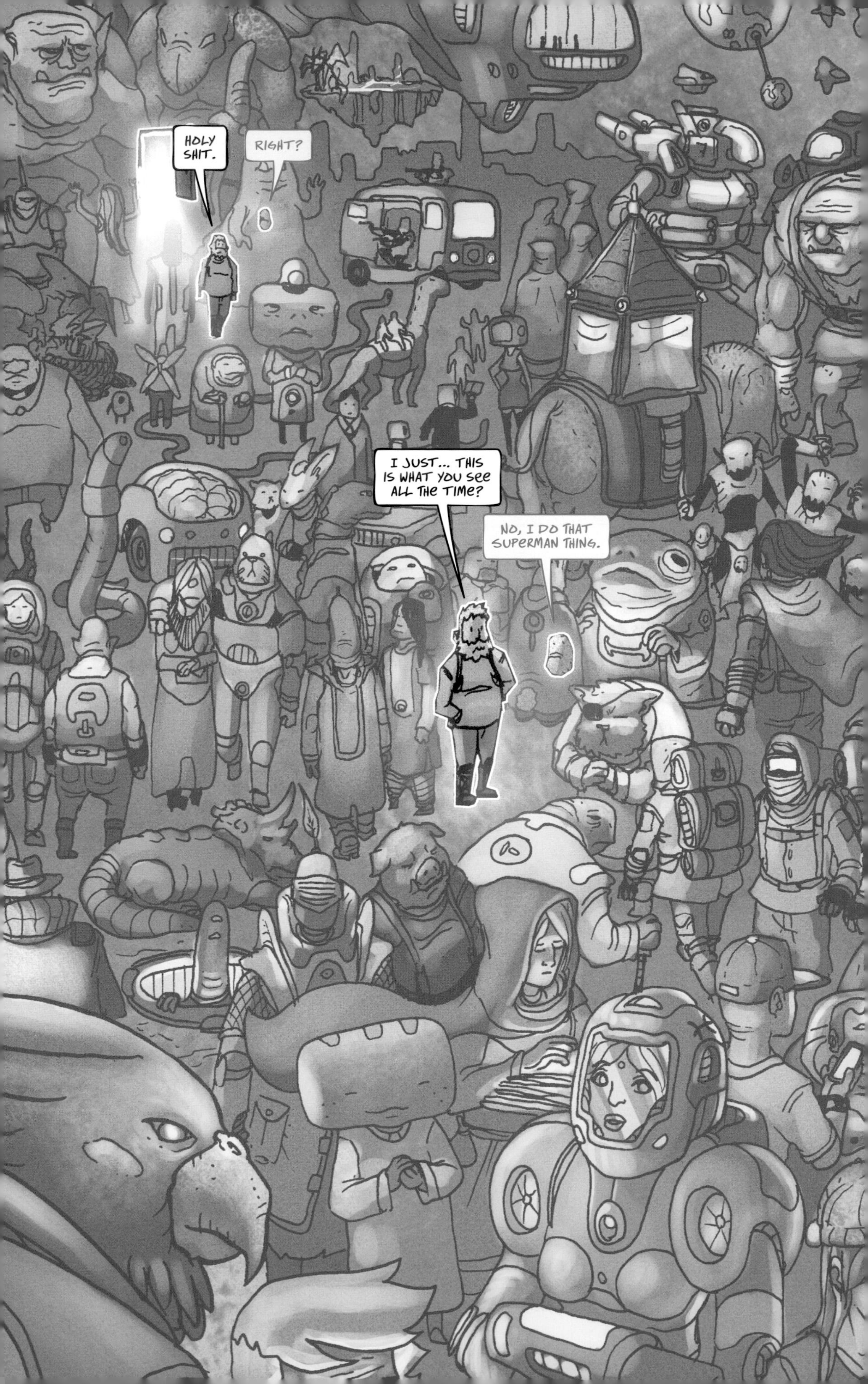
HOLY SHIT.
RIGHT?
I JUST... THIS IS WHAT YOU SEE ALL THE TIME?
NO, I DO THAT SUPERMAN THING.

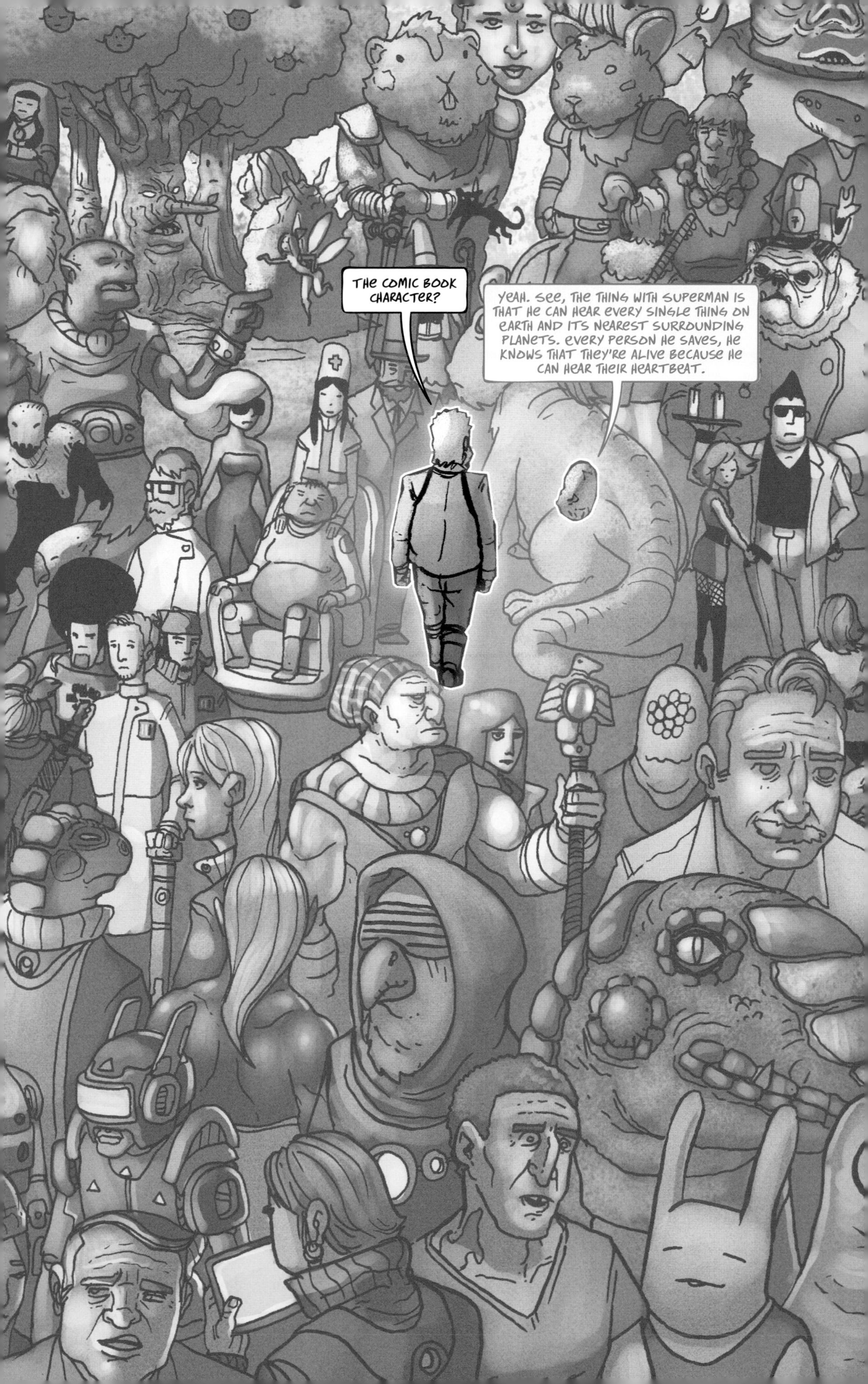
THE COMIC BOOK CHARACTER?
YEAH. SEE, THE THING WITH SUPERMAN IS THAT HE CAN HEAR EVERY SINGLE THING ON EARTH AND ITS NEAREST SURROUNDING PLANETS. EVERY PERSON HE SAVES, HE KNOWS THAT THEY'RE ALIVE BECAUSE HE CAN HEAR THEIR HEARTBEAT.

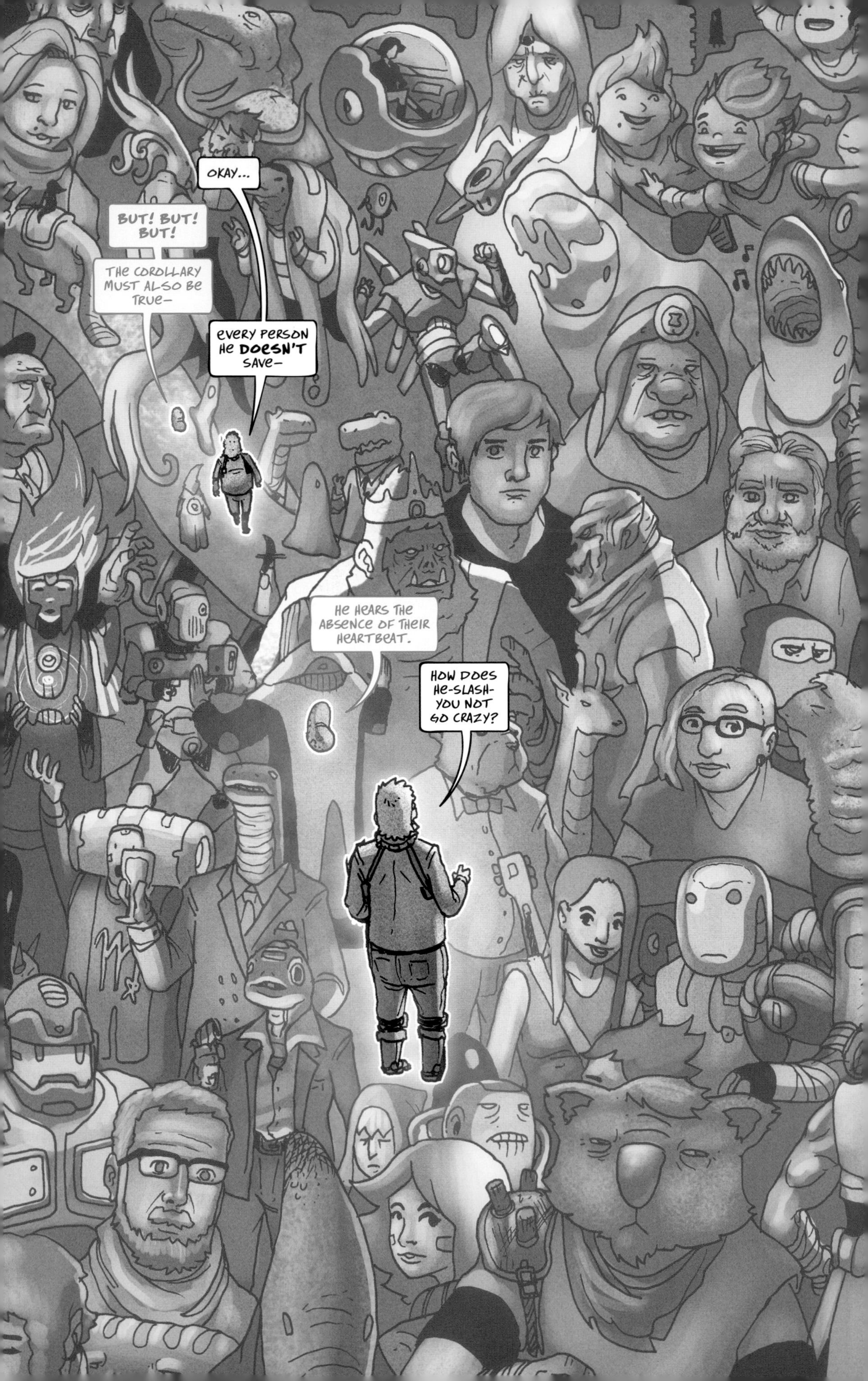
OKAY...
BUT! BUT! BUT!
THE COROLLARY MUST ALSO BE TRUE–
EVERY PERSON HE **DOESN'T** SAVE–
HE HEARS THE ABSENCE OF THEIR HEARTBEAT.
HOW DOES HE-SLASH-YOU NOT GO CRAZY?

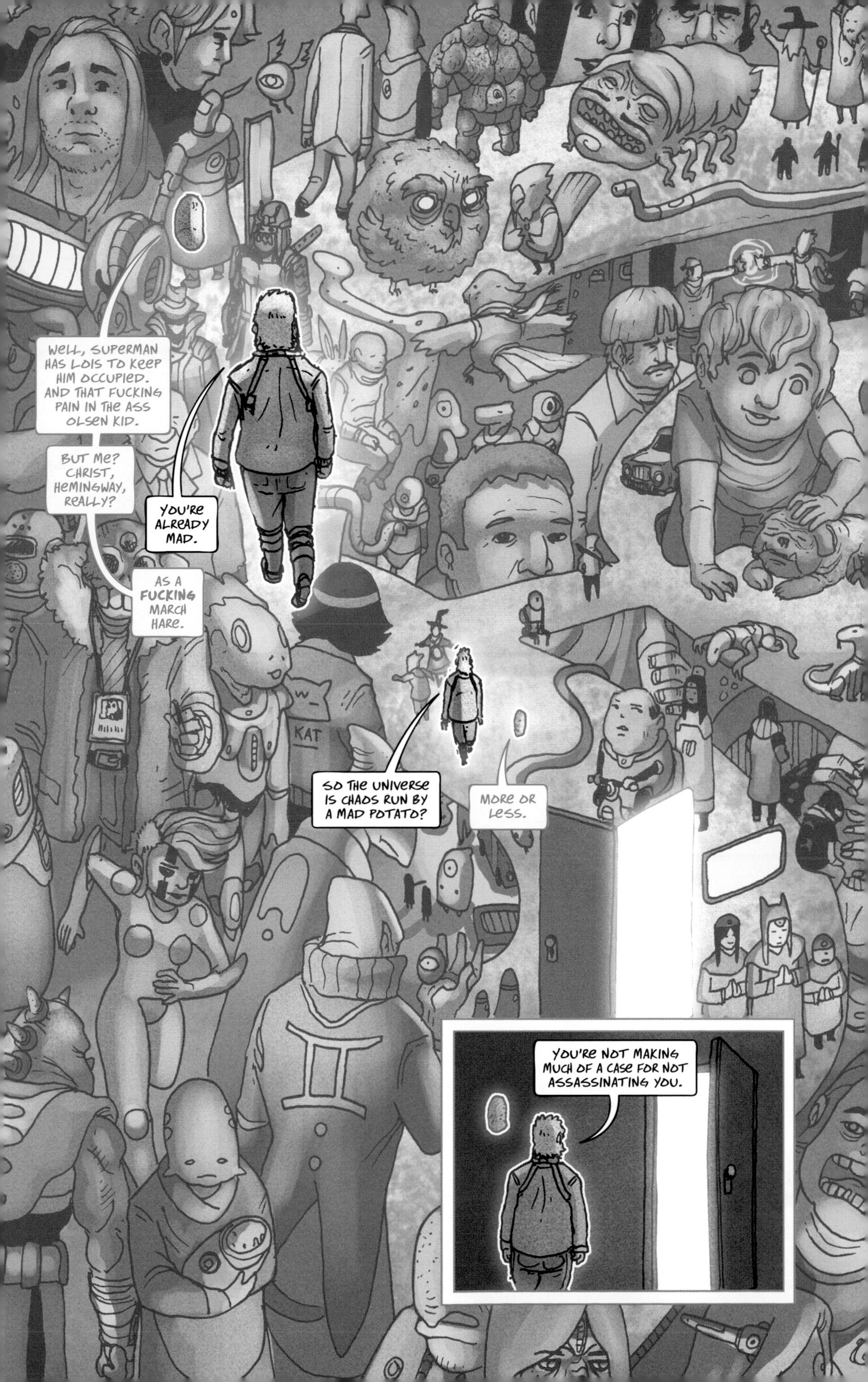
WELL, SUPERMAN HAS LOIS TO KEEP HIM OCCUPIED. AND THAT FUCKING PAIN IN THE ASS OLSEN KID.
BUT ME? CHRIST, HEMINGWAY, REALLY?
YOU'RE ALREADY MAD.
AS A FUCKING MARCH HARE.
KAT
SO THE UNIVERSE IS CHAOS RUN BY A MAD POTATO?
MORE OR LESS.
YOU'RE NOT MAKING MUCH OF A CASE FOR NOT ASSASSINATING YOU.

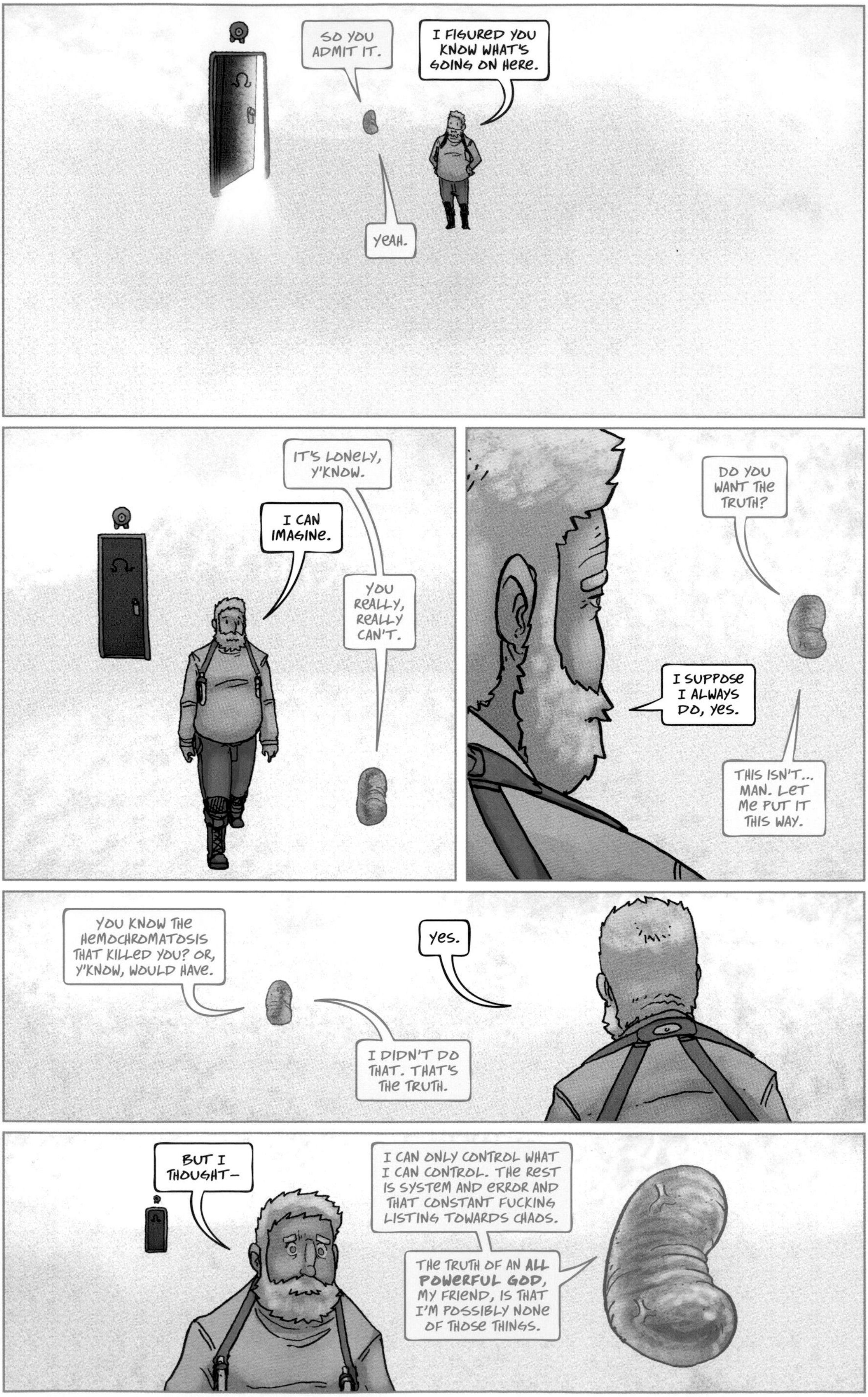
SO YOU ADMIT IT.
I FIGURED YOU KNOW WHAT'S GOING ON HERE.
YEAH.
IT'S LONELY, Y'KNOW.
I CAN IMAGINE.
YOU REALLY, REALLY CAN'T.
DO YOU WANT THE TRUTH?
I SUPPOSE I ALWAYS DO, YES.
THIS ISN'T... MAN. LET ME PUT IT THIS WAY.
YOU KNOW THE HEMOCHROMATOSIS THAT KILLED YOU? OR, Y'KNOW, WOULD HAVE.
YES.
I DIDN'T DO THAT. THAT'S THE TRUTH.
BUT I THOUGHT—
I CAN ONLY CONTROL WHAT I CAN CONTROL. THE REST IS SYSTEM AND ERROR AND THAT CONSTANT FUCKING LISTING TOWARDS CHAOS.
THE TRUTH OF AN **ALL POWERFUL GOD**, MY FRIEND, IS THAT I'M POSSIBLY NONE OF THOSE THINGS.

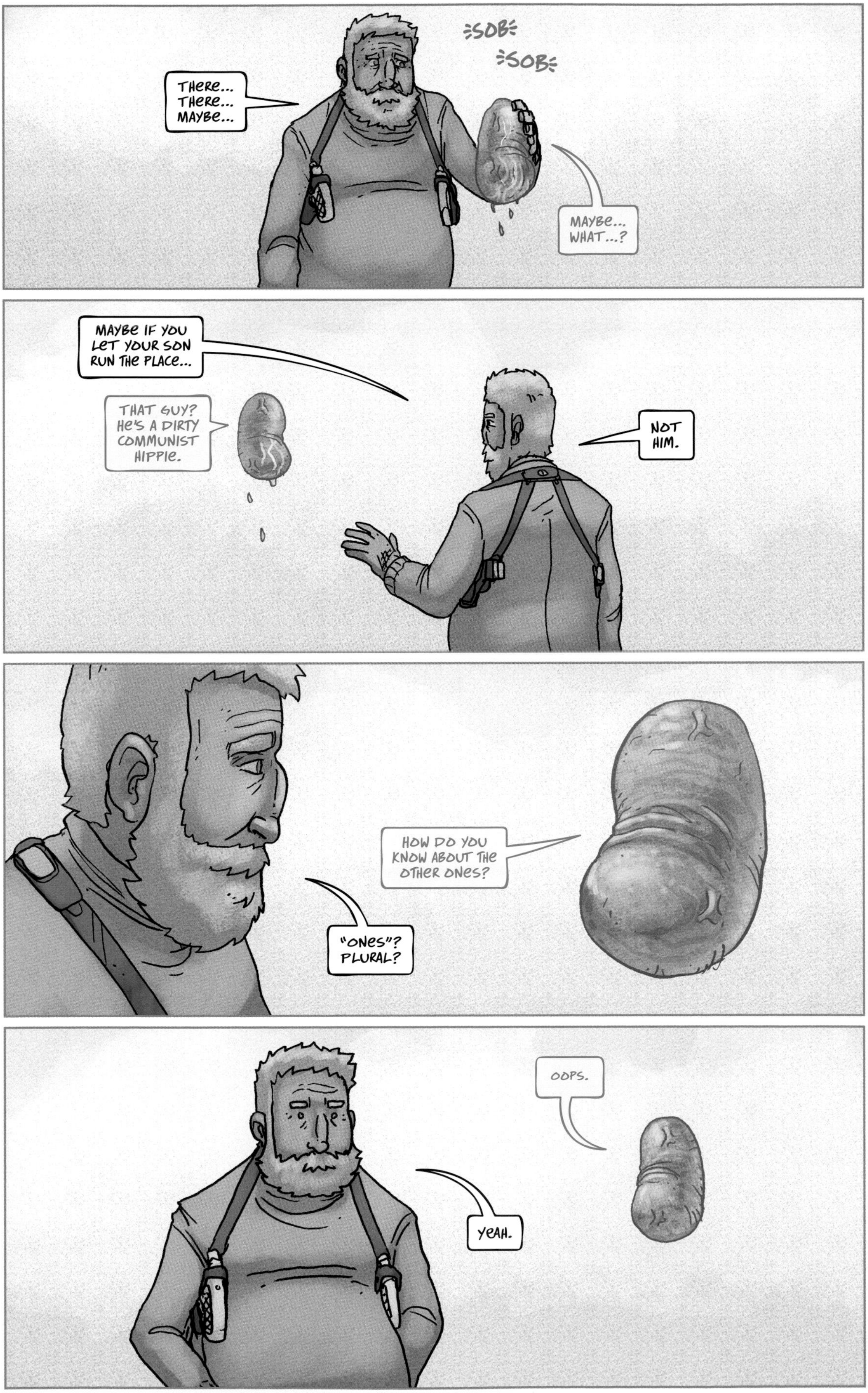
SOB
SOB
THERE... THERE... MAYBE...
MAYBE... WHAT...?
MAYBE IF YOU LET YOUR SON RUN THE PLACE...
THAT GUY? HE'S A DIRTY COMMUNIST HIPPIE.
NOT HIM.
HOW DO YOU KNOW ABOUT THE OTHER ONES?
"ONES"? PLURAL?
OOPS.
YEAH.

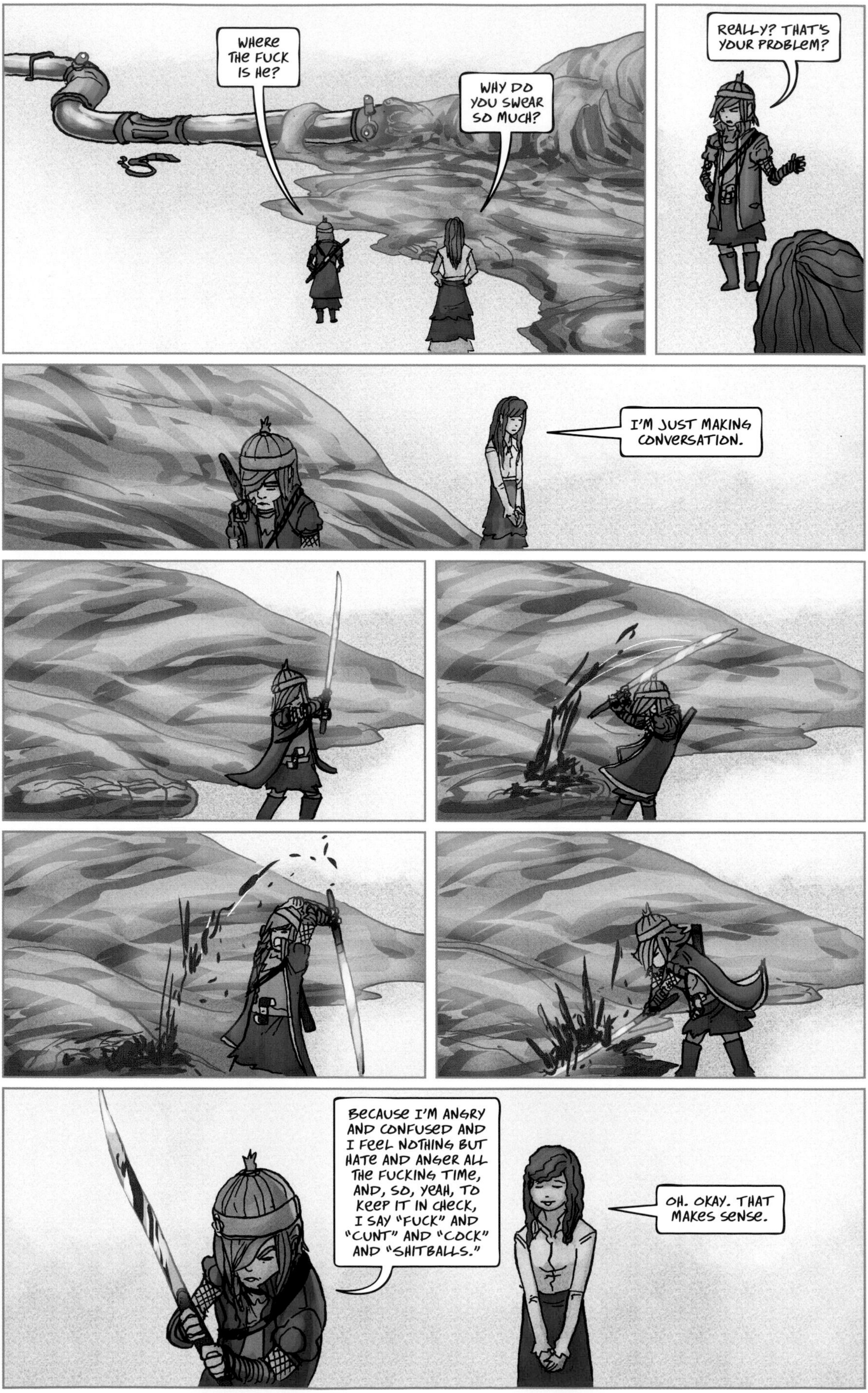
WHERE THE FUCK IS HE?
WHY DO YOU SWEAR SO MUCH?
REALLY? THAT'S YOUR PROBLEM?
I'M JUST MAKING CONVERSATION.
BECAUSE I'M ANGRY AND CONFUSED AND I FEEL NOTHING BUT HATE AND ANGER ALL THE FUCKING TIME, AND, SO, YEAH, TO KEEP IT IN CHECK, I SAY "FUCK" AND "CUNT" AND "COCK" AND "SHITBALLS."
OH. OKAY. THAT MAKES SENSE.

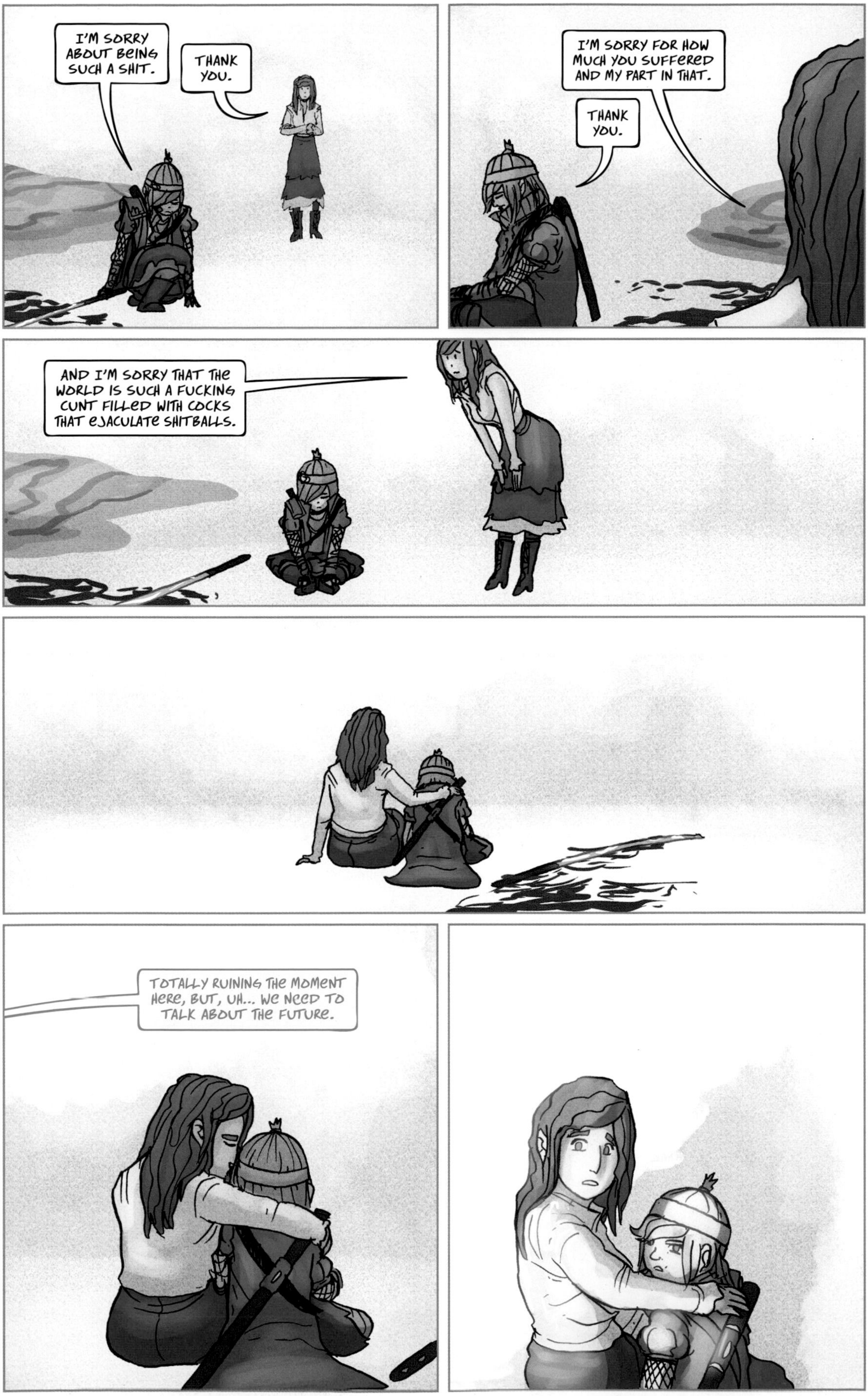
I'M SORRY ABOUT BEING SUCH A SHIT.
THANK YOU.
I'M SORRY FOR HOW MUCH YOU SUFFERED AND MY PART IN THAT.
THANK YOU.
AND I'M SORRY THAT THE WORLD IS SUCH A FUCKING CUNT FILLED WITH COCKS THAT EJACULATE SHITBALLS.
TOTALLY RUINING THE MOMENT HERE, BUT, UH... WE NEED TO TALK ABOUT THE FUTURE.

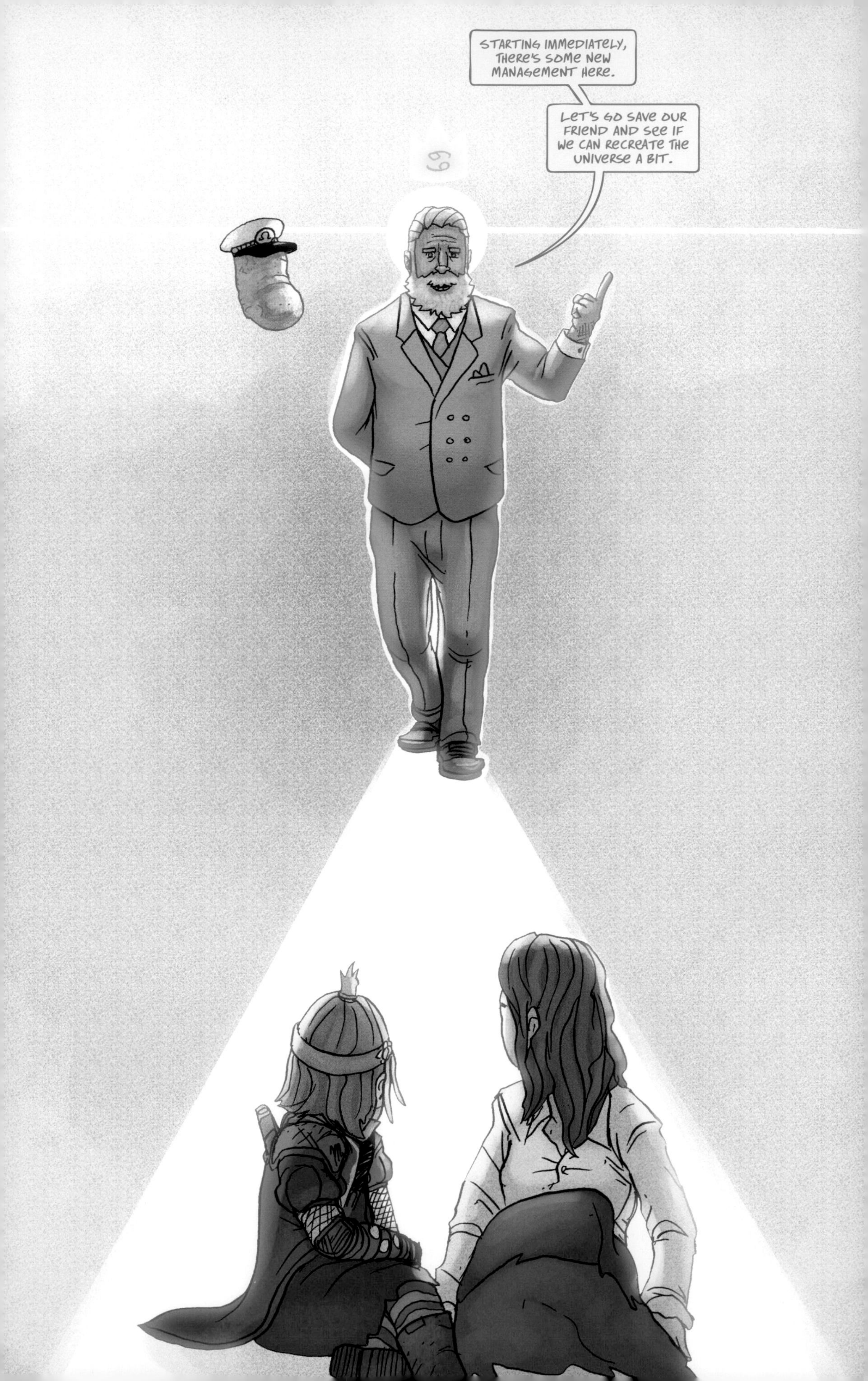
STARTING IMMEDIATELY, THERE'S SOME NEW MANAGEMENT HERE.
LET'S GO SAVE OUR FRIEND AND SEE IF WE CAN RECREATE THE UNIVERSE A BIT.

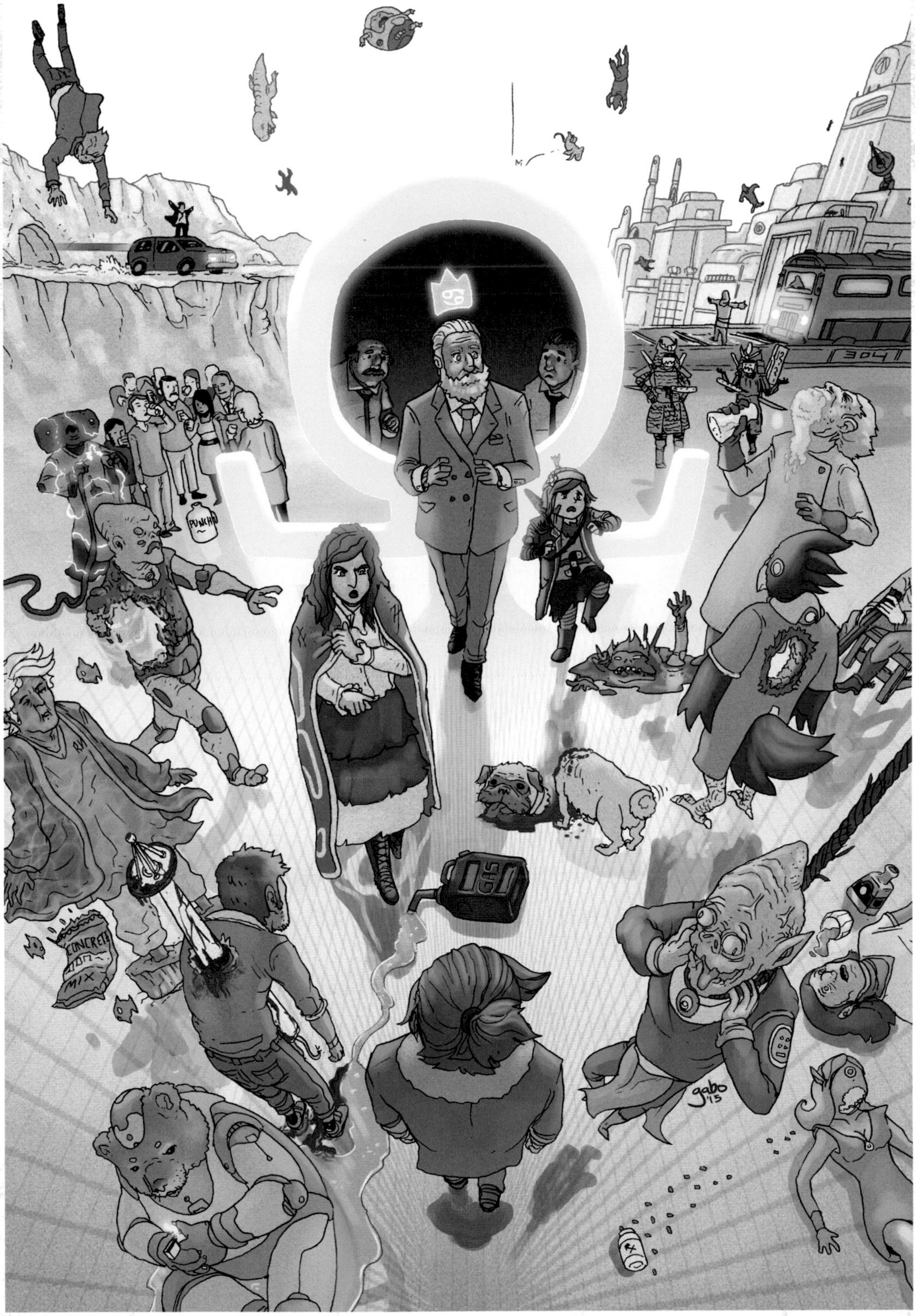
304
gabo '15

Chapter Fourteen

THE LIFE
AFTER

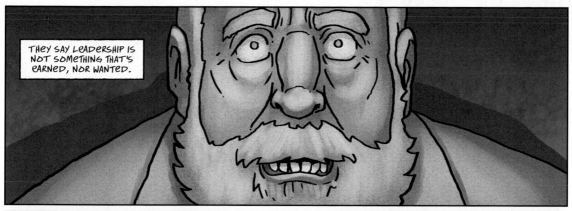

THEY SAY LEADERSHIP IS NOT SOMETHING THAT'S EARNED, NOR WANTED.

IT'S SOMETHING THAT'S FORCED UPON YOU.

AND YOU SINK OR SWIM BASED ON THE CONTENT OF YOUR CHARACTER.

I'VE FOUND MYSELF FIGHTING FOR MY LIFE, FOR THE LIVES OF THE PEOPLE AROUND ME, AND FOR THE LIFE OF MY COUNTRY, DAMNED AS IT MAY HAVE BEEN.

AND THE THING YOU TAKE HOME FROM THAT IS ALWAYS THE SAME.

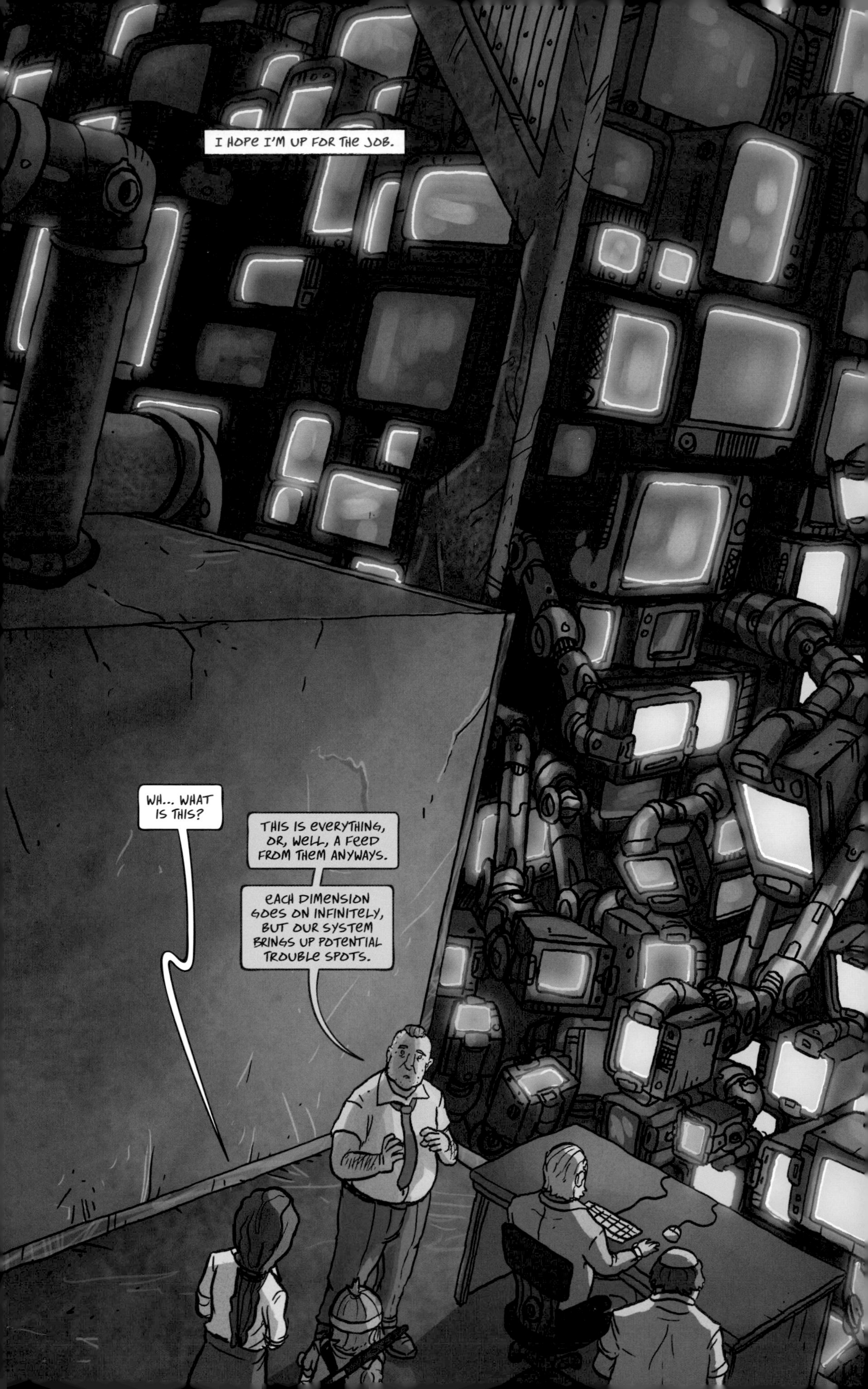
I HOPE I'M UP FOR THE JOB.
WH... WHAT IS THIS?
THIS IS EVERYTHING, OR, WELL, A FEED FROM THEM ANYWAYS.
EACH DIMENSION GOES ON INFINITELY, BUT OUR SYSTEM BRINGS UP POTENTIAL TROUBLE SPOTS.

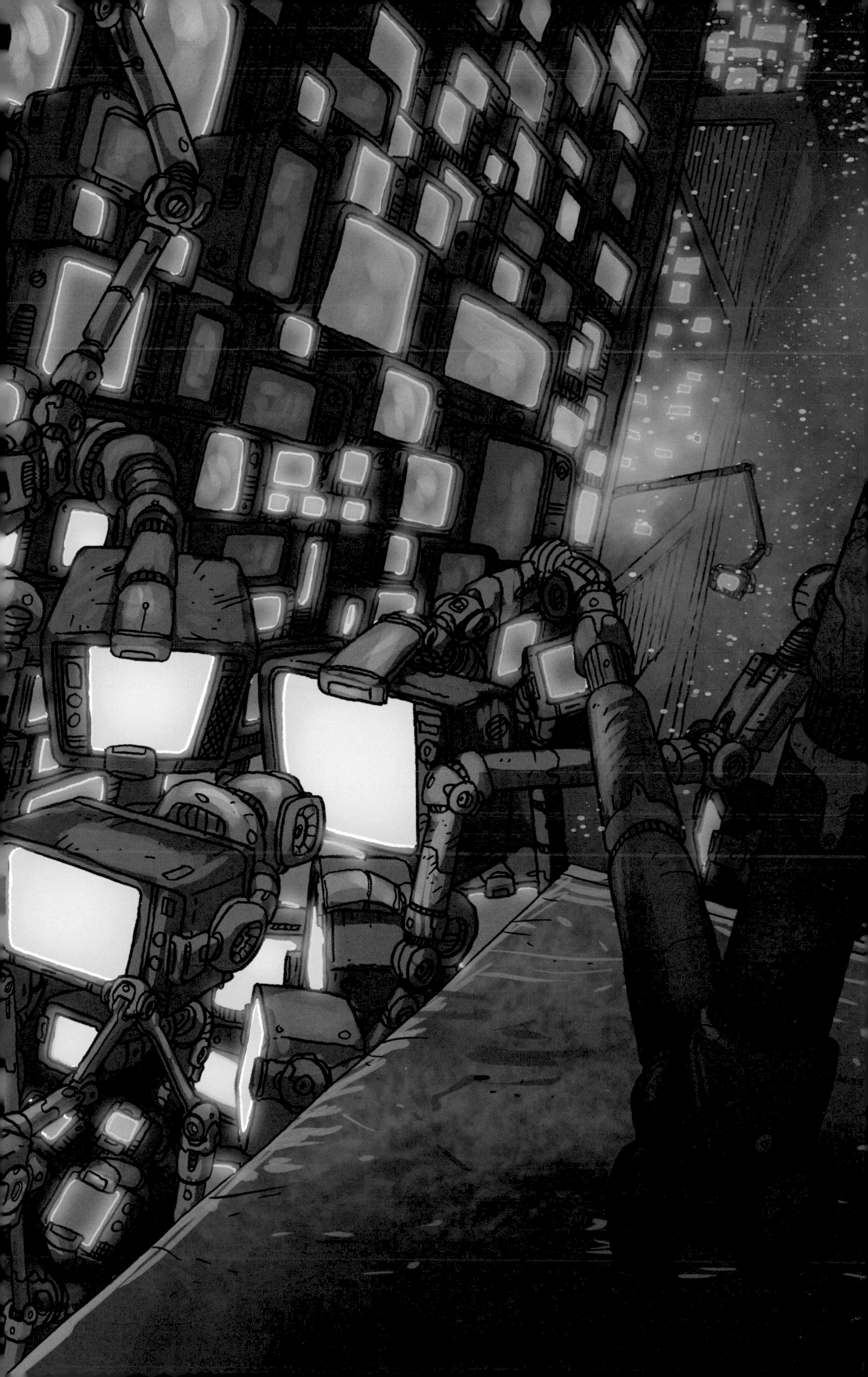

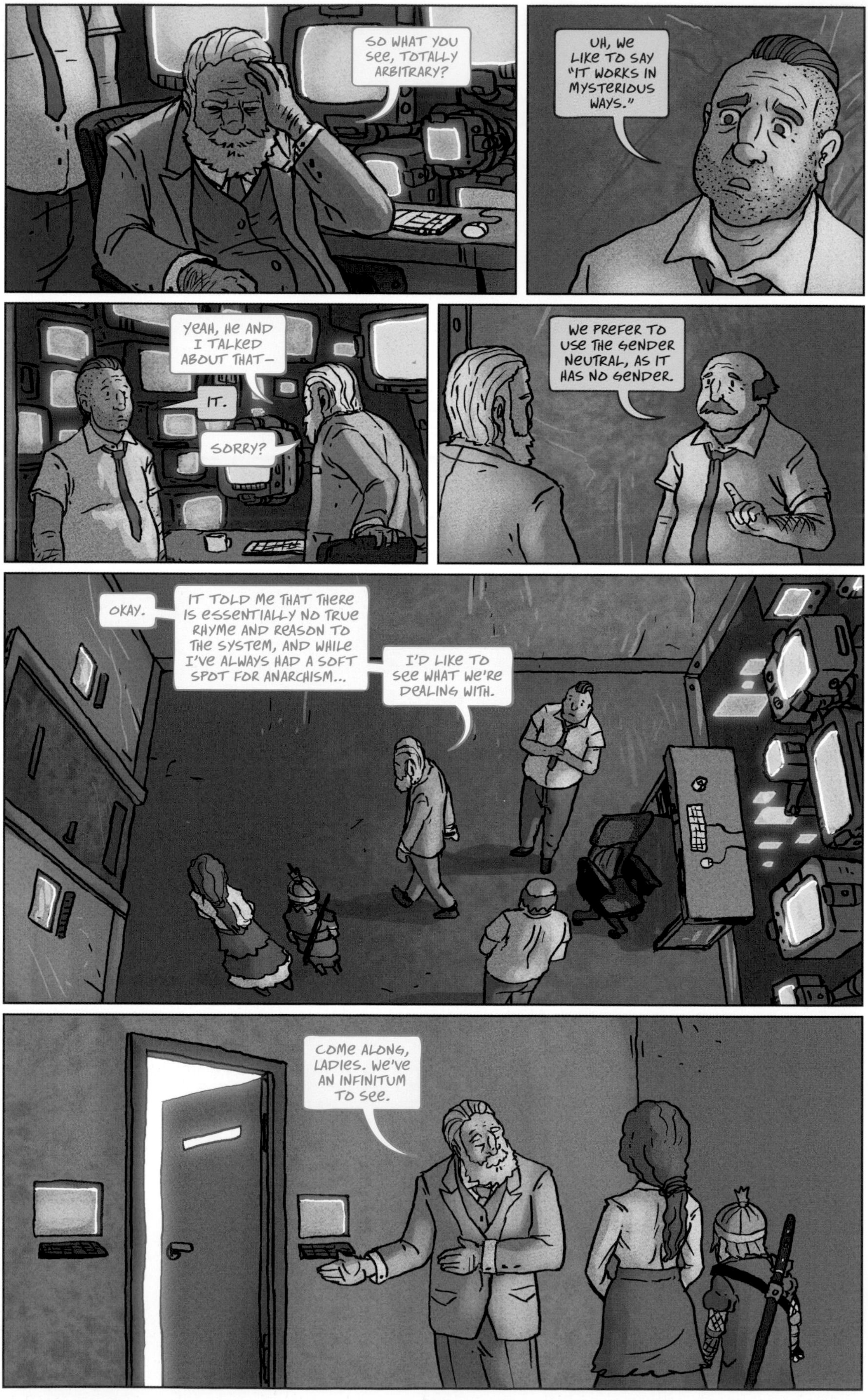
SO WHAT YOU SEE, TOTALLY ARBITRARY?
UH, WE LIKE TO SAY "IT WORKS IN MYSTERIOUS WAYS."
YEAH, HE AND I TALKED ABOUT THAT—
IT.
SORRY?
WE PREFER TO USE THE GENDER NEUTRAL, AS IT HAS NO GENDER.
OKAY.
IT TOLD ME THAT THERE IS ESSENTIALLY NO TRUE RHYME AND REASON TO THE SYSTEM, AND WHILE I'VE ALWAYS HAD A SOFT SPOT FOR ANARCHISM...
I'D LIKE TO SEE WHAT WE'RE DEALING WITH.
COME ALONG, LADIES. WE'VE AN INFINITUM TO SEE.

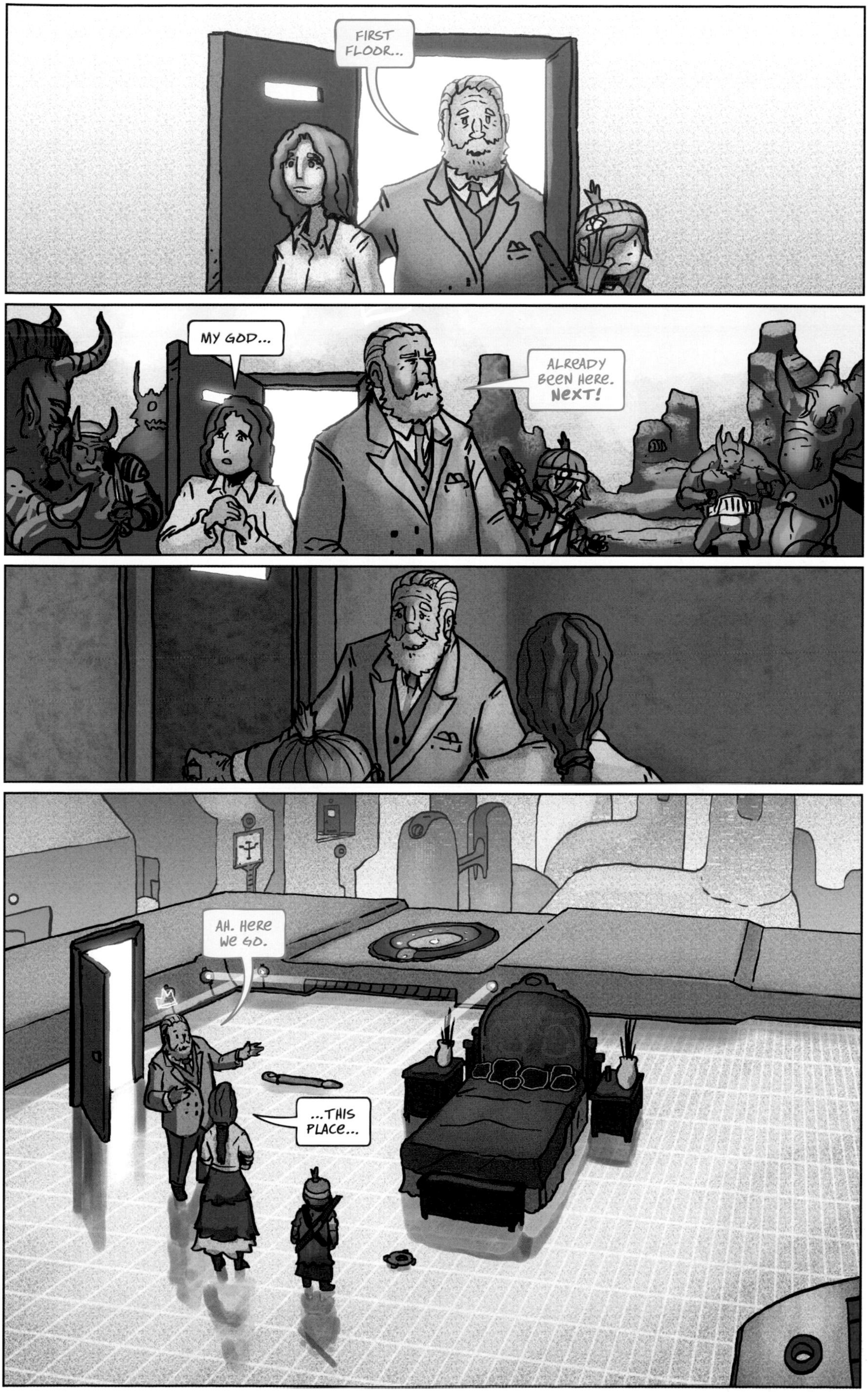

FIRST FLOOR...
MY GOD...
ALREADY BEEN HERE. NEXT!
AH. HERE WE GO.
...THIS PLACE...

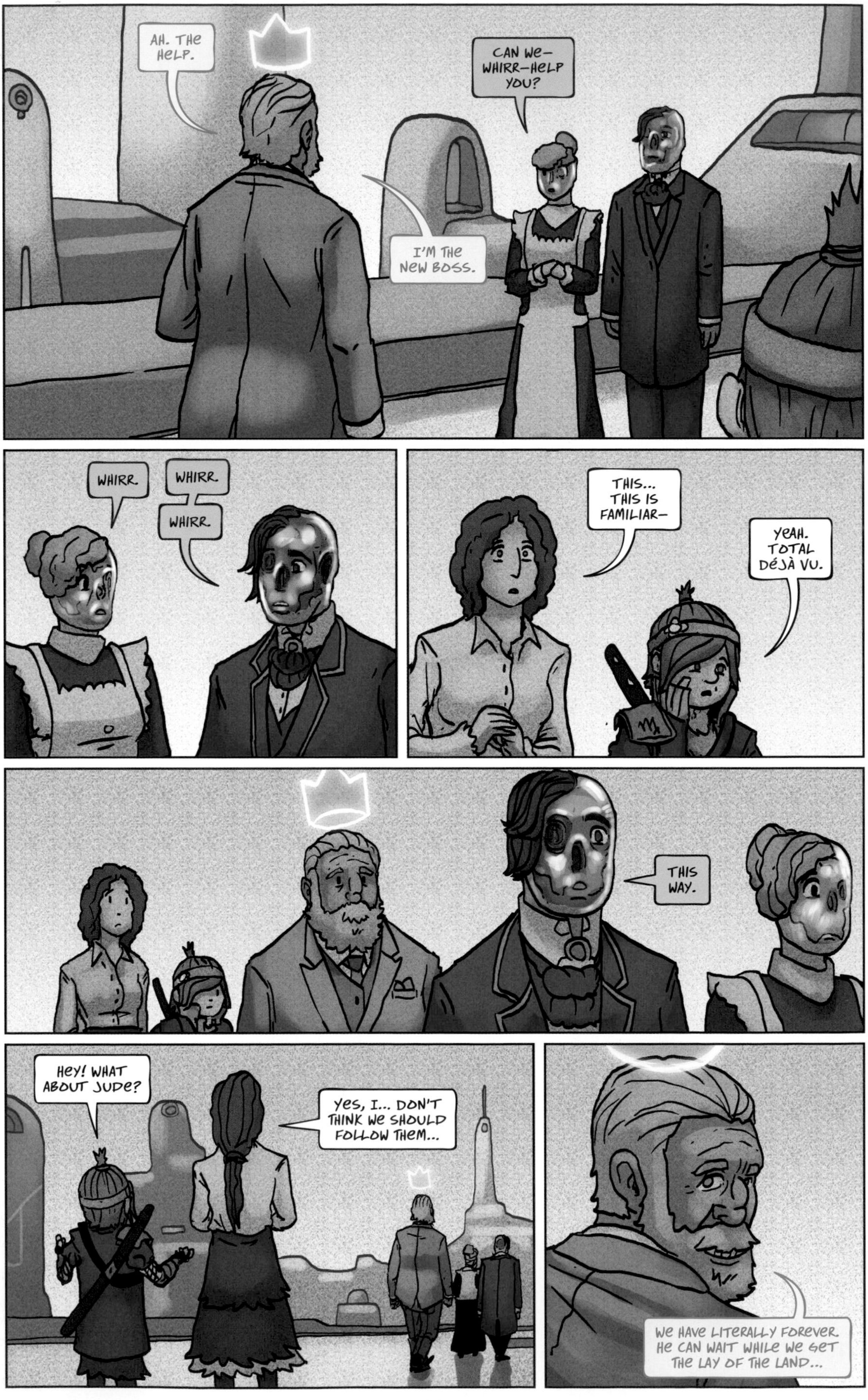
AH. THE HELP.
CAN WE—WHIRR—HELP YOU?
I'M THE NEW BOSS.
WHIRR.
WHIRR.
WHIRR.
THIS... THIS IS FAMILIAR—
YEAH. TOTAL DÉJÀ VU.
THIS WAY.
HEY! WHAT ABOUT JUDE?
YES, I... DON'T THINK WE SHOULD FOLLOW THEM...
WE HAVE LITERALLY FOREVER. HE CAN WAIT WHILE WE GET THE LAY OF THE LAND...

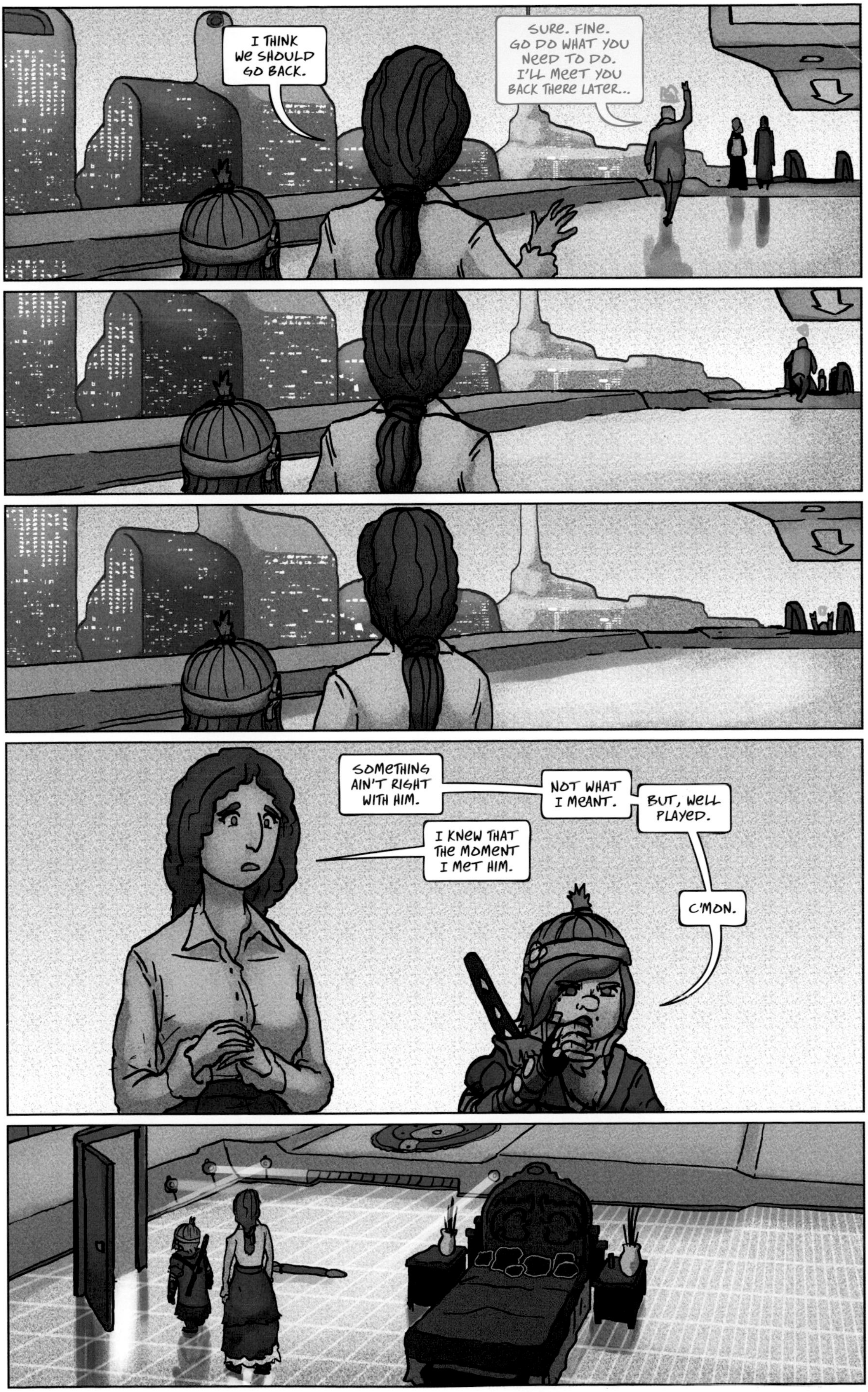
I THINK WE SHOULD GO BACK.
SURE. FINE. GO DO WHAT YOU NEED TO DO. I'LL MEET YOU BACK THERE LATER...
SOMETHING AIN'T RIGHT WITH HIM.
I KNEW THAT THE MOMENT I MET HIM.
NOT WHAT I MEANT.
BUT, WELL PLAYED.
C'MON.

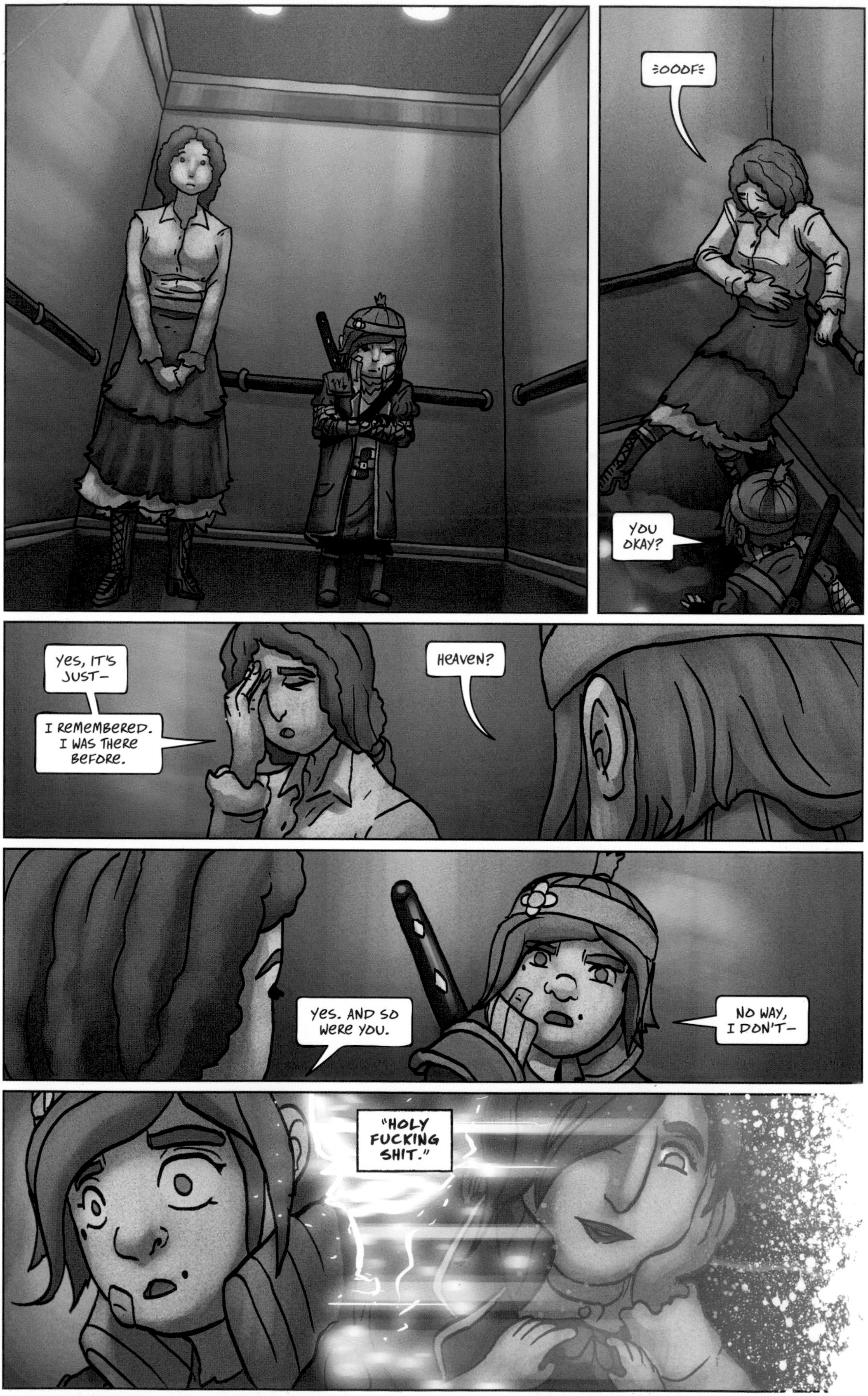

OOOF
YOU OKAY?
YES, IT'S JUST—
I REMEMBERED. I WAS THERE BEFORE.
HEAVEN?
YES. AND SO WERE YOU.
NO WAY, I DON'T—
"HOLY FUCKING SHIT."

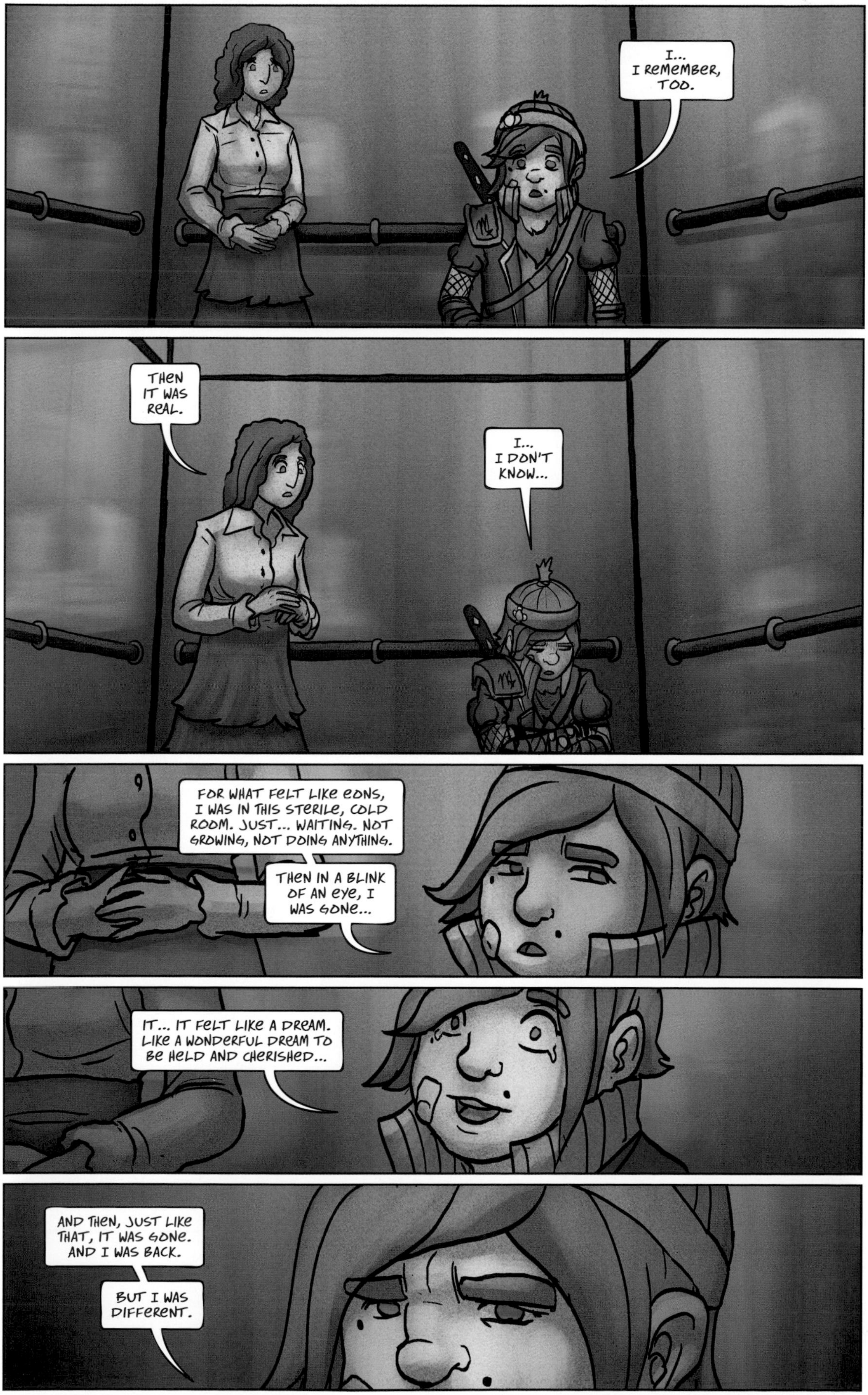
I... I REMEMBER, TOO.
THEN IT WAS REAL.
I... I DON'T KNOW...
FOR WHAT FELT LIKE EONS, I WAS IN THIS STERILE, COLD ROOM. JUST... WAITING. NOT GROWING, NOT DOING ANYTHING.
THEN IN A BLINK OF AN EYE, I WAS GONE...
IT... IT FELT LIKE A DREAM. LIKE A WONDERFUL DREAM TO BE HELD AND CHERISHED...
AND THEN, JUST LIKE THAT, IT WAS GONE. AND I WAS BACK.
BUT I WAS DIFFERENT.

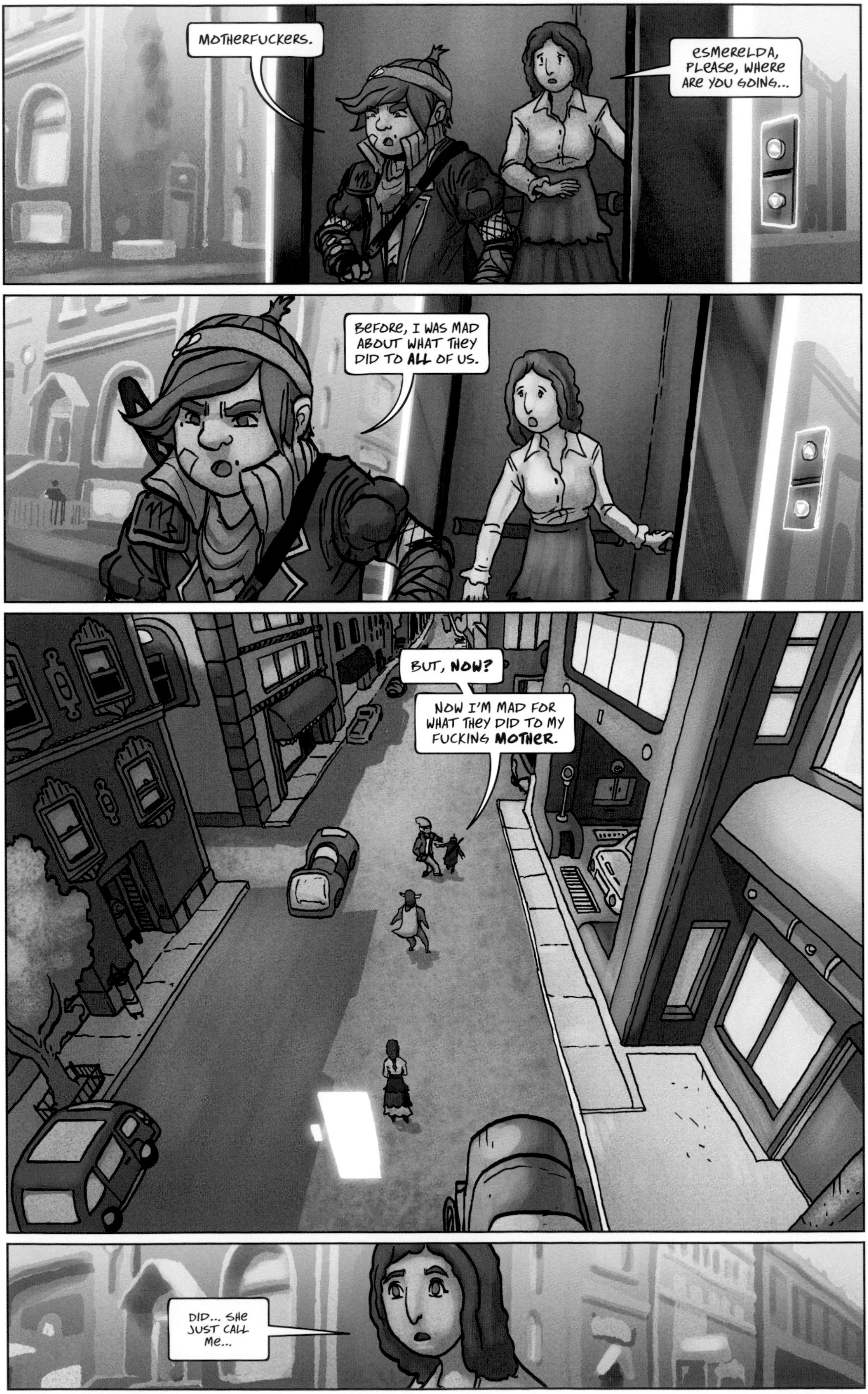
MOTHERFUCKERS.
ESMERELDA, PLEASE, WHERE ARE YOU GOING...
BEFORE, I WAS MAD ABOUT WHAT THEY DID TO **ALL** OF US.
BUT, **NOW?**
NOW I'M MAD FOR WHAT THEY DID TO MY FUCKING **MOTHER**.
DID... SHE JUST CALL ME...

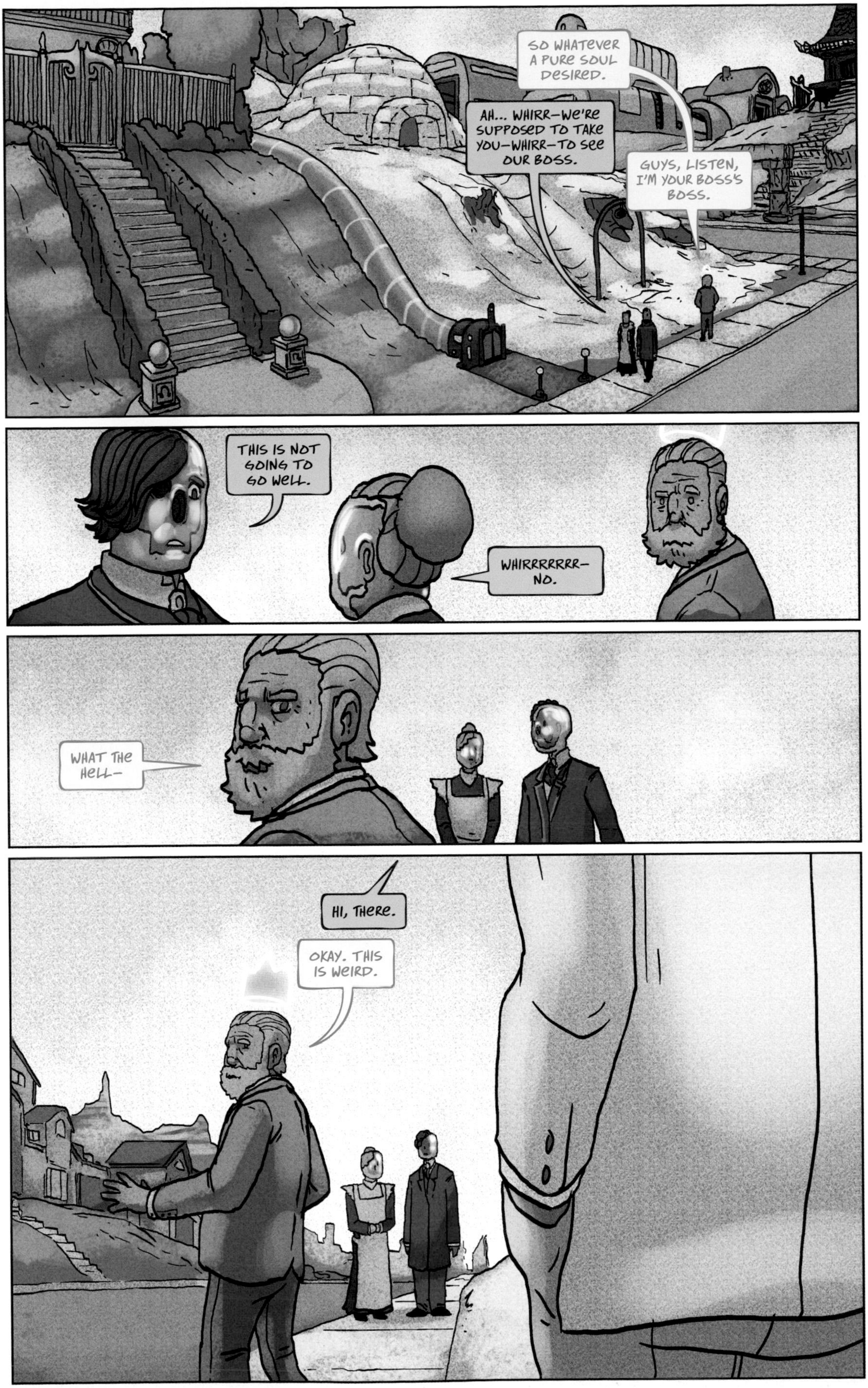
SO WHATEVER A PURE SOUL DESIRED.
AH... WHIRR—WE'RE SUPPOSED TO TAKE YOU—WHIRR—TO SEE OUR BOSS.
GUYS, LISTEN, I'M YOUR BOSS'S BOSS.
THIS IS NOT GOING TO GO WELL.
WHIRRRRRRR— NO.
WHAT THE HELL—
HI, THERE.
OKAY. THIS IS WEIRD.

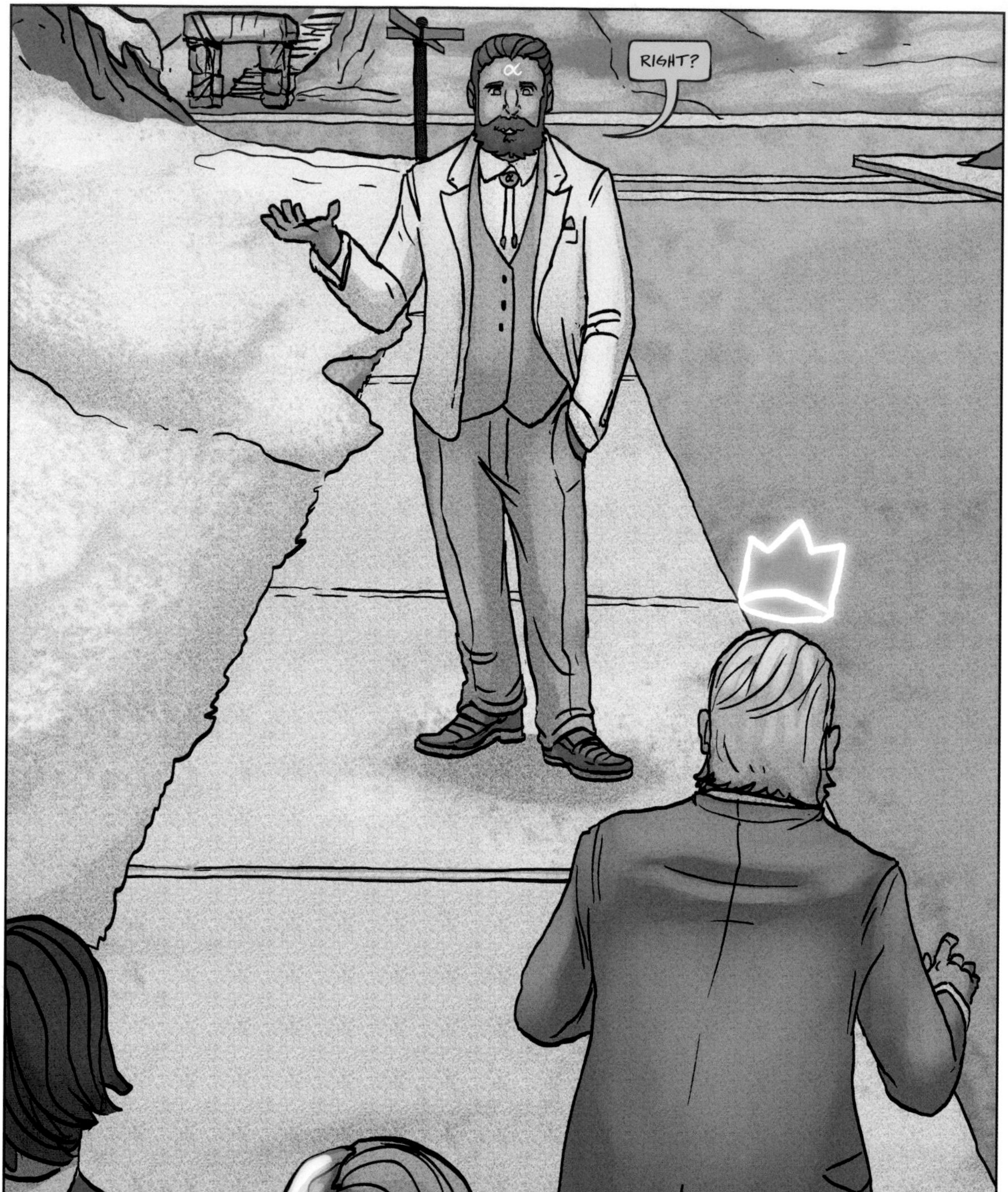
RIGHT?

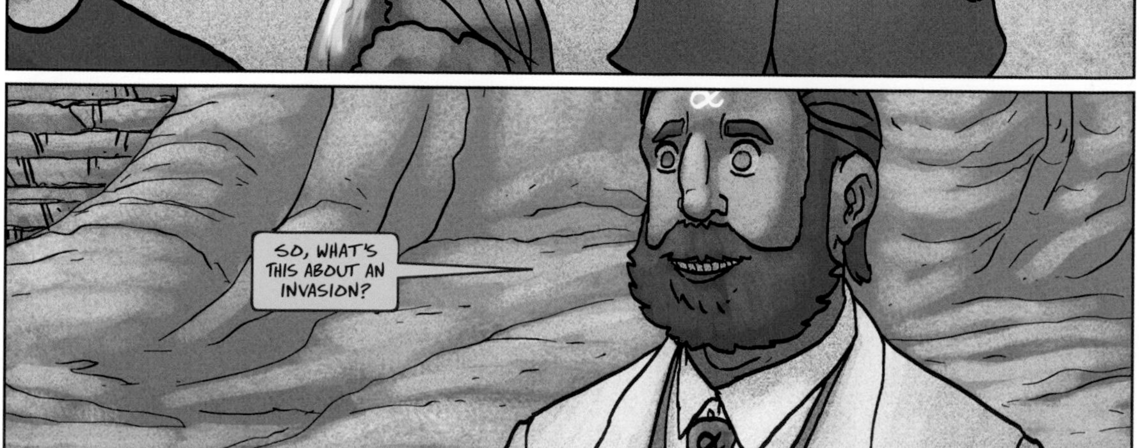
SO, WHAT'S THIS ABOUT AN INVASION?

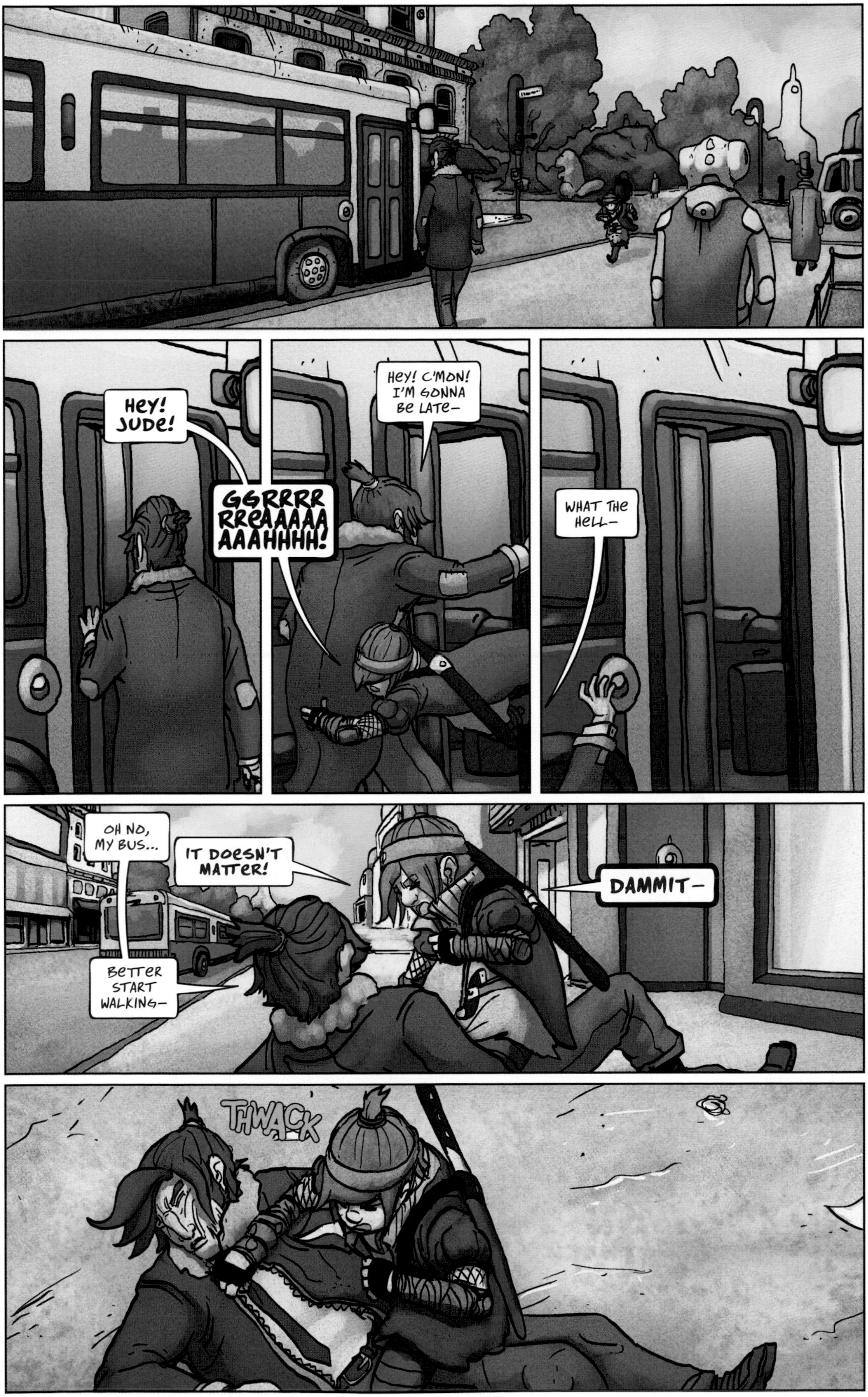
HEY! JUDE!
GGRRRRRREAAAAAAAAHHHH!
HEY! C'MON! I'M GONNA BE LATE–
WHAT THE HELL–
OH NO, MY BUS...
IT DOESN'T MATTER!
DAMMIT–
BETTER START WALKING–
THWACK

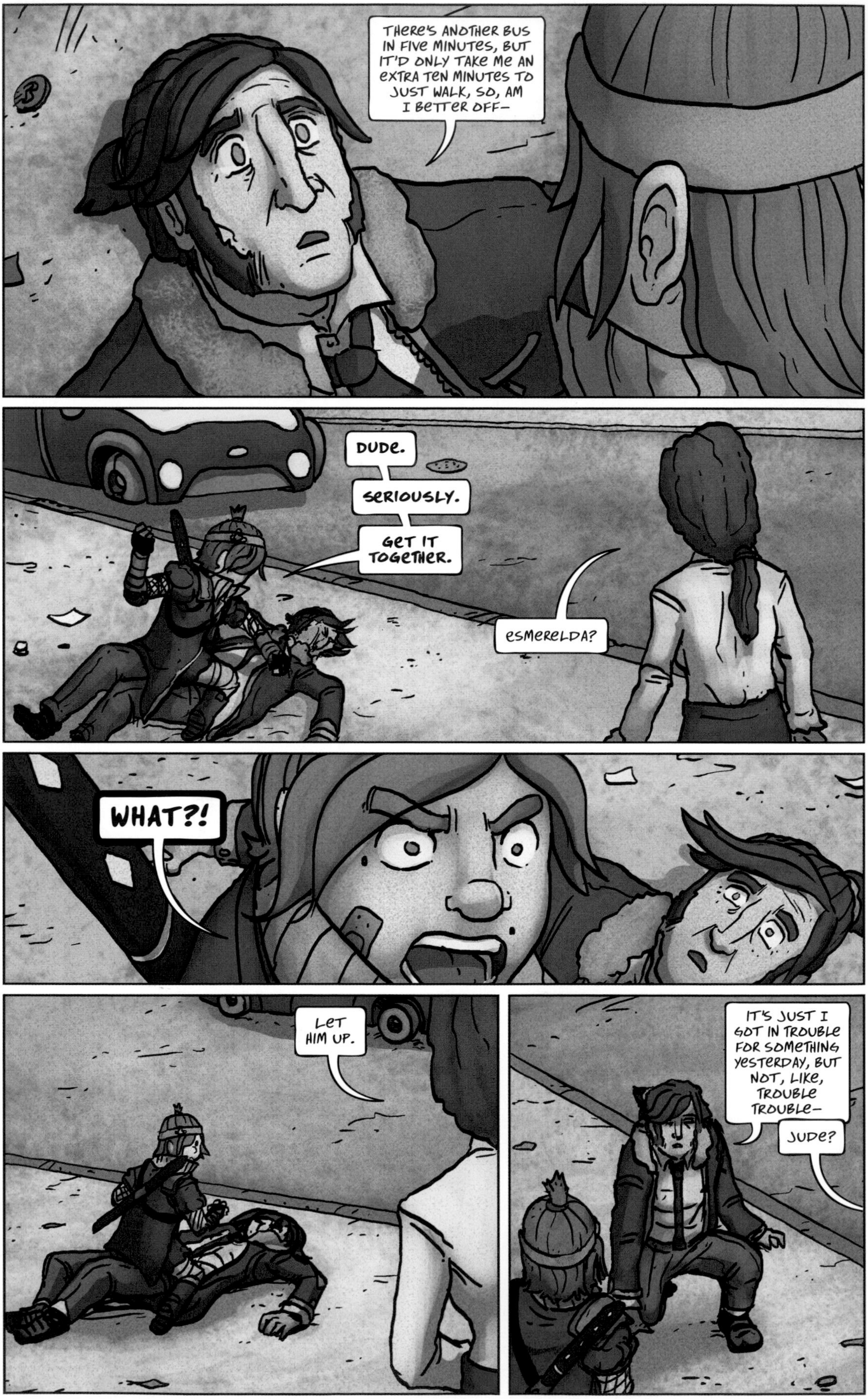
THERE'S ANOTHER BUS IN FIVE MINUTES, BUT IT'D ONLY TAKE ME AN EXTRA TEN MINUTES TO JUST WALK, SO, AM I BETTER OFF—
DUDE.
SERIOUSLY.
GET IT TOGETHER.
ESMERELDA?
WHAT?!
LET HIM UP.
IT'S JUST I GOT IN TROUBLE FOR SOMETHING YESTERDAY, BUT NOT, LIKE, TROUBLE TROUBLE—
JUDE?

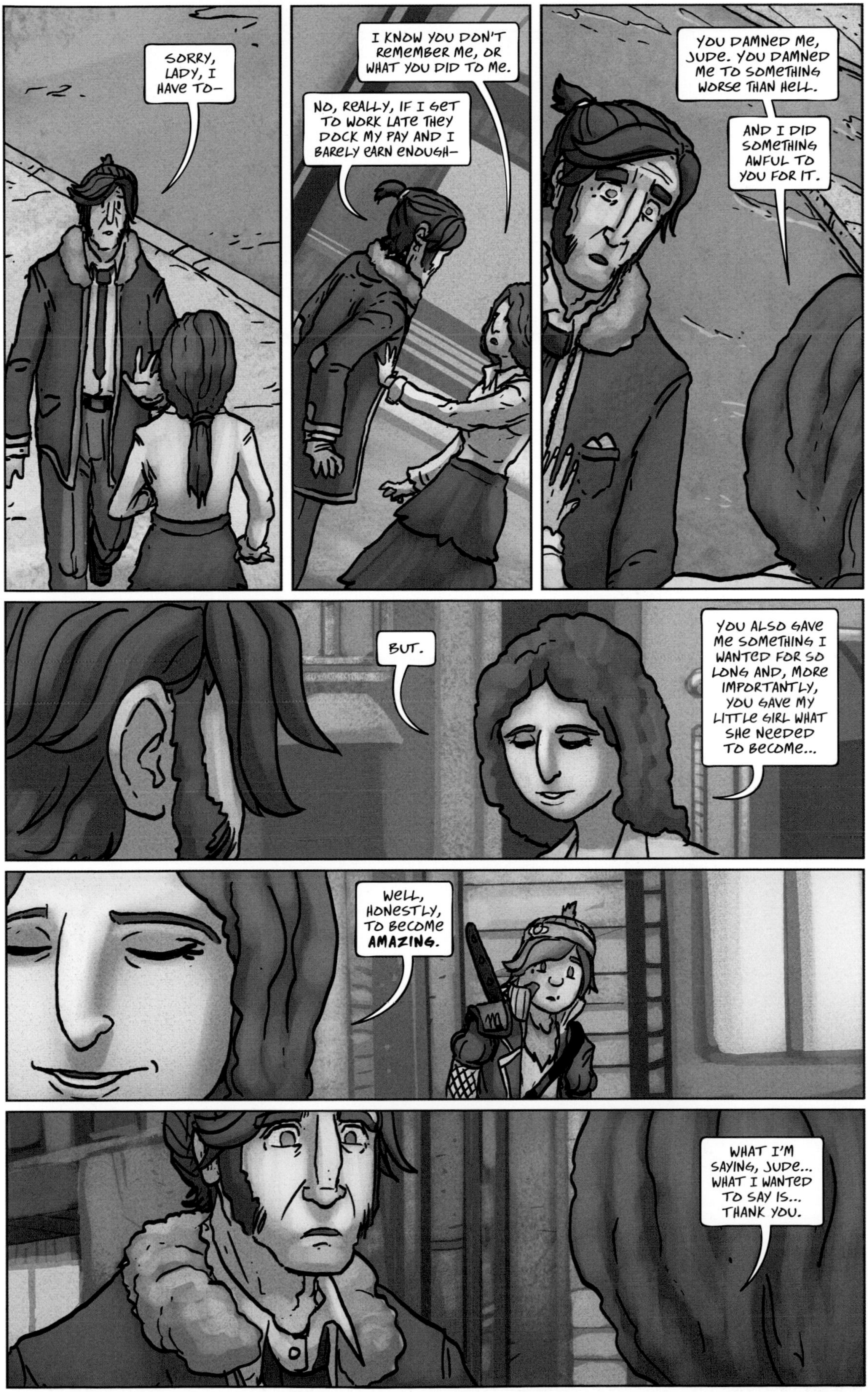

SORRY, LADY, I HAVE TO–
I KNOW YOU DON'T REMEMBER ME, OR WHAT YOU DID TO ME.
NO, REALLY, IF I GET TO WORK LATE THEY DOCK MY PAY AND I BARELY EARN ENOUGH–
YOU DAMNED ME, JUDE. YOU DAMNED ME TO SOMETHING WORSE THAN HELL.
AND I DID SOMETHING AWFUL TO YOU FOR IT.
BUT.
YOU ALSO GAVE ME SOMETHING I WANTED FOR SO LONG AND, MORE IMPORTANTLY, YOU GAVE MY LITTLE GIRL WHAT SHE NEEDED TO BECOME...
WELL, HONESTLY, TO BECOME **AMAZING**.
WHAT I'M SAYING, JUDE... WHAT I WANTED TO SAY IS... THANK YOU.

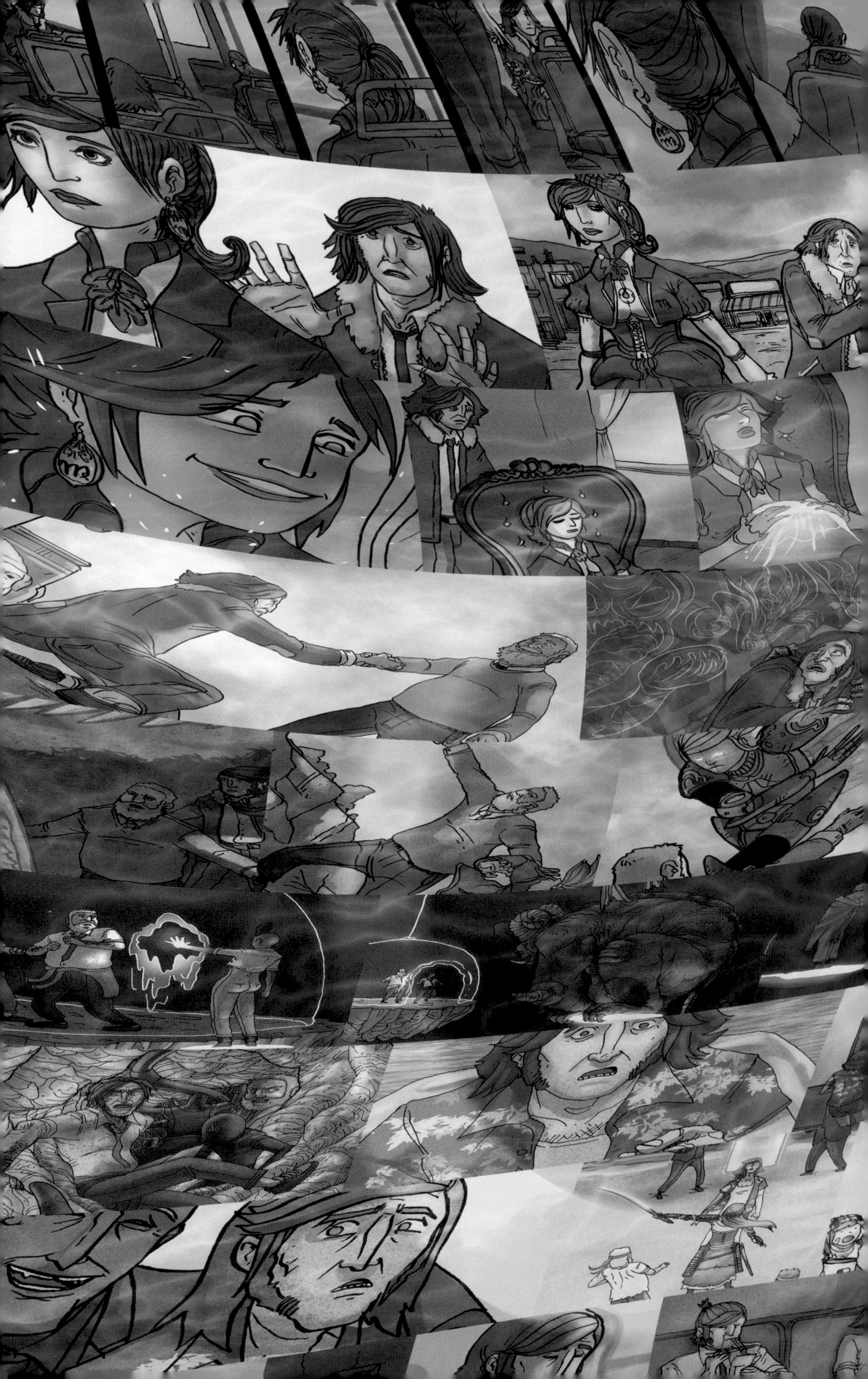

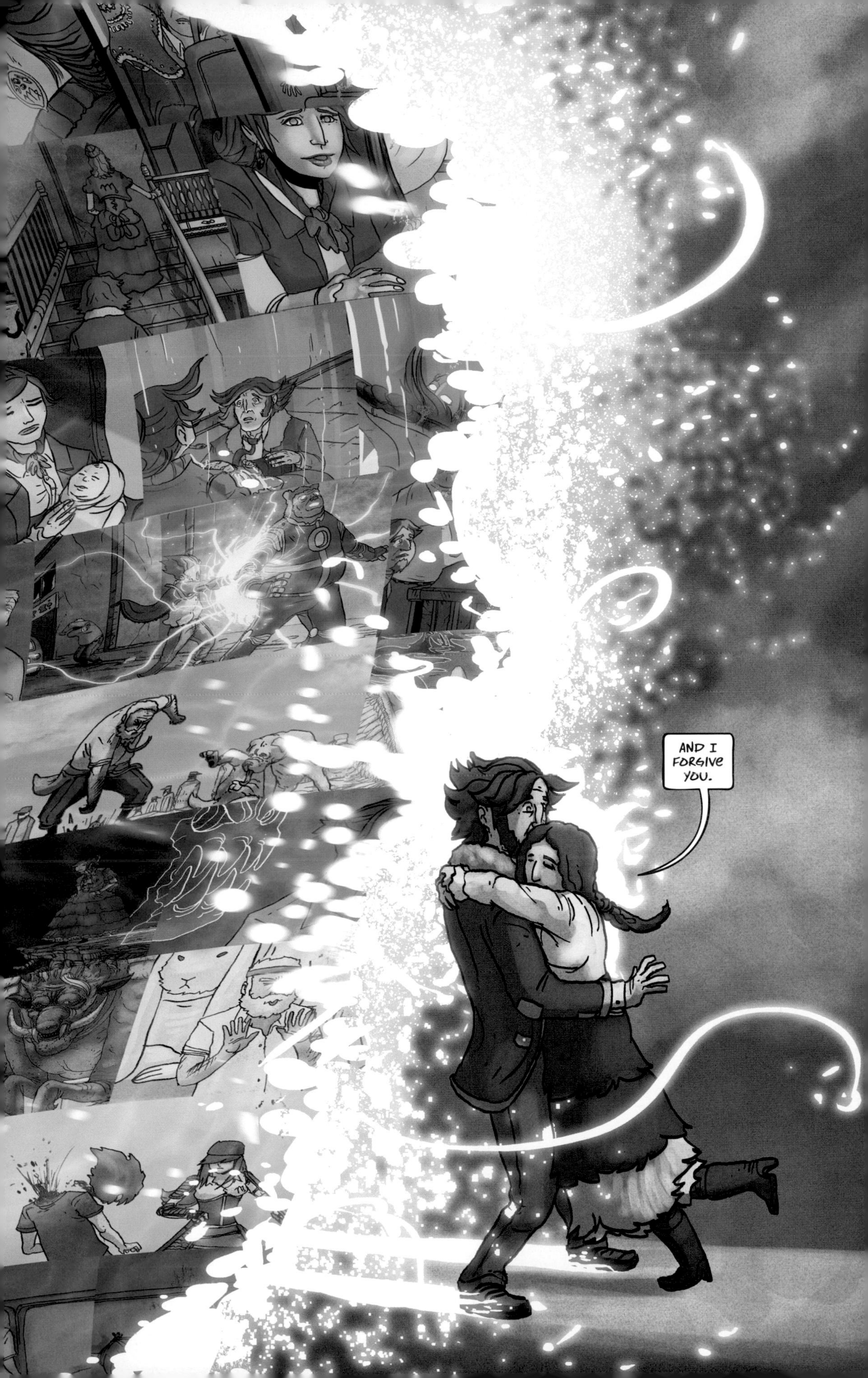
AND I FORGIVE YOU.

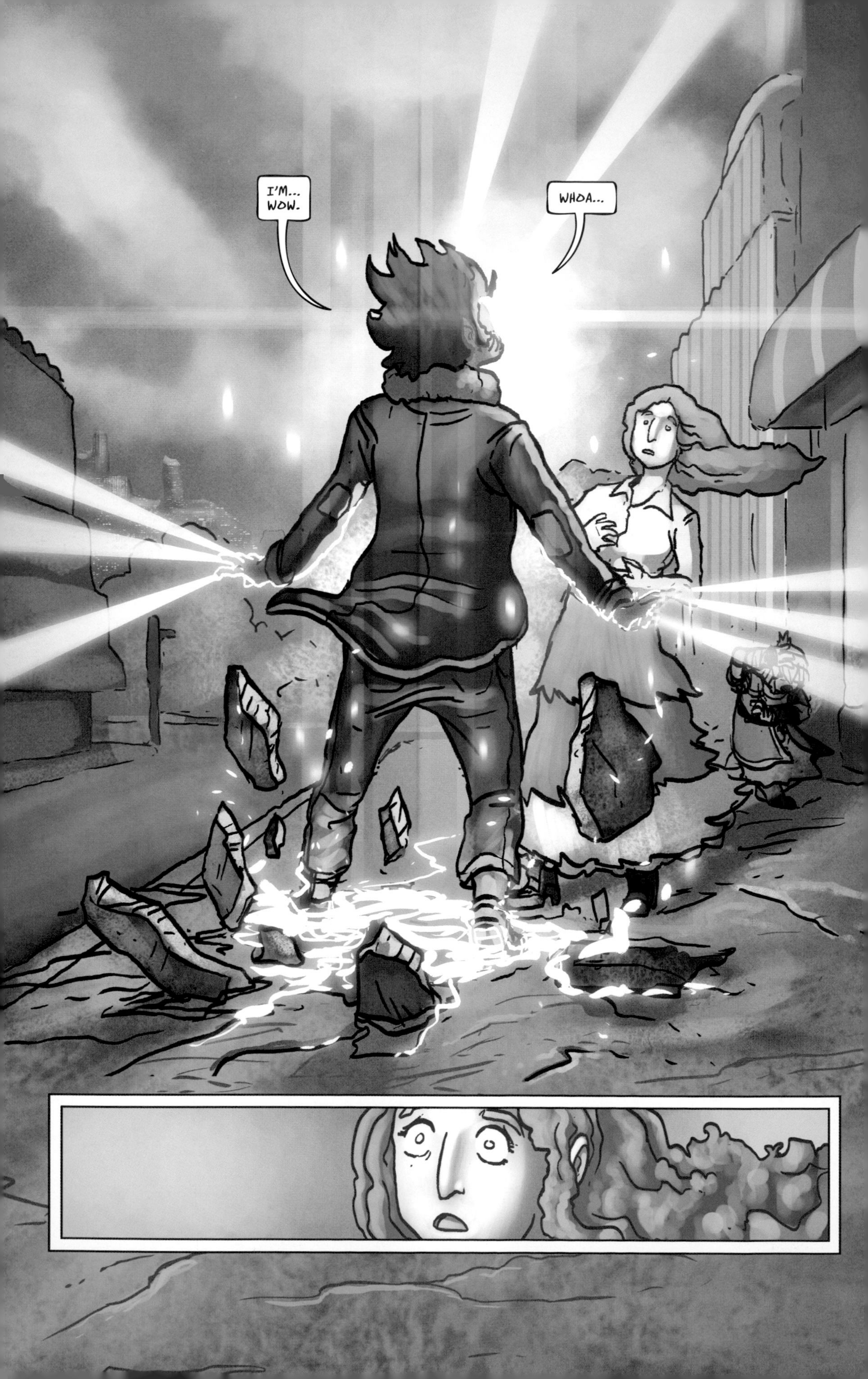
I'M... WOW.
WHOA...

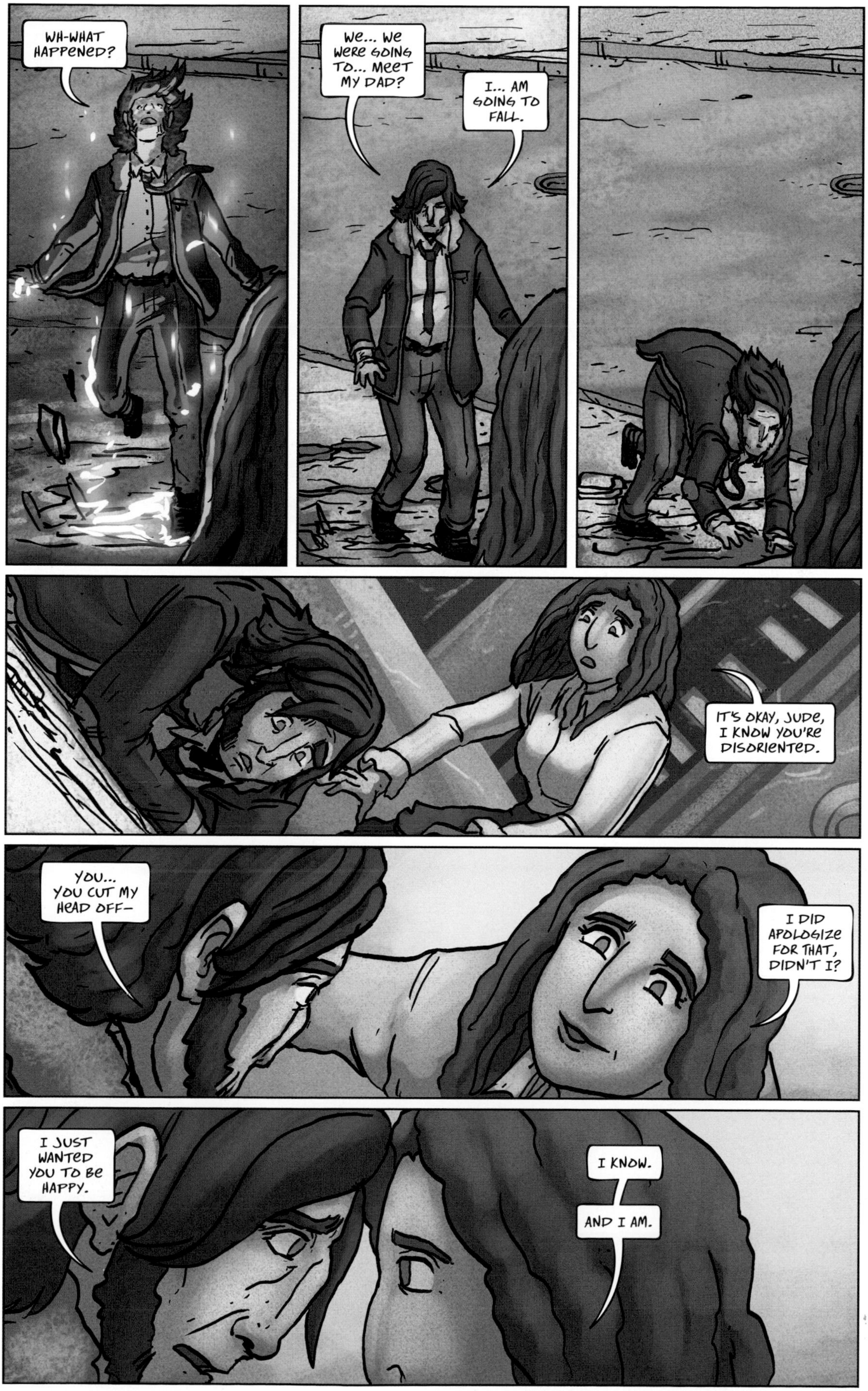
WH-WHAT HAPPENED?
WE... WE WERE GOING TO... MEET MY DAD?
I... AM GOING TO FALL.
IT'S OKAY, JUDE, I KNOW YOU'RE DISORIENTED.
YOU... YOU CUT MY HEAD OFF—
I DID APOLOGIZE FOR THAT, DIDN'T I?
I JUST WANTED YOU TO BE HAPPY.
I KNOW.
AND I AM.

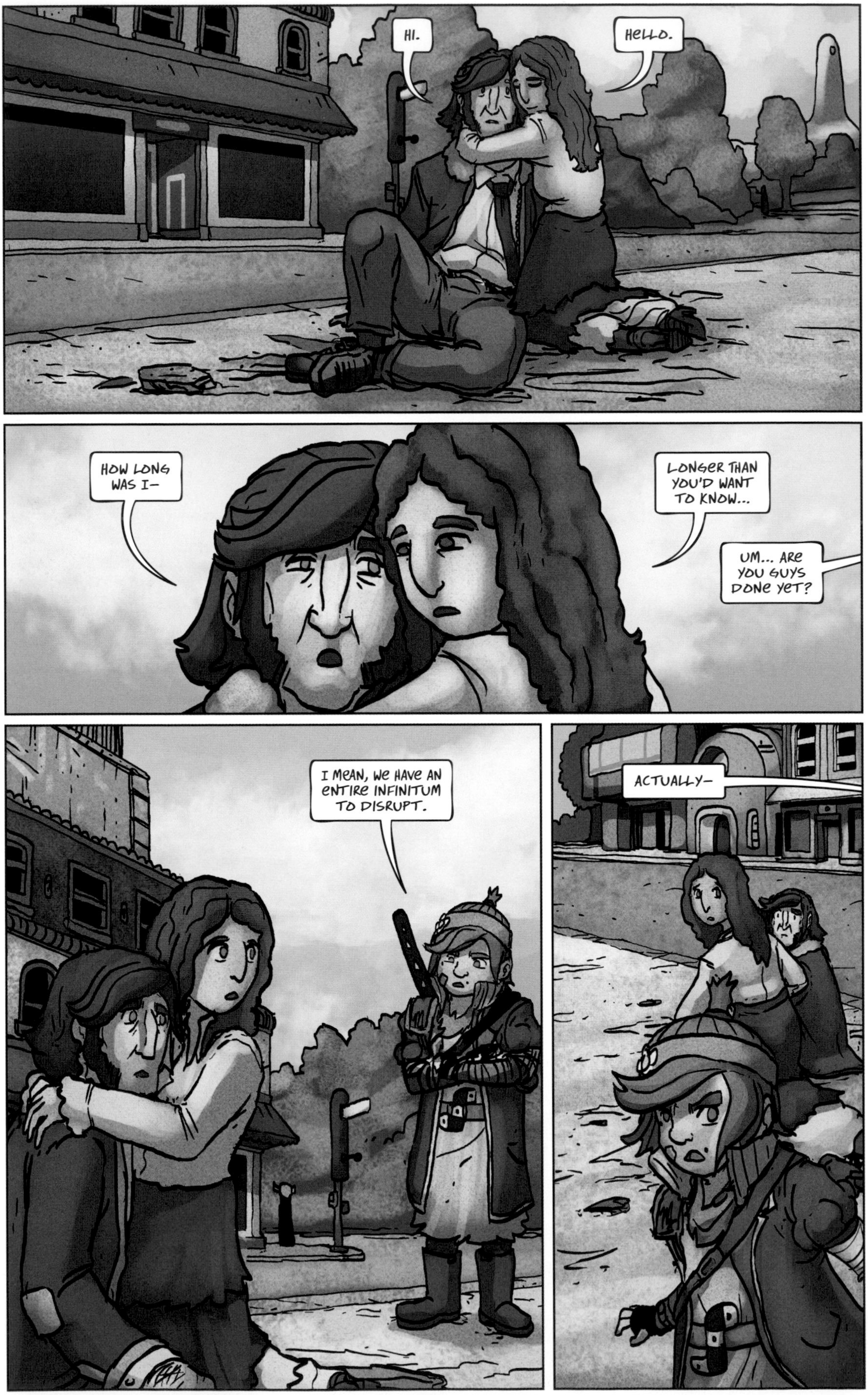
HI.
HELLO.
HOW LONG WAS I—
LONGER THAN YOU'D WANT TO KNOW...
UM... ARE YOU GUYS DONE YET?
I MEAN, WE HAVE AN ENTIRE INFINITUM TO DISRUPT.
ACTUALLY—

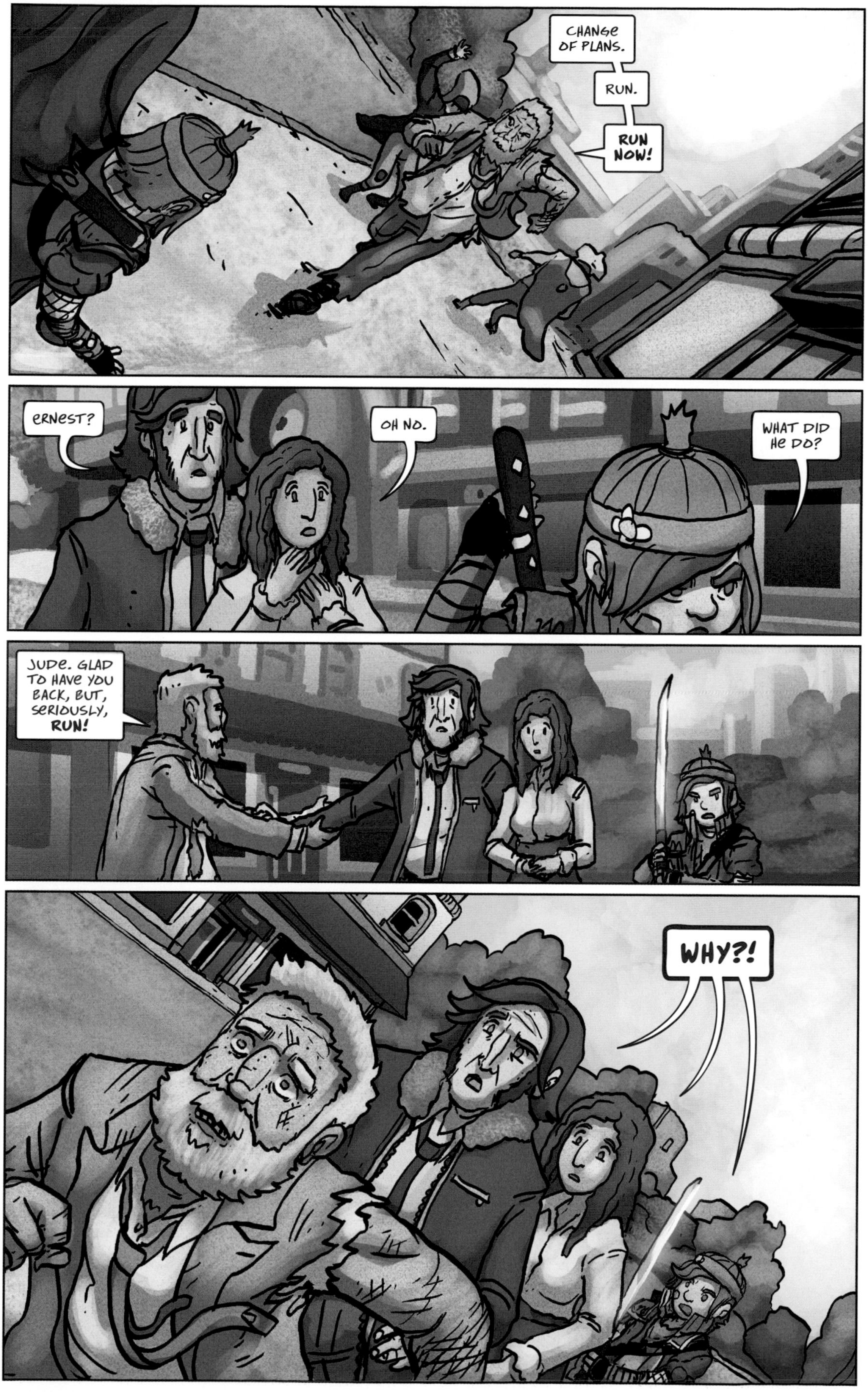
CHANGE OF PLANS.
RUN.
RUN NOW!
ERNEST?
OH NO.
WHAT DID HE DO?
JUDE. GLAD TO HAVE YOU BACK, BUT, SERIOUSLY, **RUN!**
WHY?!

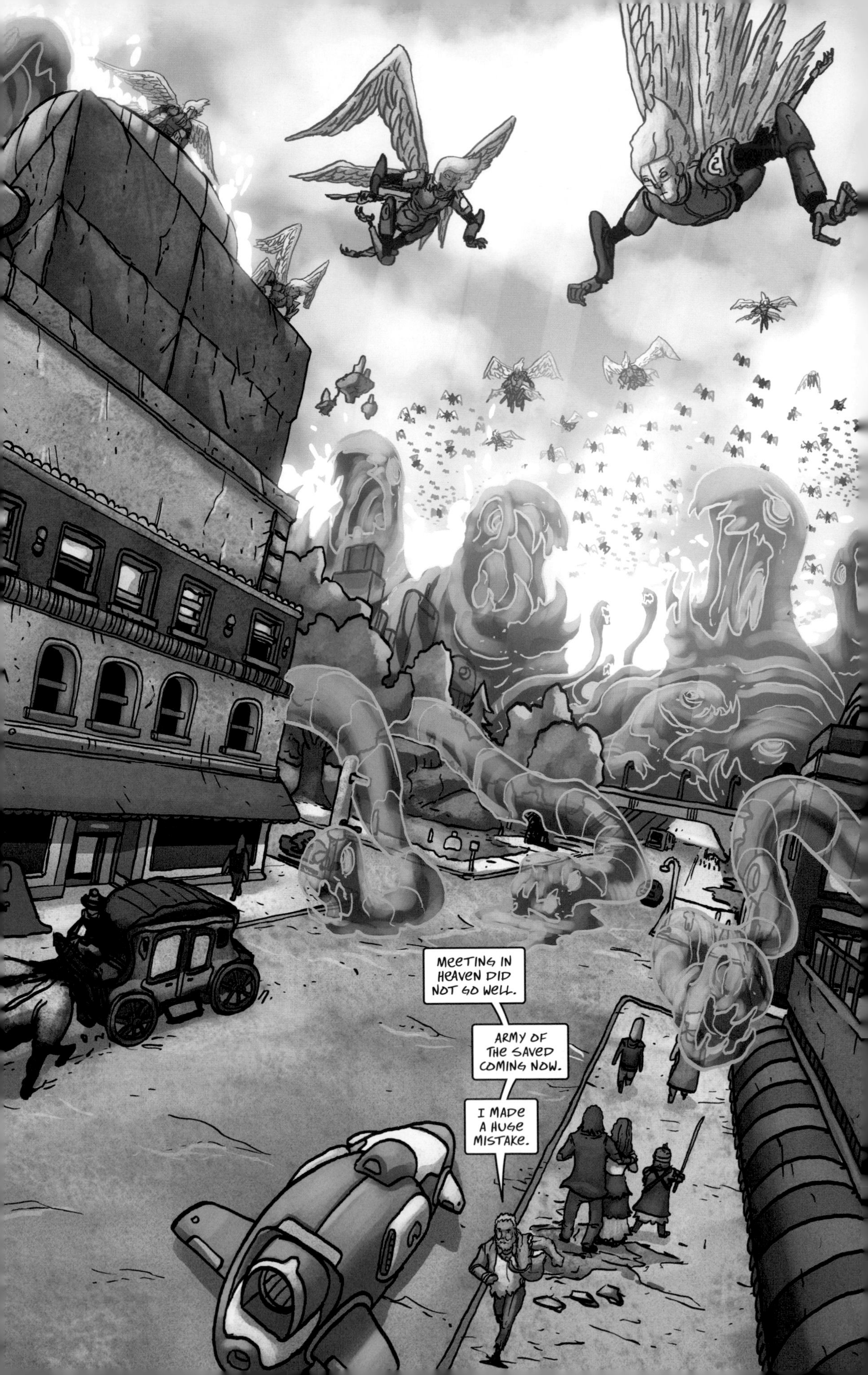
MEETING IN HEAVEN DID NOT GO WELL.
ARMY OF THE SAVED COMING NOW.
I MADE A HUGE MISTAKE.

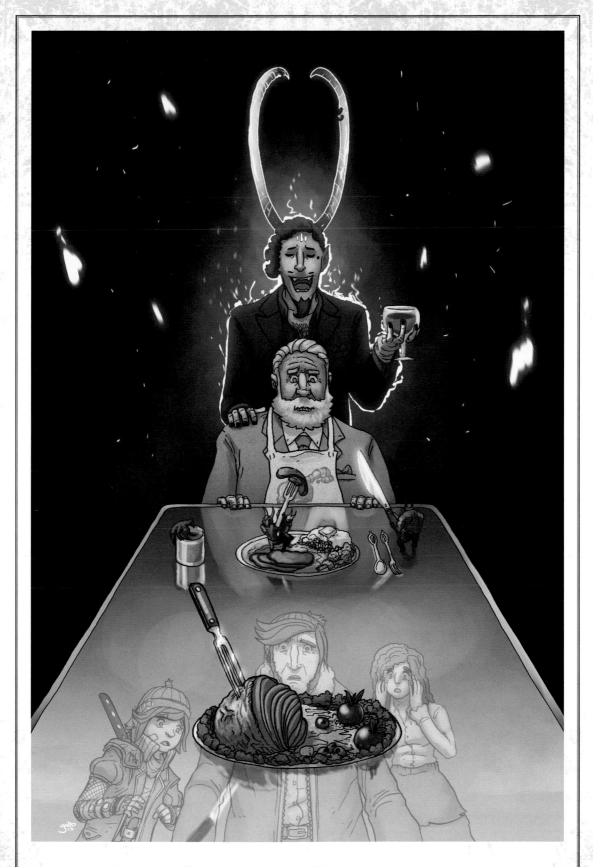

CHAPTER FIFTEEN

THE LIFE AFTER

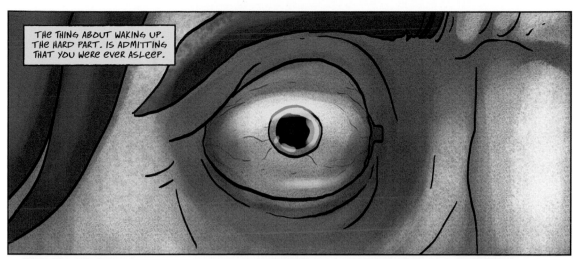

THE THING ABOUT WAKING UP. THE HARD PART. IS ADMITTING THAT YOU WERE EVER ASLEEP.

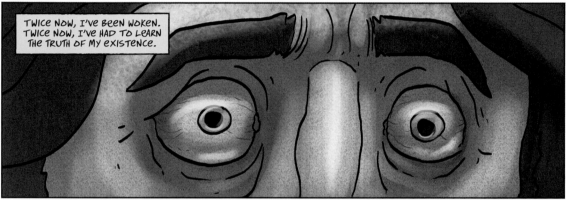

TWICE NOW, I'VE BEEN WOKEN. TWICE NOW, I'VE HAD TO LEARN THE TRUTH OF MY EXISTENCE.

THAT THIS WOMAN THAT I'D NEVER MET AND YET LOVED WAS JUST AS TRAPPED AS I WAS.

I'VE BEEN A PRISONER IN THE AFTERLIFE FOR AN ETERNITY. AND NOW, I WANT OUT.

I'D RECOMMEND **MOVING YOUR ASSES!**

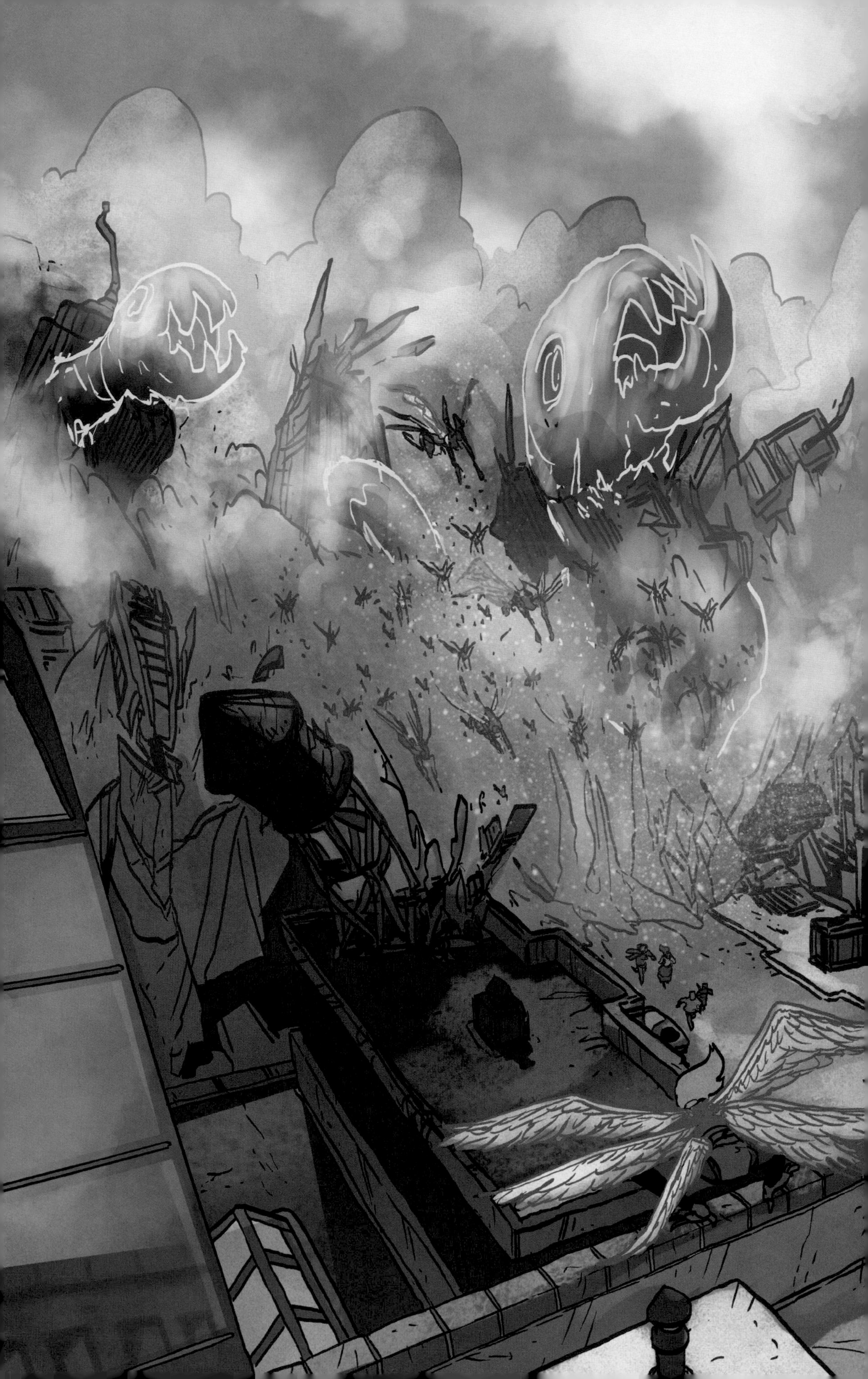

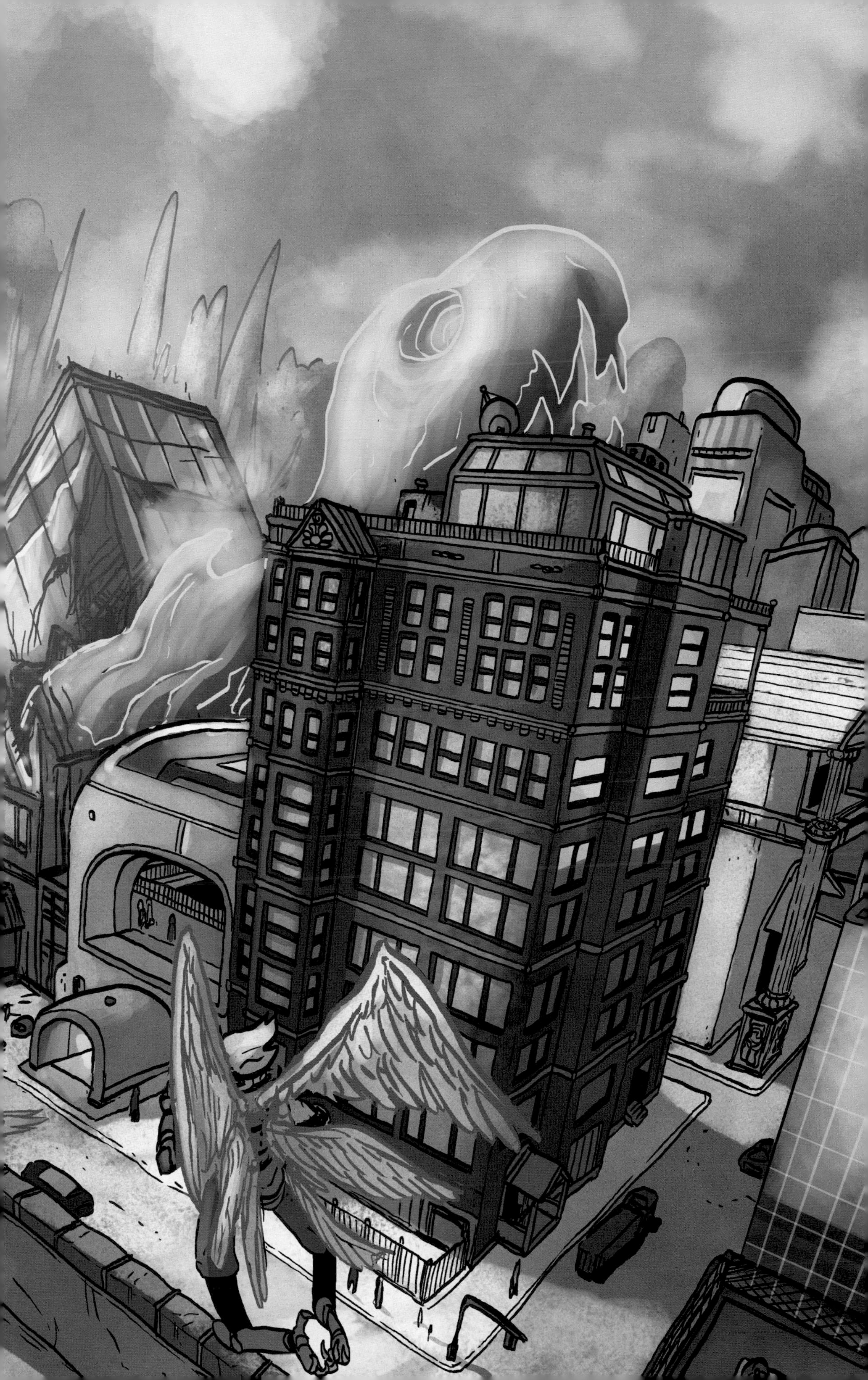

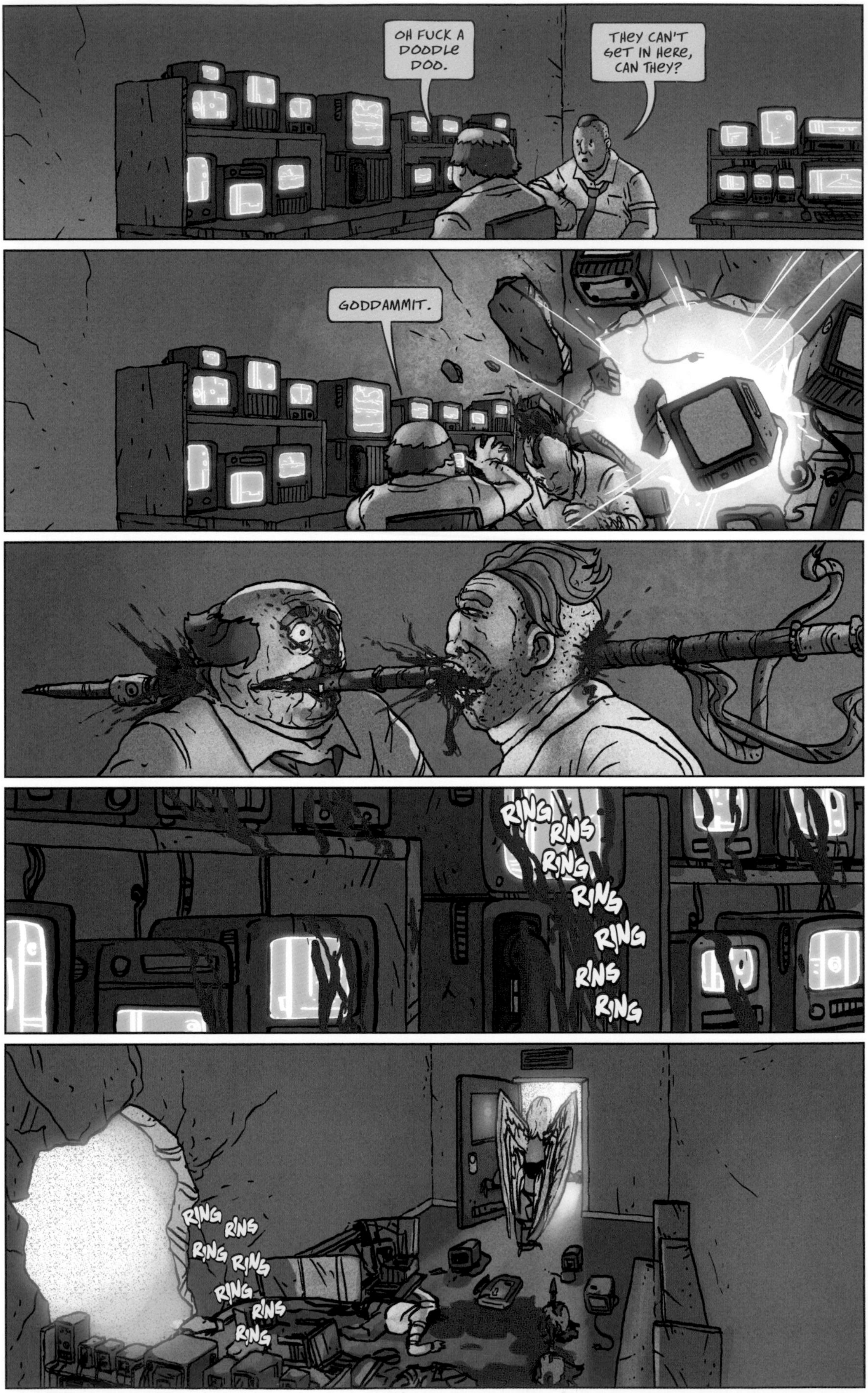
OH FUCK A DODDLE DOO.
THEY CAN'T GET IN HERE, CAN THEY?
GODDAMMIT.
RING RING RING RING RING RING RING
RING RING RING RING RING RING RING

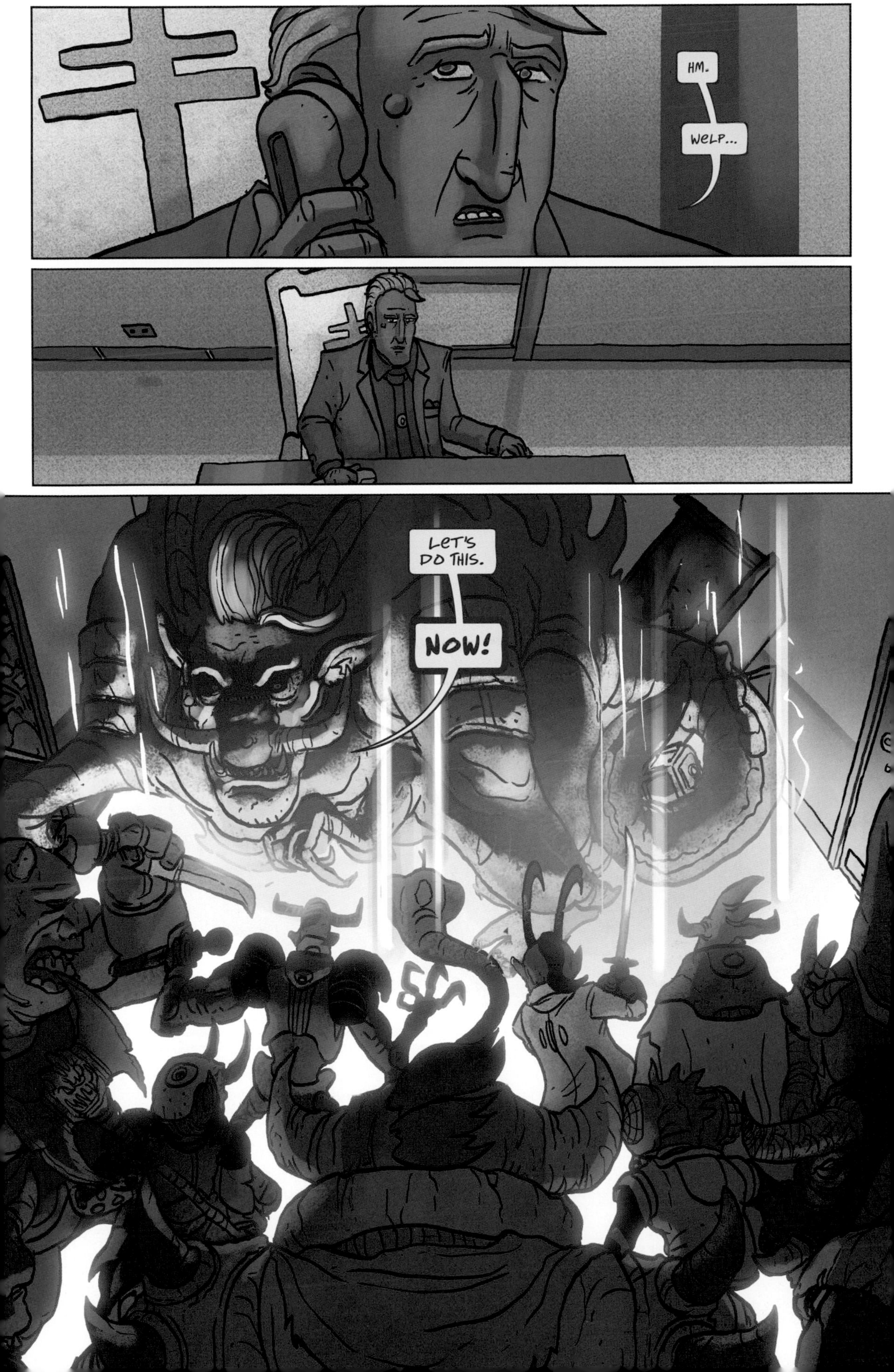
HM.
WELP...
LET'S DO THIS.
NOW!

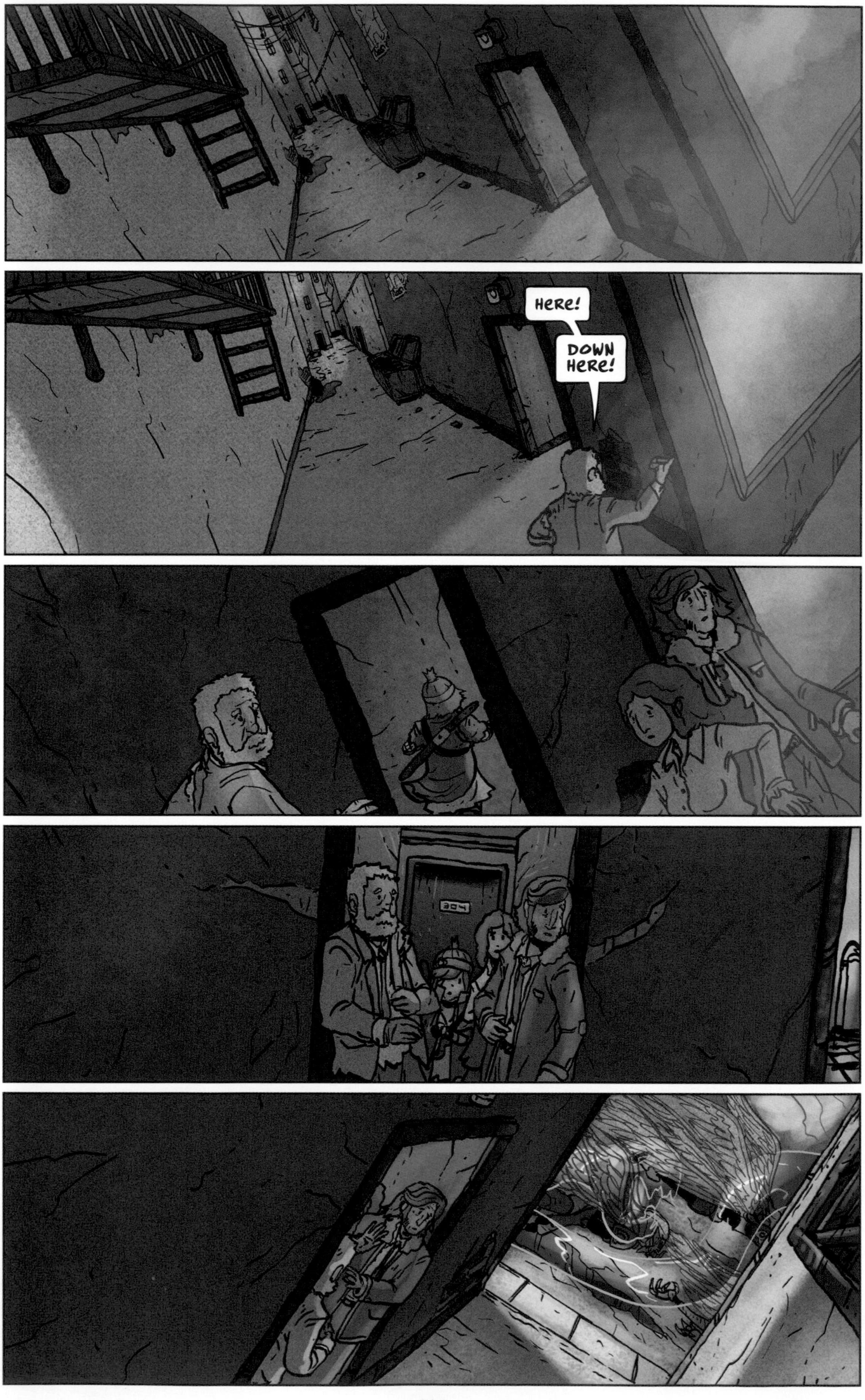
HERE!
DOWN HERE!
304

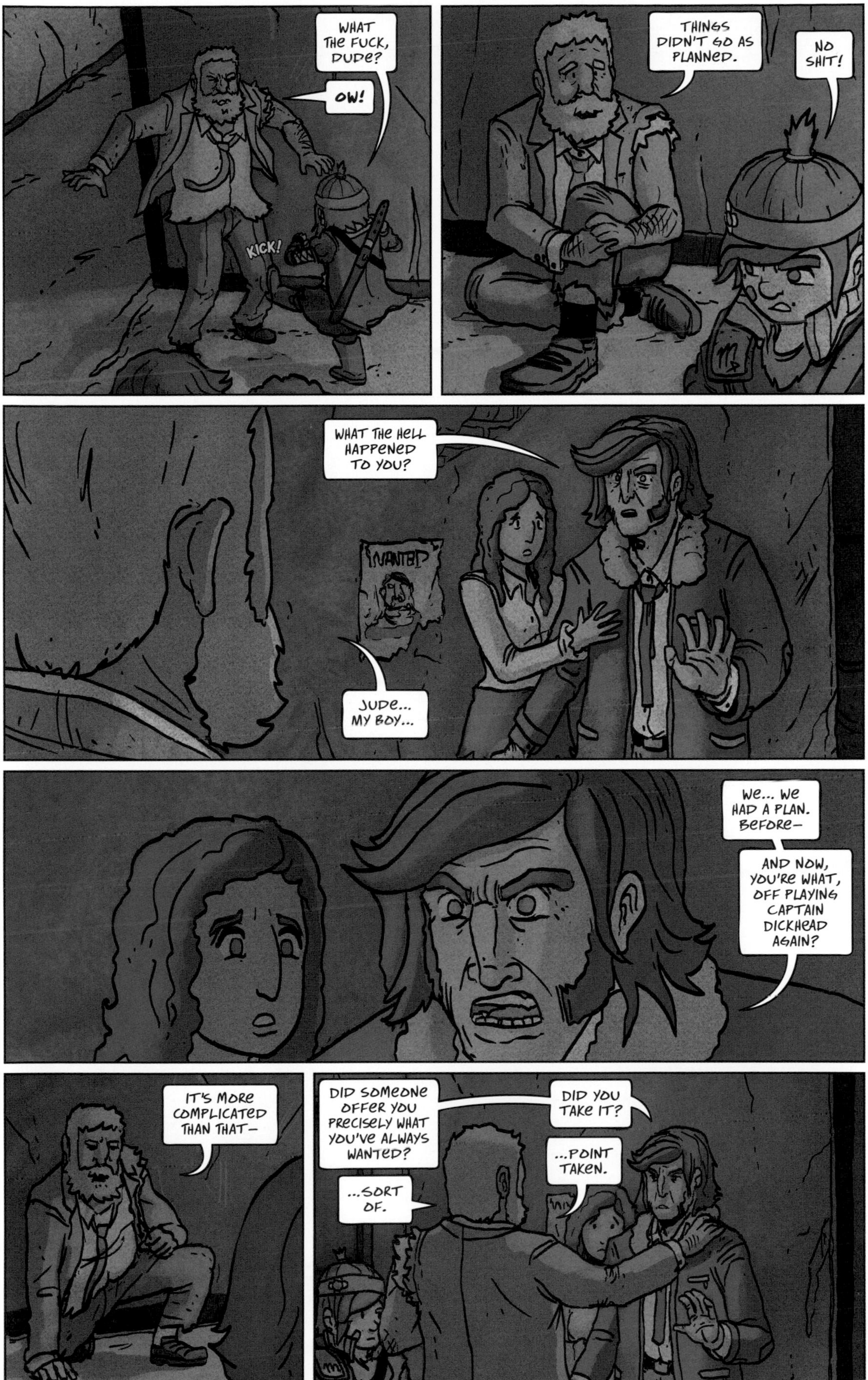
WHAT THE FUCK, DUDE?
OW!
KICK!
THINGS DIDN'T GO AS PLANNED.
NO SHIT!
WHAT THE HELL HAPPENED TO YOU?
WANTED
JUDE... MY BOY...
WE... WE HAD A PLAN. BEFORE–
AND NOW, YOU'RE WHAT, OFF PLAYING CAPTAIN DICKHEAD AGAIN?
IT'S MORE COMPLICATED THAN THAT–
DID SOMEONE OFFER YOU PRECISELY WHAT YOU'VE ALWAYS WANTED?
...SORT OF.
DID YOU TAKE IT?
...POINT TAKEN.

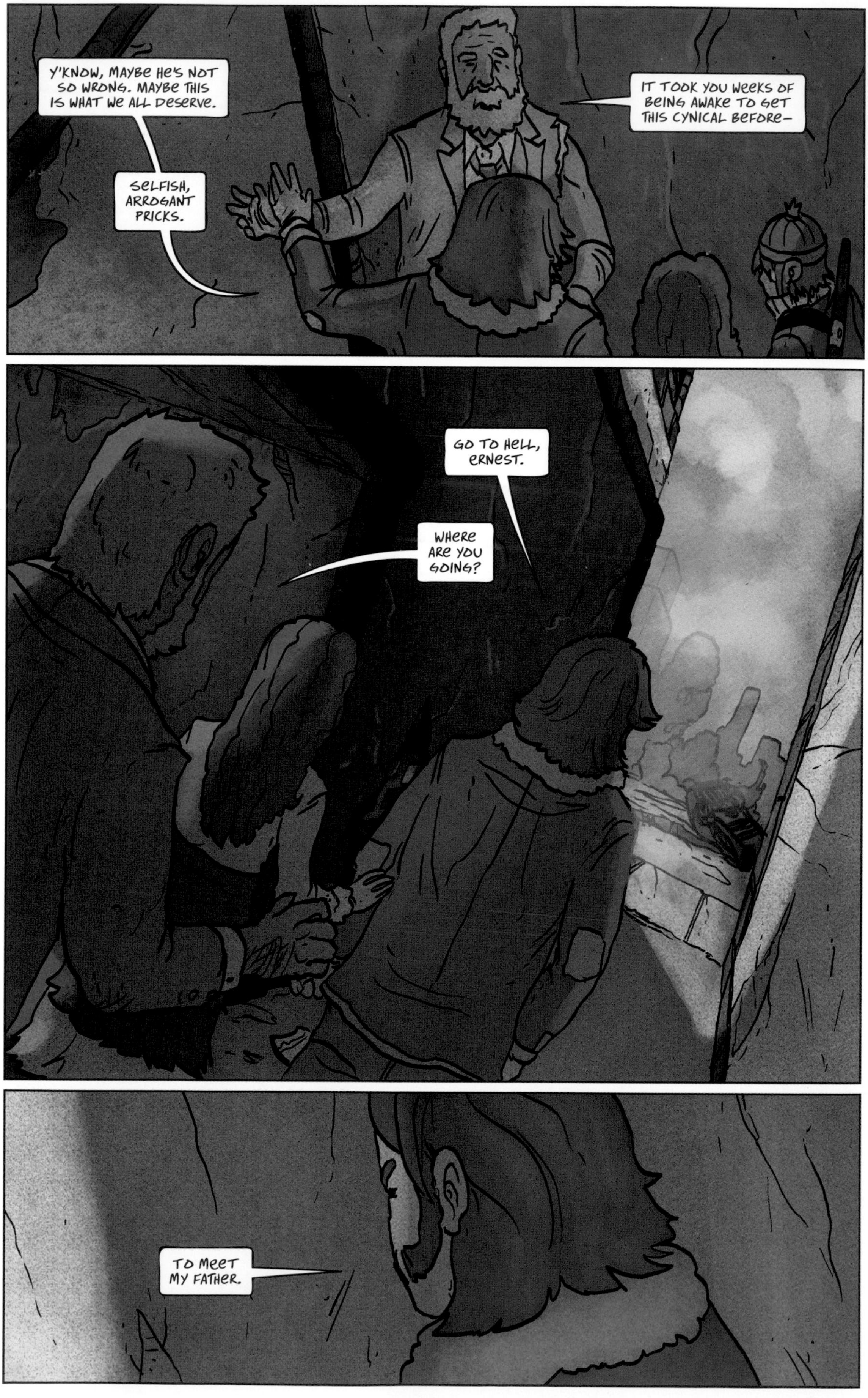
Y'KNOW, MAYBE HE'S NOT SO WRONG. MAYBE THIS IS WHAT WE ALL DESERVE.
SELFISH, ARROGANT PRICKS.
IT TOOK YOU WEEKS OF BEING AWAKE TO GET THIS CYNICAL BEFORE–
GO TO HELL, ERNEST.
WHERE ARE YOU GOING?
TO MEET MY FATHER.

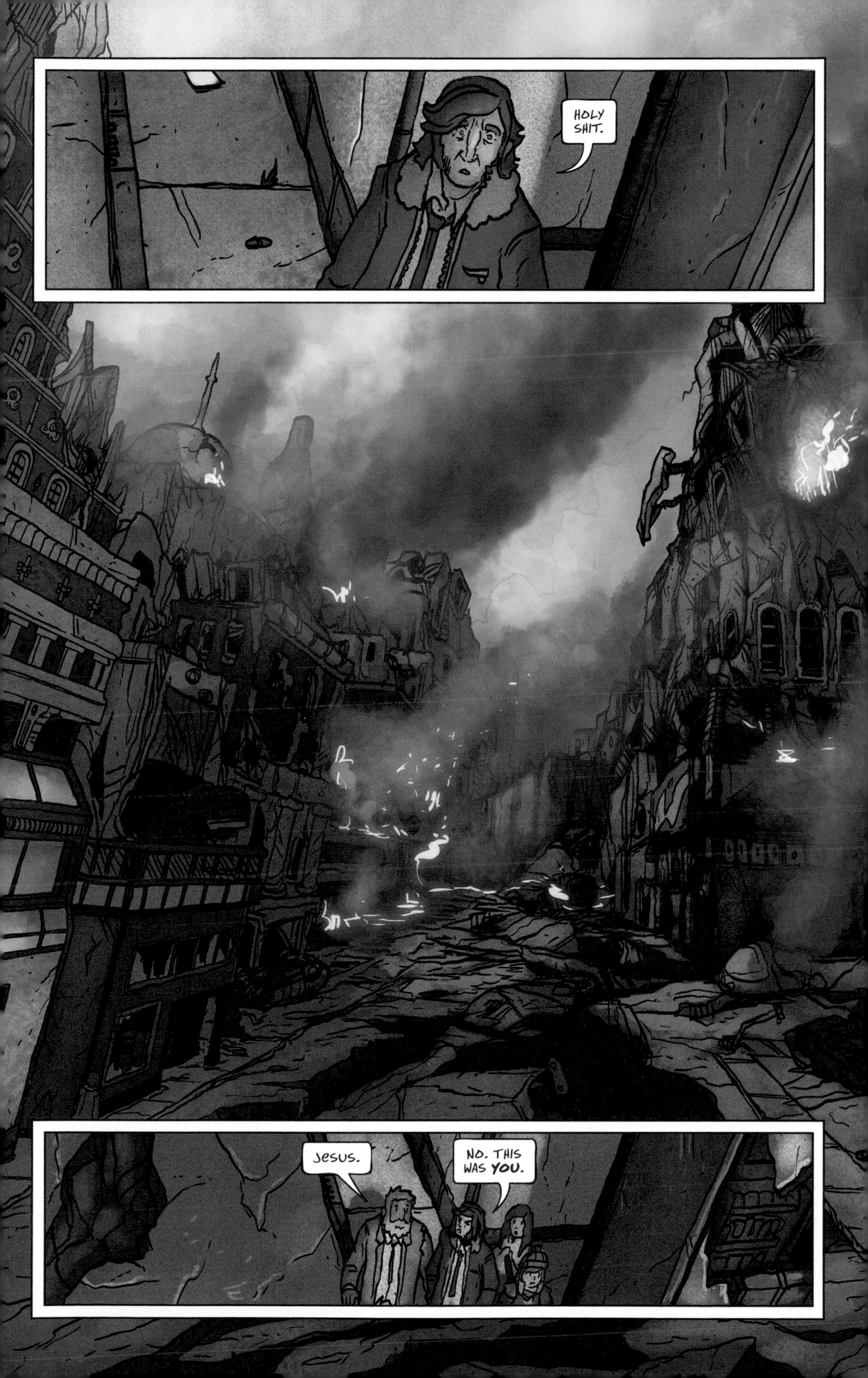
HOLY SHIT.
JESUS.
NO. THIS WAS YOU.

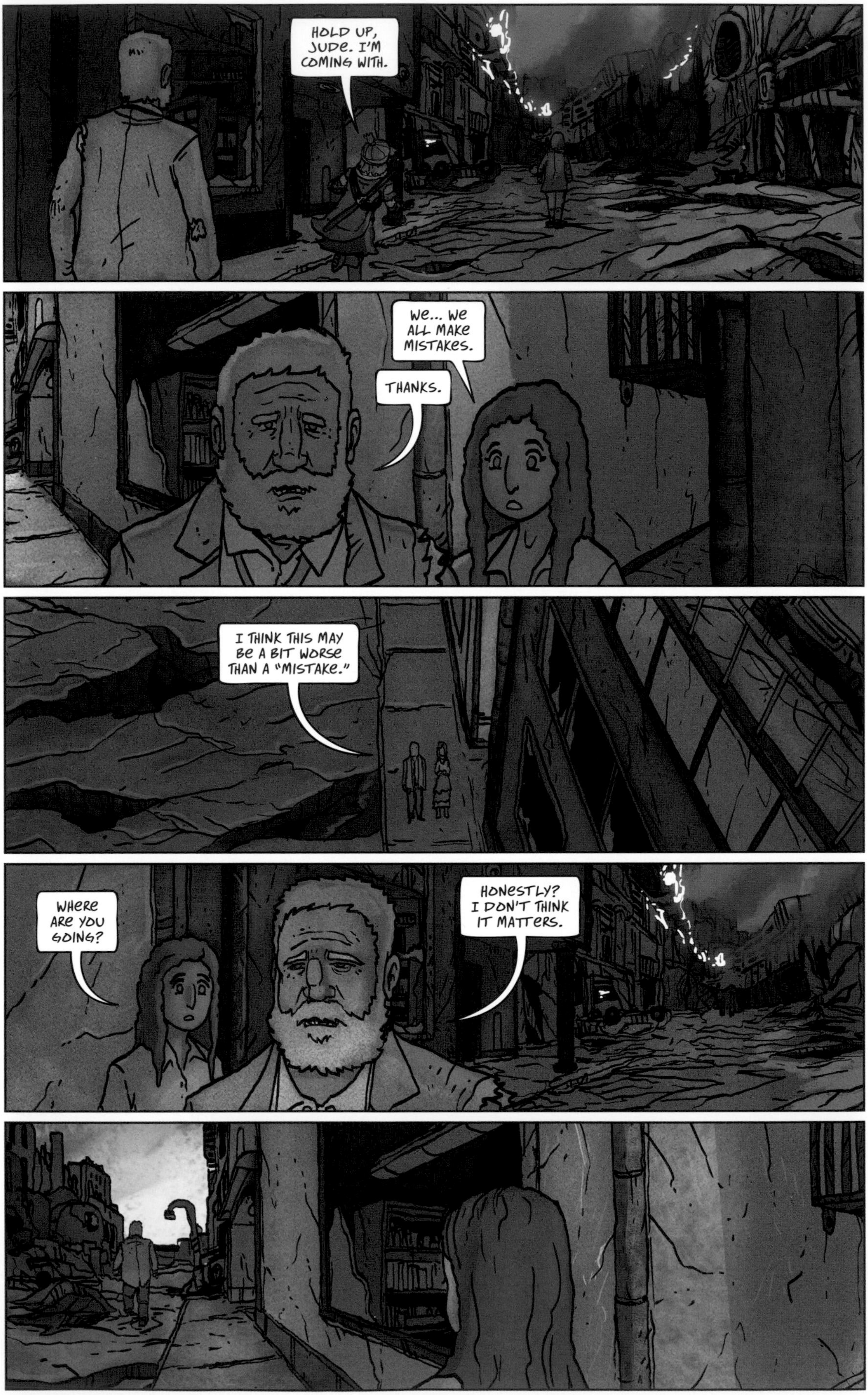
HOLD UP, JUDE. I'M COMING WITH.
WE... WE ALL MAKE MISTAKES.
THANKS.
I THINK THIS MAY BE A BIT WORSE THAN A "MISTAKE."
WHERE ARE YOU GOING?
HONESTLY? I DON'T THINK IT MATTERS.

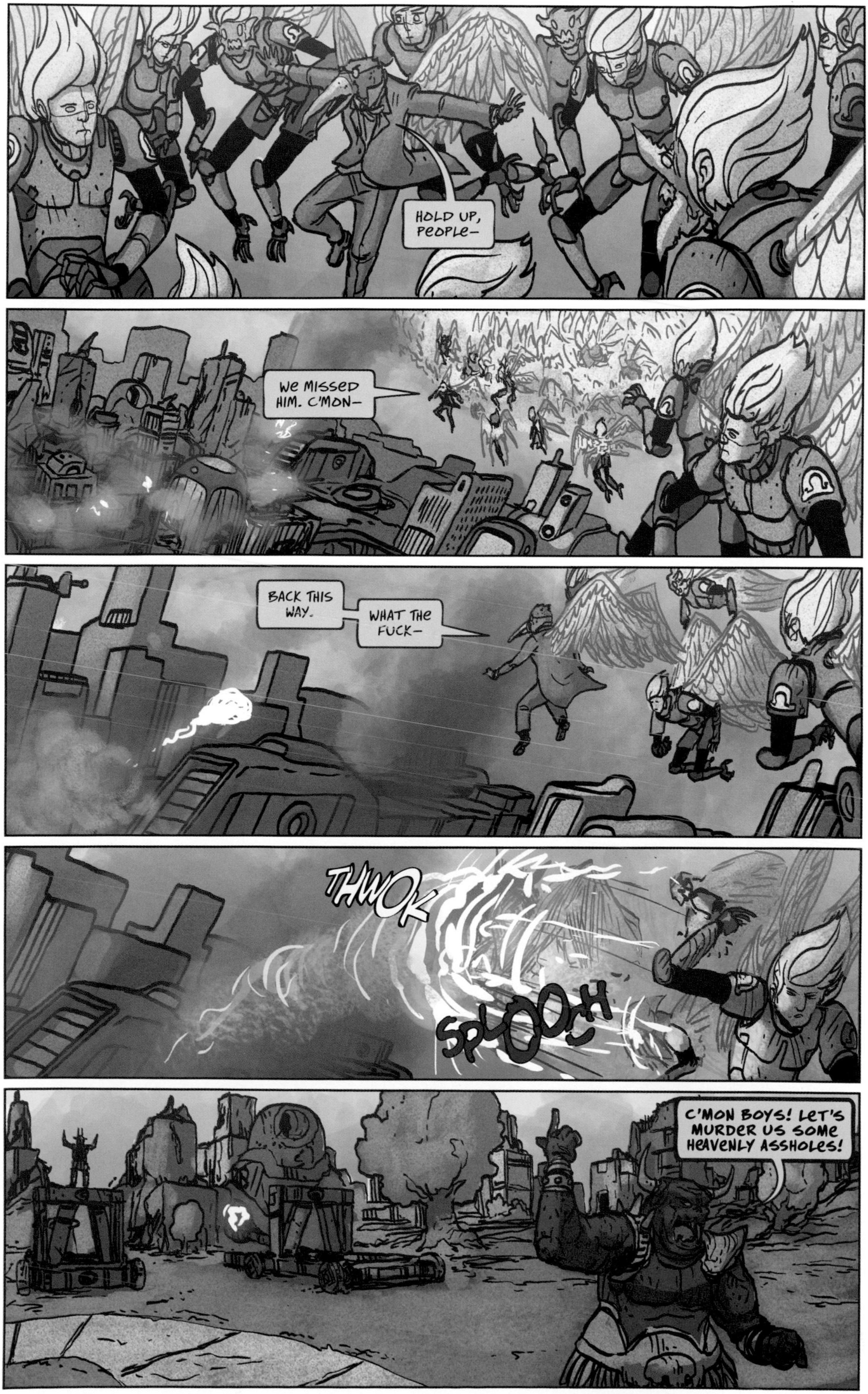
HOLD UP, PEOPLE—
WE MISSED HIM. C'MON—
BACK THIS WAY.
WHAT THE FUCK—
THWOK
SPLOOOCH
C'MON BOYS! LET'S MURDER US SOME HEAVENLY ASSHOLES!

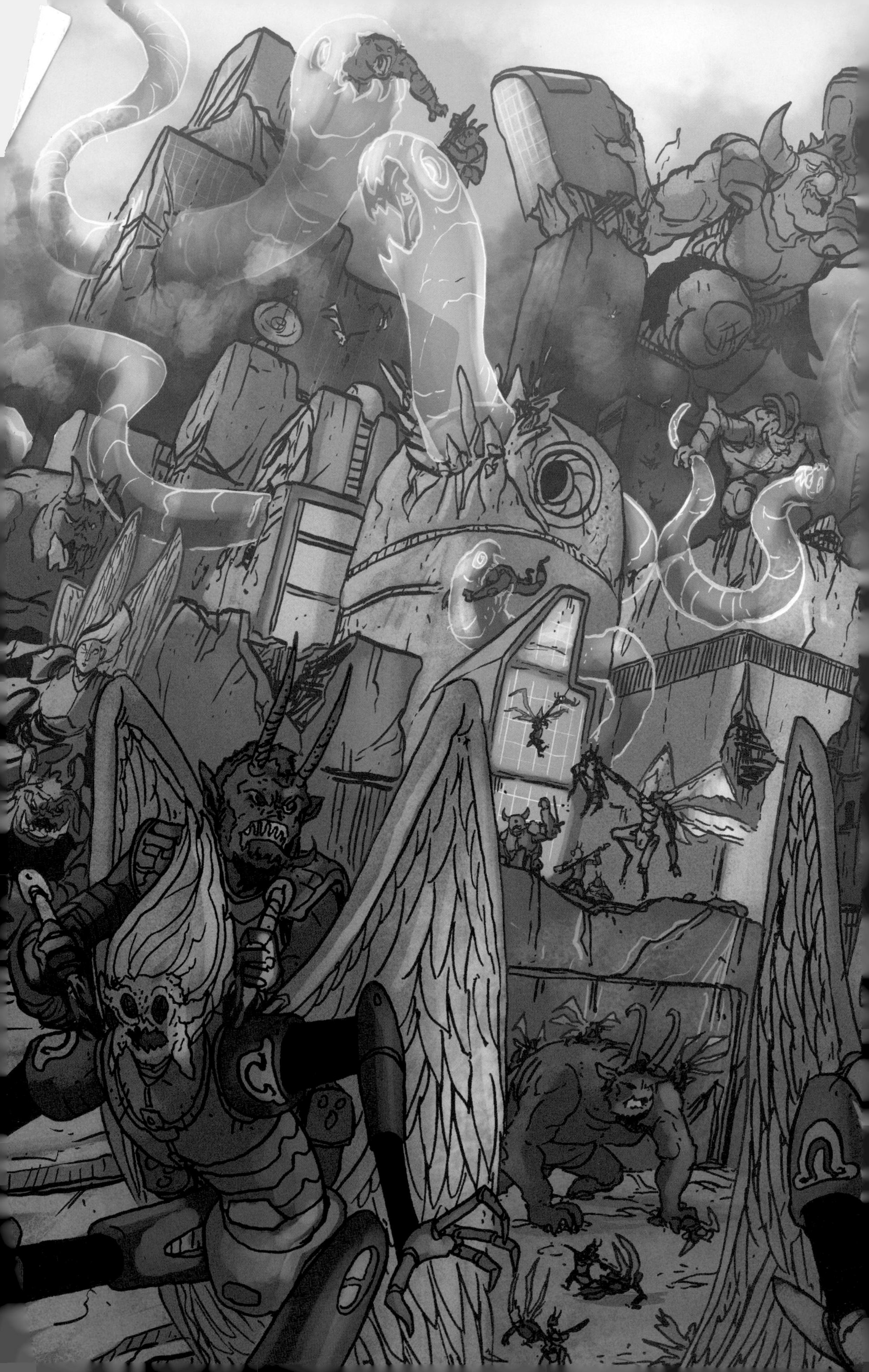

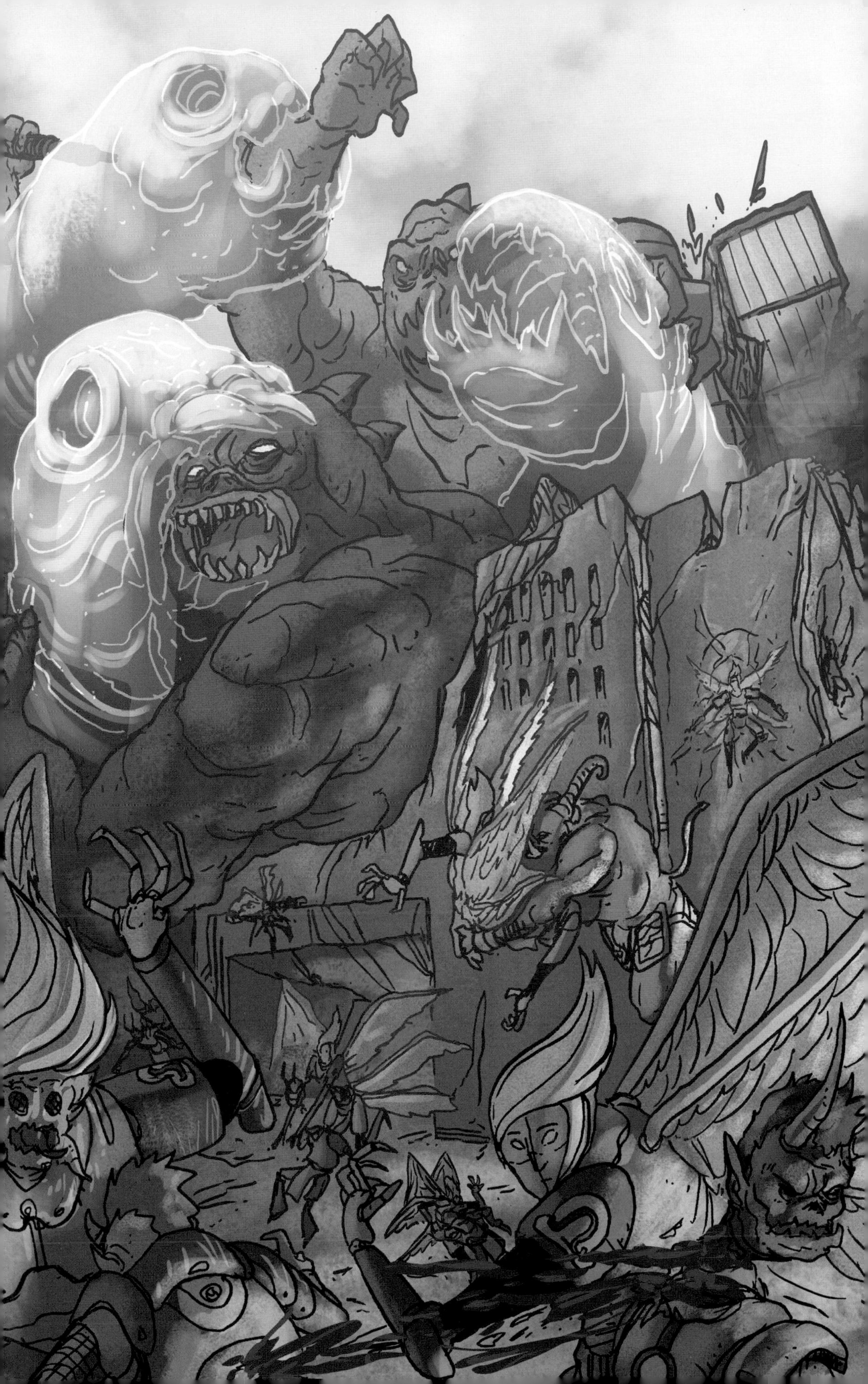

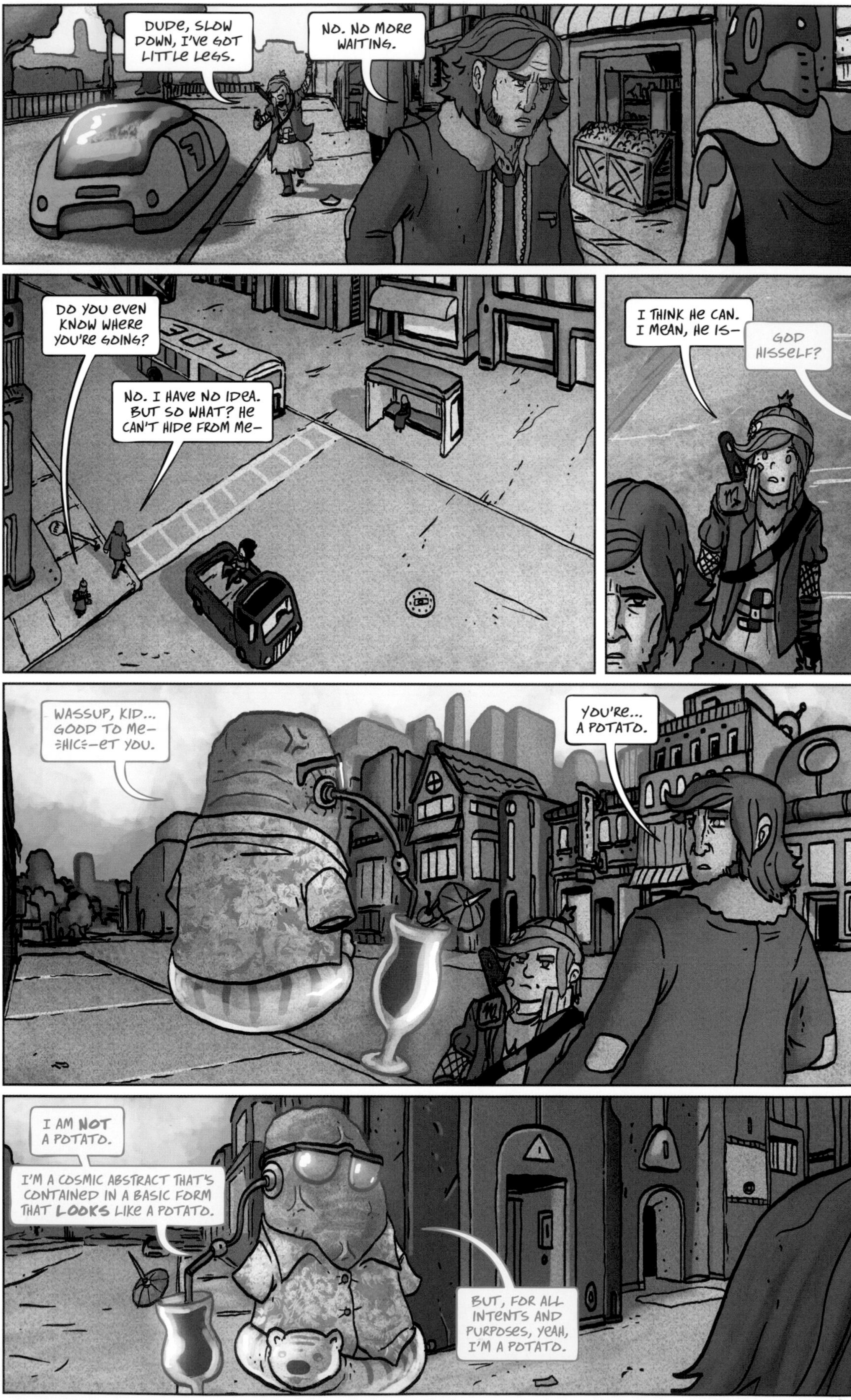
DUDE, SLOW DOWN, I'VE GOT LITTLE LEGS.
NO. NO MORE WAITING.
DO YOU EVEN KNOW WHERE YOU'RE GOING?
NO. I HAVE NO IDEA. BUT SO WHAT? HE CAN'T HIDE FROM ME—
304
I THINK HE CAN. I MEAN, HE IS—
GOD HISSELF?
WASSUP, KID... GOOD TO ME— *HIC*—ET YOU.
YOU'RE... A POTATO.
I AM NOT A POTATO.
I'M A COSMIC ABSTRACT THAT'S CONTAINED IN A BASIC FORM THAT LOOKS LIKE A POTATO.
BUT, FOR ALL INTENTS AND PURPOSES, YEAH, I'M A POTATO.

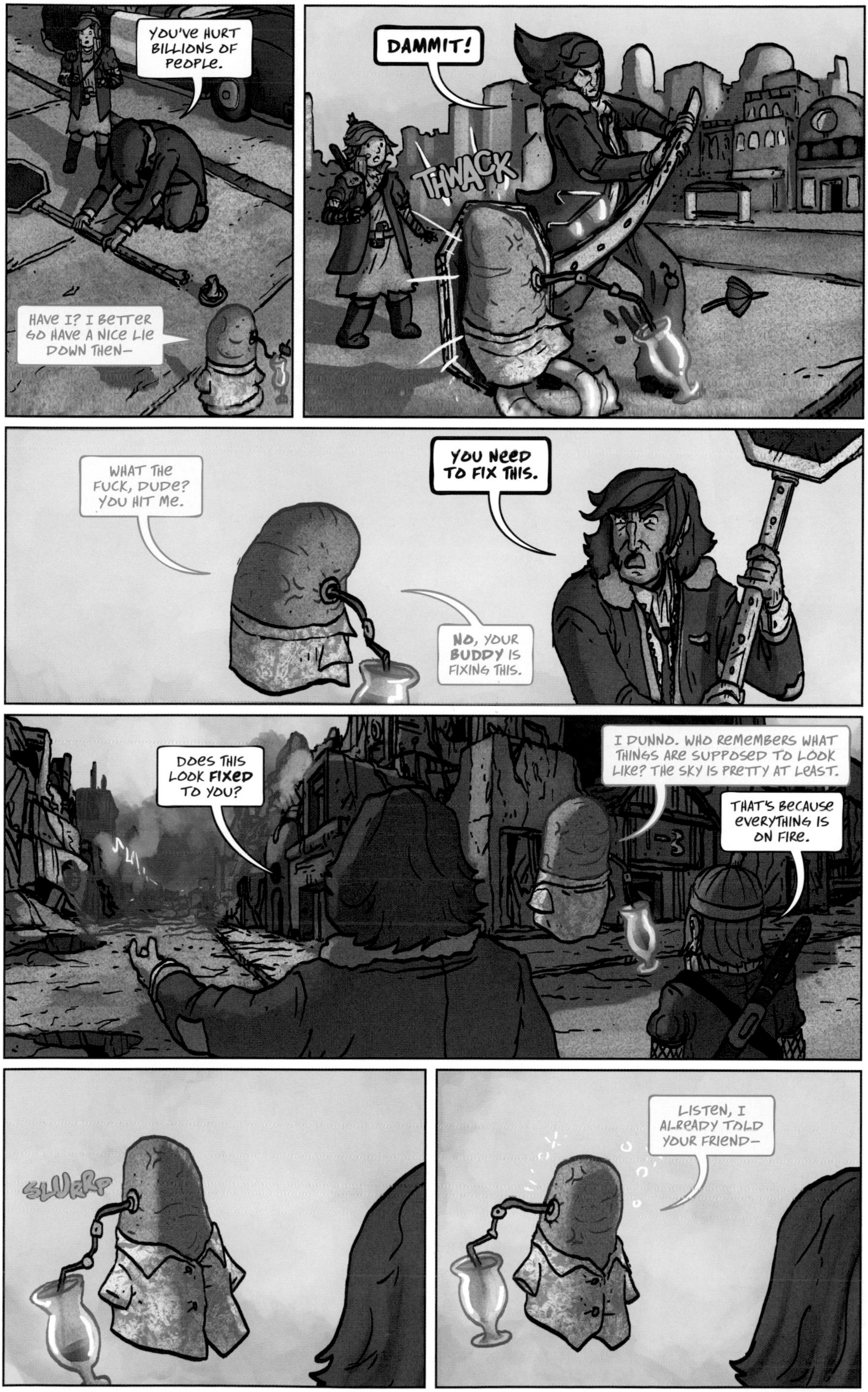
YOU'VE HURT BILLIONS OF PEOPLE.
HAVE I? I BETTER GO HAVE A NICE LIE DOWN THEN—
DAMMIT!
THWACK
WHAT THE FUCK, DUDE? YOU HIT ME.
YOU NEED TO FIX THIS.
NO, YOUR BUDDY IS FIXING THIS.
DOES THIS LOOK FIXED TO YOU?
I DUNNO. WHO REMEMBERS WHAT THINGS ARE SUPPOSED TO LOOK LIKE? THE SKY IS PRETTY AT LEAST.
THAT'S BECAUSE EVERYTHING IS ON FIRE.
SLURRP
LISTEN, I ALREADY TOLD YOUR FRIEND—

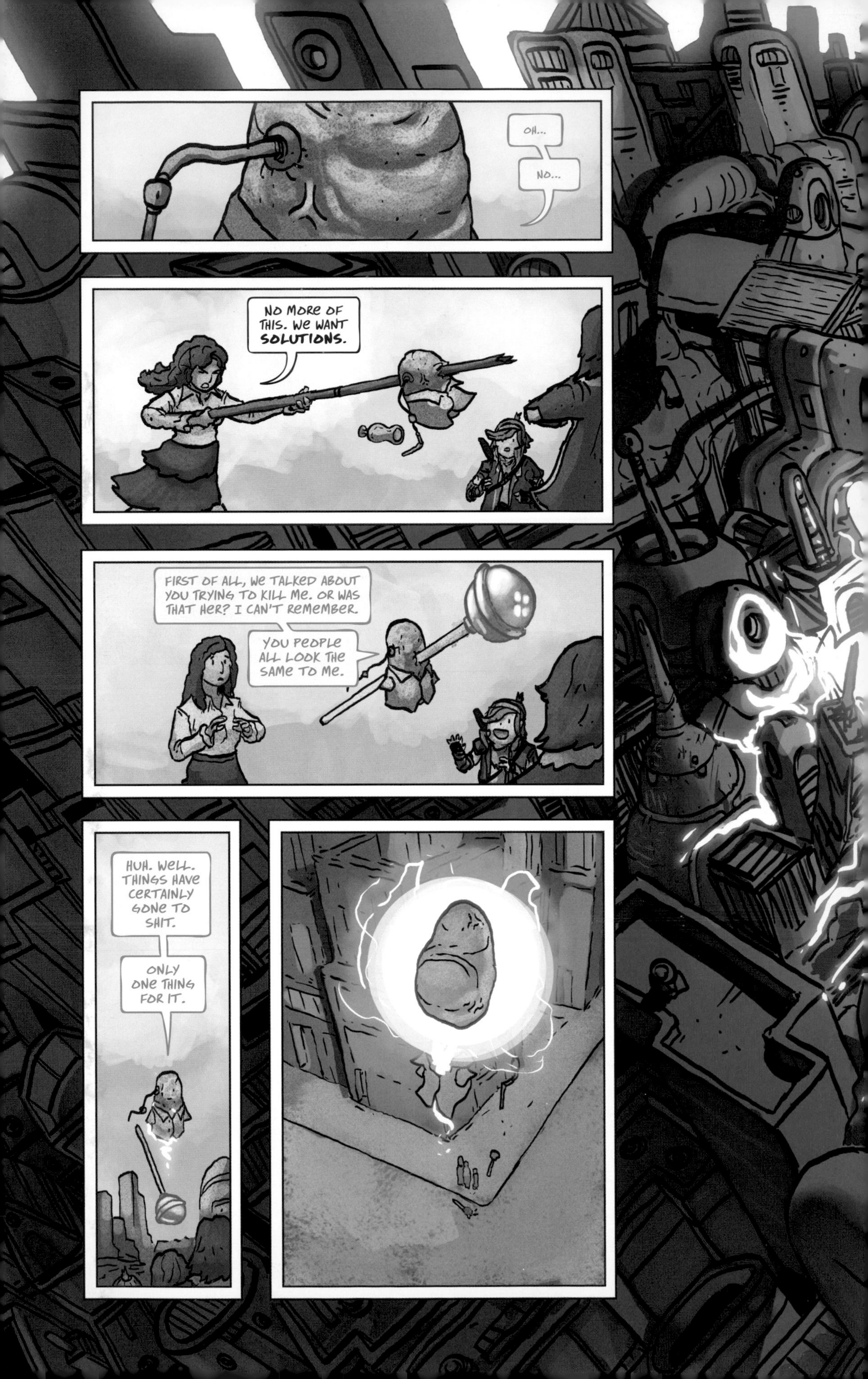
OH...
NO...
NO MORE OF THIS. WE WANT SOLUTIONS.
FIRST OF ALL, WE TALKED ABOUT YOU TRYING TO KILL ME. OR WAS THAT HER? I CAN'T REMEMBER.
YOU PEOPLE ALL LOOK THE SAME TO ME.
HUH. WELL. THINGS HAVE CERTAINLY GONE TO SHIT.
ONLY ONE THING FOR IT.

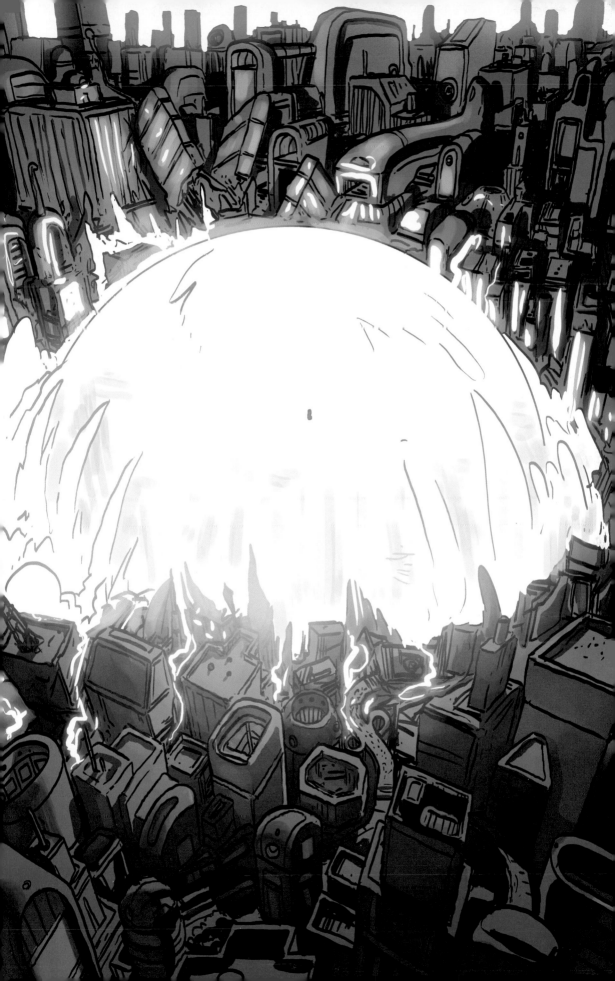

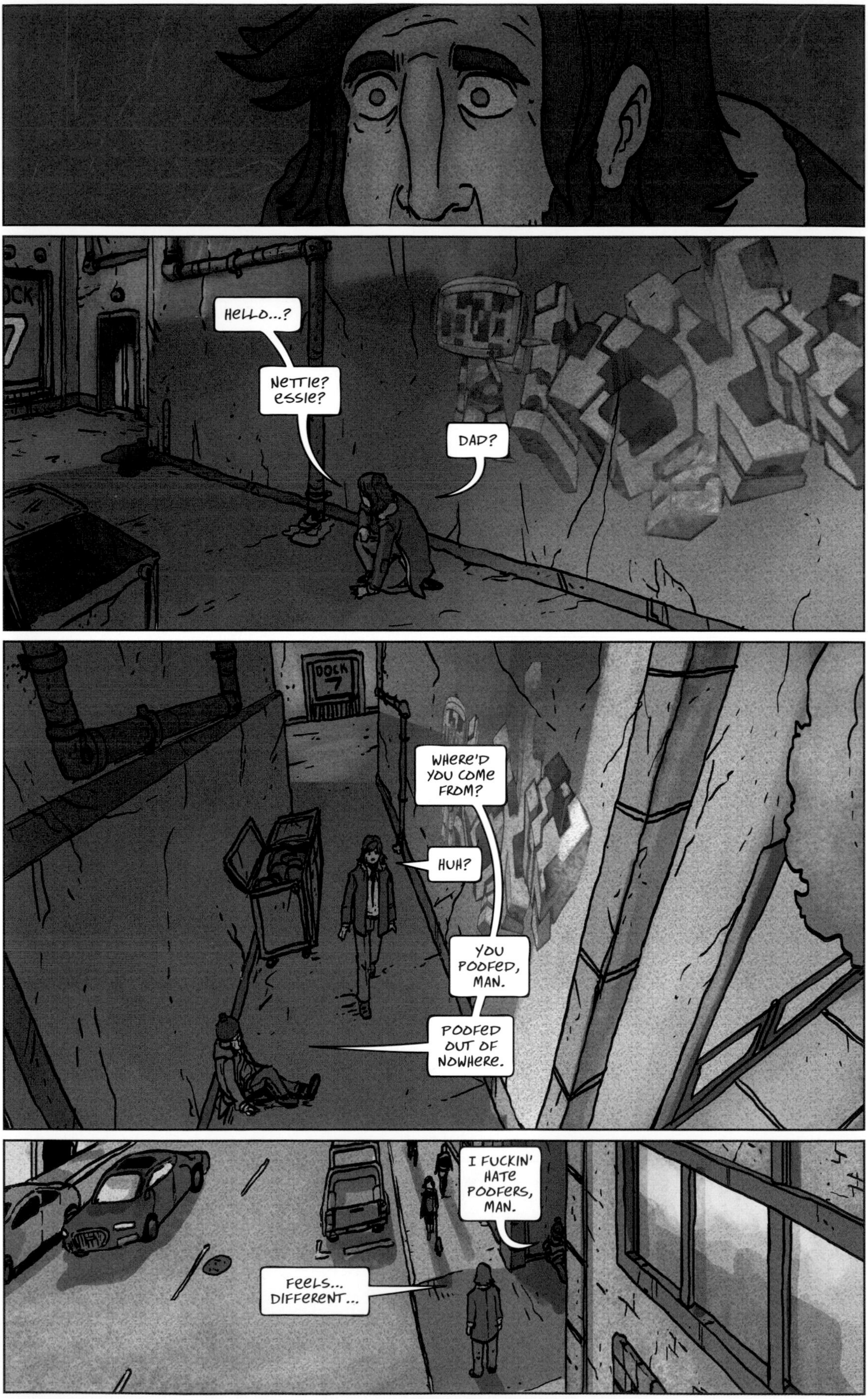
DOCK 7
HELLO...?
NETTIE? ESSIE?
DAD?
DOCK 7
WHERE'D YOU COME FROM?
HUH?
YOU POOFED, MAN.
POOFED OUT OF NOWHERE.
I FUCKIN' HATE POOFERS, MAN.
FEELS... DIFFERENT...

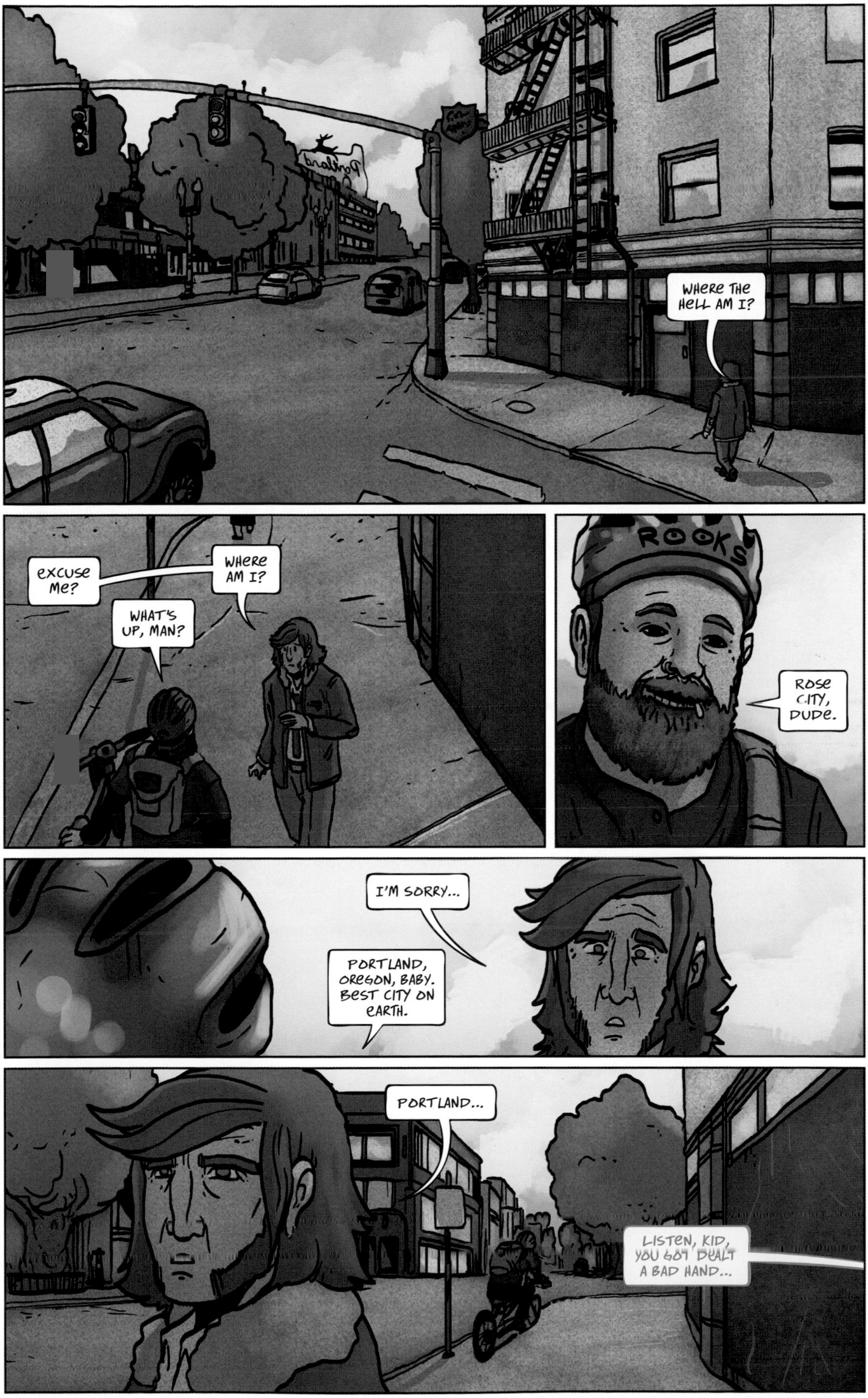
WHERE THE HELL AM I?
EXCUSE ME?
WHERE AM I?
WHAT'S UP, MAN?
ROOKS
ROSE CITY, DUDE.
I'M SORRY...
PORTLAND, OREGON, BABY. BEST CITY ON EARTH.
PORTLAND...
LISTEN, KID, YOU GOT DEALT A BAD HAND...

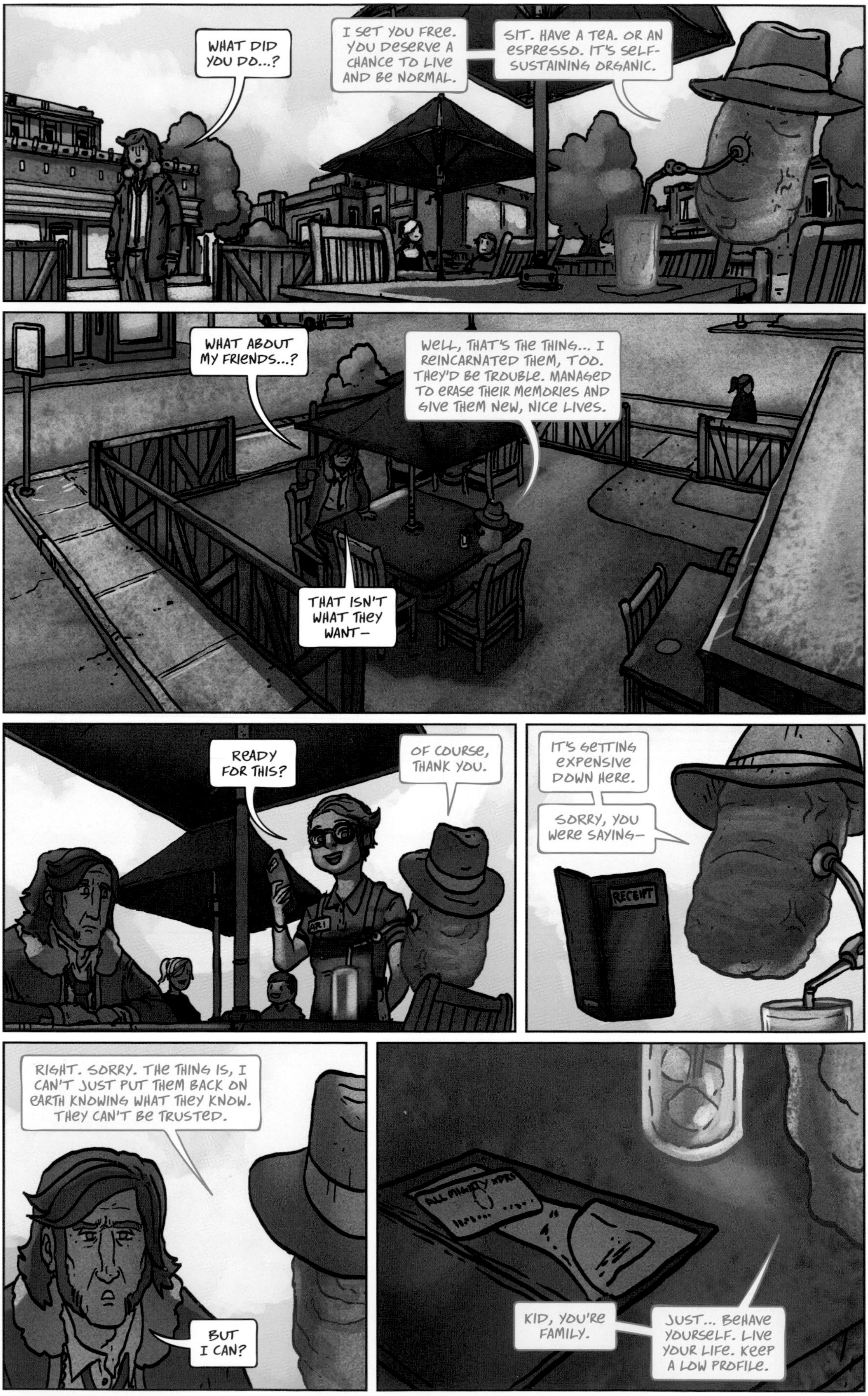
WHAT DID YOU DO...?
I SET YOU FREE. YOU DESERVE A CHANCE TO LIVE AND BE NORMAL.
SIT. HAVE A TEA. OR AN ESPRESSO. IT'S SELF-SUSTAINING ORGANIC.
WHAT ABOUT MY FRIENDS...?
WELL, THAT'S THE THING... I REINCARNATED THEM, TOO. THEY'D BE TROUBLE. MANAGED TO ERASE THEIR MEMORIES AND GIVE THEM NEW, NICE LIVES.
THAT ISN'T WHAT THEY WANT–
READY FOR THIS?
OF COURSE, THANK YOU.
IT'S GETTING EXPENSIVE DOWN HERE.
SORRY, YOU WERE SAYING–
RECEIPT
RIGHT. SORRY. THE THING IS, I CAN'T JUST PUT THEM BACK ON EARTH KNOWING WHAT THEY KNOW. THEY CAN'T BE TRUSTED.
BUT I CAN?
KID, YOU'RE FAMILY.
JUST... BEHAVE YOURSELF. LIVE YOUR LIFE. KEEP A LOW PROFILE.

SIX MONTHS LATER

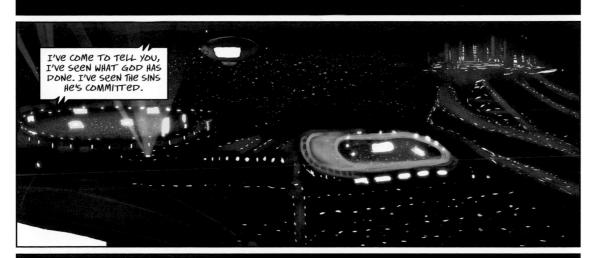

I'VE COME TO TELL YOU, I'VE SEEN WHAT GOD HAS DONE. I'VE SEEN THE SINS HE'S COMMITTED.

AND HE DOESN'T CARE. WHEN I CONFRONTED HIM, WHEN I BEGGED HIM TO END THE SUFFERING.

HE SENT ME HERE. **BACK** HERE.

AT FIRST I THOUGHT IT WAS A SLIGHT. AN ATTACK. A GENUINE ATTEMPT TO DESTROY ME.

BUT NOW. I KNOW WHY HE DID IT.

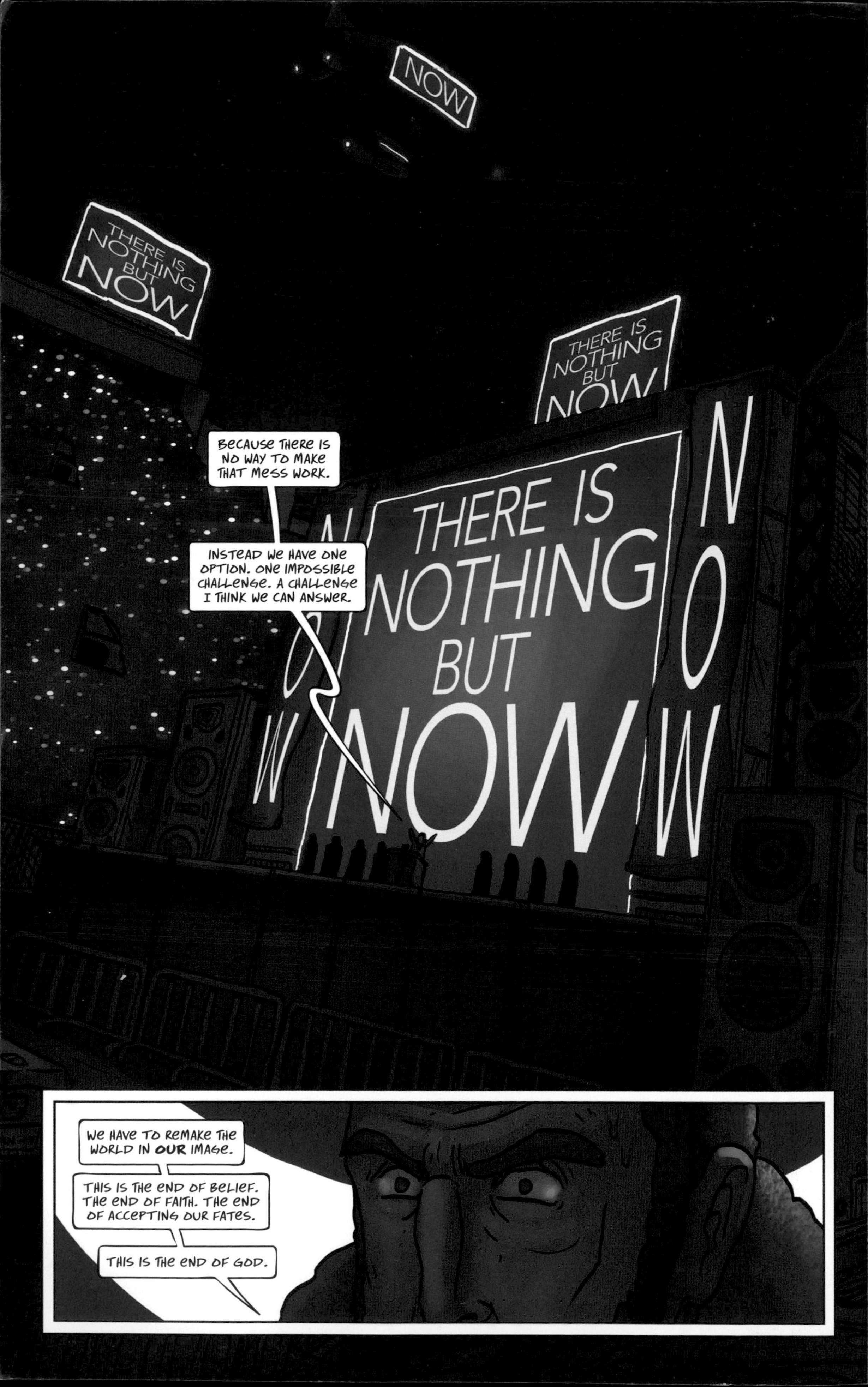
NOW
THERE IS NOTHING BUT NOW
THERE IS NOTHING BUT NOW
BECAUSE THERE IS NO WAY TO MAKE THAT MESS WORK.
INSTEAD WE HAVE ONE OPTION. ONE IMPOSSIBLE CHALLENGE. A CHALLENGE I THINK WE CAN ANSWER.
THERE IS NOTHING BUT NOW
NOW
NOW
WE HAVE TO REMAKE THE WORLD IN **OUR** IMAGE.
THIS IS THE END OF BELIEF. THE END OF FAITH. THE END OF ACCEPTING OUR FATES.
THIS IS THE END OF GOD.

THE LIFE AFTER

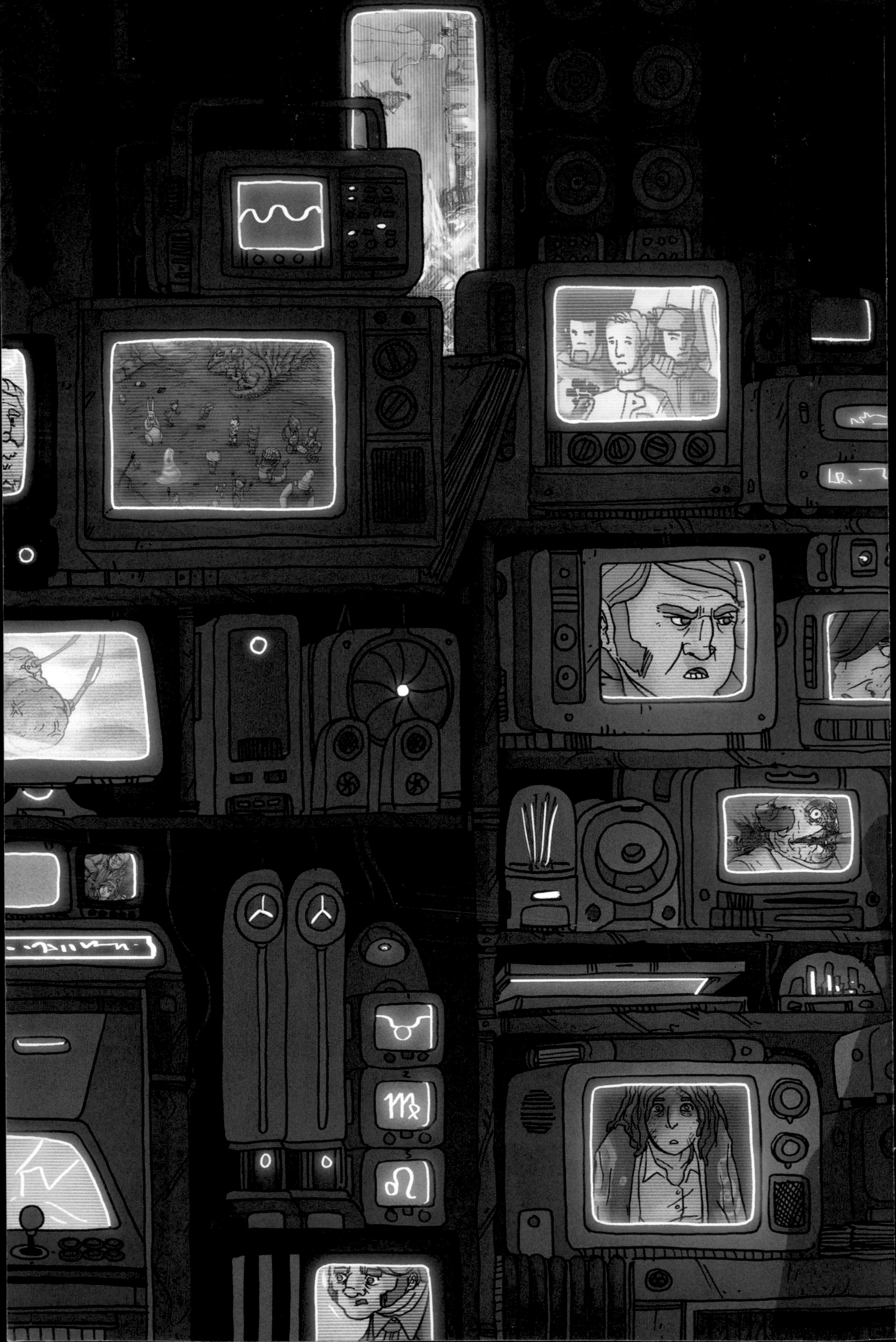

THE LIFE AFTER

THE EPIC CONTINUES EVERY MONTH!

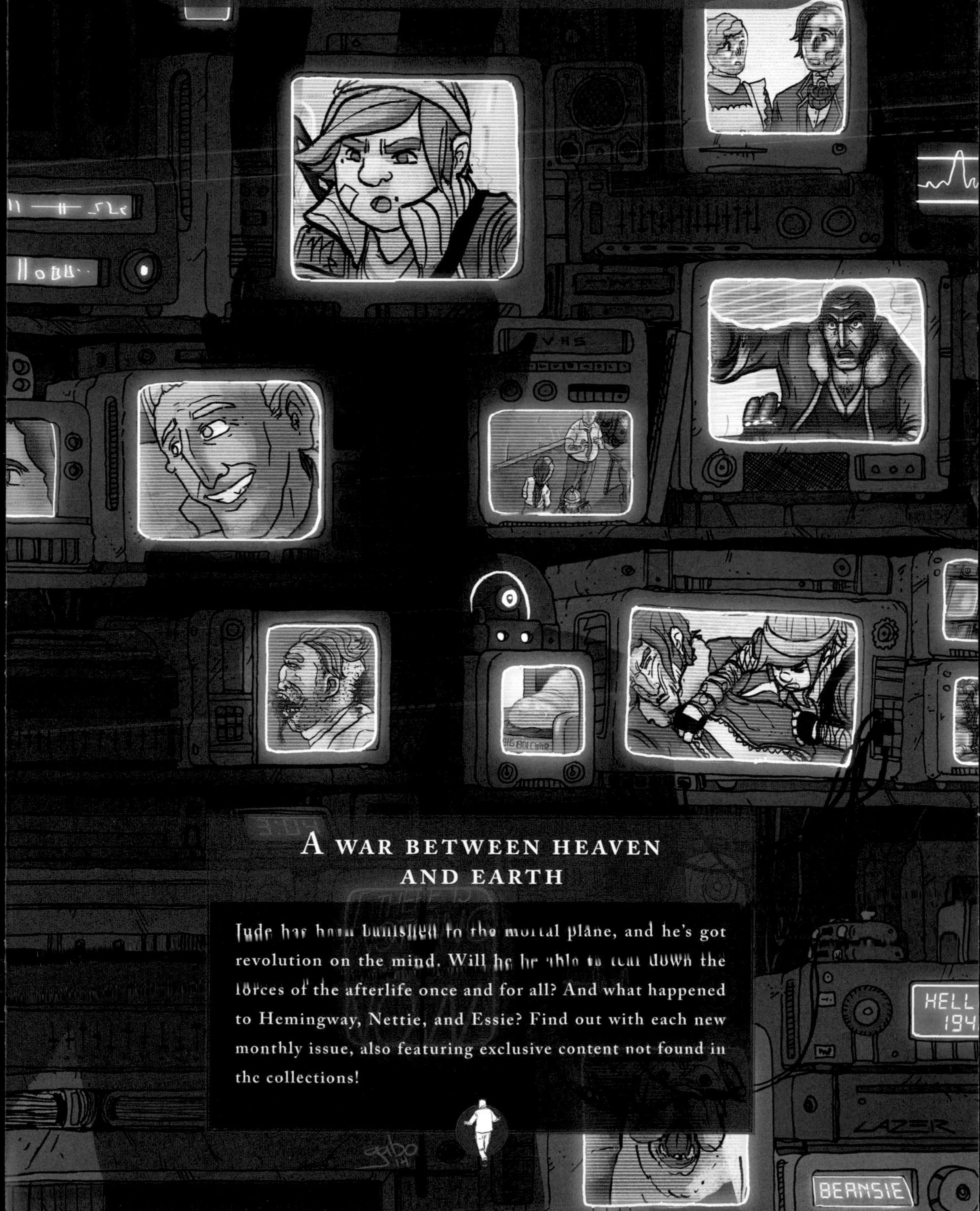

A WAR BETWEEN HEAVEN AND EARTH

Jude has been banished to the mortal plane, and he's got revolution on the mind. Will he be able to tear down the forces of the afterlife once and for all? And what happened to Hemingway, Nettie, and Essie? Find out with each new monthly issue, also featuring exclusive content not found in the collections!

JOSHUA HALE FIALKOV

Joshua Hale Fialkov is the Harvey-, Eisner-, and Emmy-nominated creator of graphic novels, including *The Bunker*, *Punks*, *Tumor*, *Echoes*, and *Elk's Run*. He has written *The Ultimates* for Marvel and *I, Vampire* for DC Comics. He lives in Los Angeles with his wife, author Christina Rice, their daughter, who will remain anonymous (and adorable), their dogs Cole and Olaf. Their cat Smokey has moved on to afterlife 3480-B6, where she's likely playing with her also late sister, The Bandit.

GABO

The Chicago-based Mexican-American known as Gabo eats a bowl of layouts for breakfast, sips ink soup for lunch and has a fatty gouache steak for dinner. He was a 2015 Russ Manning Promising Newcomer award nominee, and in the past has earned an Eisner and Harvey award for his color work.

In his downtime he is the series artist on *Albert the Alien* (Thrillbent) and is the father of the world's best comic book battle website, EnterVoid.com.

He currently resides in the backwoods of Wisconsin with five other like-minded artists. Together they come together and form VONNHAUS.

ALSO BY JOSHUA HALE FIALKOV AND ONI PRESS...

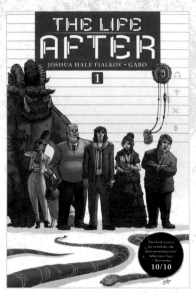

THE LIFE
AFTER
JOSHUA HALE FIALKOV • GABO
1
10/10

THE LIFE AFTER,
VOLUME ONE
By Joshua Hale Fialkov and Gabo
136 pages, softcover, color
ISBN 978-1-62010-214-5

THE LIFE
AFTER
JOSHUA HALE FIALKOV • GABO
2

THE LIFE AFTER,
VOLUME TWO
By Joshua Hale Fialkov and Gabo
144 pages, softcover, color
ISBN 978-1-62010-254-1

THE
BUNKER

THE BUNKER,
VOLUME ONE
By Joshua Hale Fialkov and Joe Infurnari
136 pages, softcover, color
ISBN 978-1-62010-164-3

THE
BUNKER

THE BUNKER,
VOLUME TWO
By Joshua Hale Fialkov and Joe Infurnari
136 pages, softcover, color
ISBN 978-1-62010-210-7

ELK'S RUN
A TALE OF SMALL TOWN HORROR
JOSHUA HALE FIALKOV
NOEL TUAZON
SCOTT KEATING

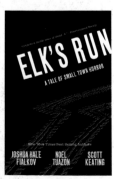

ELK'S RUN:
TENTH ANNIVERSARY EDITION
By Joshua Hale Fialkov, Noel Tuazon, and Scott Keating
248 pages, hardcover, color
ISBN 978-1-62010-279-4

TUMOR
JOSHUA HALE FIALKOV & NOEL TUAZON

TUMOR
By Joshua Hale Fialkov and Noel Tuazon
248 pages, hardcover, B&W
ISBN 978-1-62010-326-5

ONI PRESS

For more information on these and other fine Oni Press comic books and graphic novels visit www.onipress.com.
To find a comic specialty store in your area visit www.comicshops.us.